M000188742

THE

BETTER PART,

GOSPEL OF JOHN

A CHRIST-CENTERED RESOURCE
FOR PERSONAL PRAYER

BY JOHN BARTUNEK, LC, THD

SOPHIA INSTITUTE PRESS
Manchester, NH

Cover image: iStock.com

Gospel text taken from *The Jerusalem Bible* by Alexander Jones, ed., copyright © 1966 by Darton, Longman & Todd, Ltd. and Doubleday, a division of Random House, Inc. Used by permission of Doubleday, a division of Random House, Inc.

Imprimi Potest:
Francisco Mateos, LC
Nihil Obstat
Imprimatur
† Most Reverend Henry J. Mansell
Archbishop of Hartford
June 14, 2007

ISBN: 978-1-64413-148-0

First Printing

CONTENTS

INTRODUCTION

The Importance of Personal Prayer

Conscientious Christians pray. Their typical days, weeks, months, and years are seasoned with prayer—traditional prayers, liturgical prayers, spontaneous prayers. They make prayer commitments, giving structure and consistency to their faith journey. Prayer keeps Christians united to the Vine, so their lives can bear the fruit both they and Christ long for.[1]

Among the most basic prayer commitments is one that can have more bearing on your life than any other because it is more personalized: the daily meditation. Certainly you can't mature as a Christian without the sacramental life, just as crops can't mature without sunlight and soil. And the various devotional and vocal prayers that punctuate your day keep you strong and focused amid the unrelenting blows of the unchristian culture all around you. But, as generations of saints and sinners have found out, that is not enough.

Without the daily renewal and deepening of your personal relationship with Jesus Christ that happens especially through meditation, sooner or later routine sets in. You get into a rut. Your prayers get mechanical, your sacramental life slides into hollow ritualism, and before you know it, your faith gets sidelined and you get dragged back into the rat race in some form or other. The daily meditation keeps your faith, that pearl of great price,[2] lively, supple, and relevant. It irrigates the soil of your soul, making your sacramental life more fruitful, keeping your other prayer commitments meaningful, and continually opening up new vistas along the path to spiritual maturity.

This is why spiritual writers through the ages have so consistently emphasized the importance of meditation, also known as mental prayer, since it is a deeply interior way of praying. Here is what two doctors of the Church have to say about it:

> He who neglects mental prayer needs not a devil to carry him to hell, but he brings himself there with his own hands. (St. Teresa of Avila)

> It is morally impossible for him who neglects meditation to live without sin. (St. Alphonsus Ligouri)

> And by experience we see that many persons who recite a great number of vocal prayers, the Office and the Rosary, fall into sin, and continue to live

---

1 "I am the vine, and you are the branches. He who dwells in me, as I dwell in him, bears much fruit; for apart from me you can do nothing" (Jn 15:5).

2 "Again, the kingdom of Heaven is like a merchant looking for fine pearls; when he finds one of great value he goes and sells everything he owns and buys it" (Mt 13:45-46).

in sin. But he who attends to mental prayer scarcely ever falls into sin, and should he have the misfortune of falling into it, he will hardly continue to live in so miserable a state; he will either give up mental prayer, or renounce sin. Meditation and sin cannot stand together. However abandoned a soul may be, if she perseveres in meditation, God will bring her to salvation. (St. Alphonsus Ligouri)

The daily meditation, in other words, is not an optional extra for super-Christians; it's every Christian's bread and butter. Without it, your Christian identity shrivels. But it's not enough just to do a daily meditation; you need to learn to do it better and better. Maturity in the spiritual life depends to a great extent on constantly going deeper in your personal prayer life. The law of life is growth, so if your capacity for mental prayer isn't growing, your life with Christ is in danger of wasting away.[3]

The Benefits of *The Better Part*

The Better Part is meant to foster and accompany growth in mental prayer. It is not primarily instructional (like a "how-to" book on prayer), and not complete in itself (like ready-made meditations). Rather, *The Better Part* is a companion for your daily meditation, providing enough structure and content to serve as a catalyst for you to learn to pray better as you pray, to make your meditation more personal and personalized, to help you learn to follow the Holy Spirit's lead more readily.

Used well, *The Better Part* helps you discover at least three things:

1. ***HOW YOU PRAY BEST.*** Prayer is similar to walking. To walk, everyone has to follow the same principles of physics — friction, gravity, muscle propulsion, momentum. And yet, even though the principles are the same, everyone's walk is a little bit different. When babies learn to walk, they start out clumsy and awkward, until they develop the rhythm and style proper to their body type, personality, and environment. Meditation follows a similar pattern: the same principles for all, activated uniquely

---

3 This intensely personal prayer — Christian meditation — contributes significantly to the communal life of the Church. As our personal friendship with Christ develops, we become more mature and fruitful members of his Body, the Church. Therefore, although this book focuses on the personal encounter with Christ in meditation, it does not mean to belittle the ecclesial nature of the Christian vocation. The two aspects are complementary and intertwined.

by each. *The Better Part* can help you wherever you happen to be on the spectrum.

2. **THE DIMENSIONS OF CHRIST.** (These include his characteristics, actions, words, sufferings that speak most profoundly to your soul.) The heart of Christianity is each believer's friendship with Jesus Christ, and friendship is never generic. If you read the lives of the saints, you quickly discover how each one's holiness has its own, unique flavor—St. Francis' friendship with Christ was different than St. Dominic's because St. Francis and St. Dominic were different. Every person has a unique personality, so each person will relate to Christ uniquely. God created you to know him as only you can know him. *The Better Part* is designed to help you uncover and develop the distinctiveness of your friendship with Christ, without which you will always feel more restless and dissatisfied than you need to.

3. **THE INESTIMABLE VALUE OF A DEEP PRAYER LIFE.** Every Christian has a responsibility to become an expert in prayer. Without a mature prayer life, you cannot become a mature Christian, in which case you will never discover the authentic Christian joy, wisdom, and fruitfulness that flow from being fully formed in Christ.[4] This expertise in prayer comes only from the Holy Spirit, who uses two training methods:

First, he instructs you in prayer through the experience of others. Through the ages, the Church and its saints have produced a whole library of accessible, practical, and inspiring books on prayer. You'll want to read them and study them. All Christians who take their friendship with Christ seriously should regularly read good books (and plenty of good articles) on prayer or the spiritual life.[5] *The Better Part* is not one of these treatises on prayer, but Part 1: The Fundamentals of Christian Meditation will serve as a refresher course on the central principles of Christian meditation, something you can refer to in order to keep your meditation in shape.

Second, the Holy Spirit makes you an expert in prayer when you actually pray. You need to dive into the pool and splash around so that your coach can teach you to swim. Here *The Better Part* is a valuable tool.

---

4 "My dear children, for whom I am again in the pains of childbirth until Christ is formed in you..." (Gal 4:19); "...to build up the Body of Christ, until we all reach unity in faith and knowledge of the Son of God and form the perfect man, fully mature with the fullness of Christ himself. If we live by the truth and in love, **we shall grow completely into Christ**" (Eph 4:12-13, 15, emphasis added).

5 See Appendix 2 for a list of excellent books on prayer and the spiritual life.

Instead of supplying you with spiritual reflections gleaned from others' experience of God in prayer, as many spiritual books do so well, this is a truly Christ-centered resource, purposely open-ended, but in a strategically structured way. Each unit in *The Better Part* will thus serve as a springboard for your own praying, a way to aid your docility to the Holy Spirit's coaching. (Part I: The Fundamentals of Christian Meditation explains more fully how this works.)

And so, if you are just starting out in Christian meditation, *The Better Part* can help you lay a firm foundation. If you are already adept at mental prayer, its open-ended, Christ-centered structure makes it a rich and flexible source of meditation material. It is perhaps most helpful, however, for those who would label themselves neither beginners nor advanced, but somewhere in between.

Many Christians — even committed, well-formed Christians — reach a plateau in their prayer life because their meditation stays at the level of reflective spiritual reading, even when their soul is ready to go higher (this distinction is explained more fully later). *The Better Part*, used rightly, can help foster this move forward.

The rest of this Introduction will explain how *The Better Part* is composed and organized. It will show how to make this book a tool for knowing, loving, and following Christ more wholeheartedly, which is what God is hoping for, your soul is thirsting for, and all prayer is striving for. Then, Part I: The Fundamentals of Christian Meditation will review in detail the fundamental principles, steps, and difficulties of Christian meditation, and it will equip you to do a checkup on your own prayer life. The rest of the book contains the actual meditation units.

Be forewarned — *The Better Part* is not necessarily the easier part. Christ never promised that following him would be easy. In fact, he promised it wouldn't. The spiritual life is full of mystery. You find yourself on unfamiliar ground when you trust God to lead you to richer pastures. Often it is much more comfortable to keep doing what you already know how to do, like Martha, who busied herself in the kitchen when Jesus and the Apostles dropped by for dinner. Her sister Mary put normal activities on hold for a little while instead, and sat at Jesus' feet, drinking in his wisdom, his love, and his beauty. When Martha complained that Mary was being lazy and impractical, Jesus smiled at her and said:

"Martha, Martha. You worry and fret about so many things, and yet few are needed, indeed only one. It is Mary who has chosen the better part, and it is not to be taken from her." (Lk 10:41-42)

How to Use *THE BETTER PART*

No book can pray for you. No book can teach you to pray. At most, a book can be a useful tool. *The Better Part* is designed to help you engage more actively in the quest of Christian meditation so you can reap more fruits of spiritual growth.

The Better Part is divided into units. Each unit consists of five parts: a passage from the Gospel according to St. John and a four-part commentary based on the same four themes throughout the book: Christ the Lord, Christ the Teacher, Christ the Friend, and Christ in My Life. This structure is substantive, meditative, and flexible.

SUBSTANTIVE: A CHRIST-CENTERED RESOURCE *The Better Part* is substantive because it is eminently Christ-centered. Christ is the "power of God and the wisdom of God" (1 Cor 1:24). The gospel is the good news of the "boundless riches" (Eph 3:8) of Christ. The Christian life consists in knowing, loving, and imitating Christ. He is God made man — "for the sake of our salvation," as the Creed puts it. You will never be able to exhaust the Gospels. They are the heart of the Bible and the privileged place of God's revelation. The Old Testament was a preparation for the revelation of the mystery of Christ, and the rest of the New Testament shows the consequences and flowering of this revelation. The Church has always taught that because Christ is God as well as man, all of his words and actions as recorded in the Gospels are not merely edifying events from the past. Christ spoke and lived them with you in mind, so that they are alive and relevant and addressed to you and the circumstances of your life at every moment: "Jesus Christ is the same yesterday and today and forever" (Heb 13:8).

This eminently Christ-centered approach derives especially from the spirituality characterizing the Legionaries of Christ and the Regnum Christi Movement.[6] This spirituality, one of the many fragrant blossoms in the Church's rich garden of charisms, imbues the entire book.

At times in your spiritual journey you may find other sources more stimulating and helpful for your personal prayer, but after each such sojourn you will feel yourself drawn back to the Gospels, the living Word of God, the life,

---

6 For more information on the Legionaries of Christ and the Regnum Christi Movement, visit www.legionariesofchrist.org and www.regnumchristi.org.

words, actions, passion, death, and resurrection of our Lord and Savior, the inexhaustible fountain of the Christian life:

> In the beginning was the Word.... Through him all things were made; without him nothing was made that has been made. In him was life, and that life was the light of men... grace and truth came through Jesus Christ. No one has ever seen God. It is God the only Son, who is close to the Father's heart, who has made him known. (Jn 1:1, 3-4, 17-18)

MEDITATIVE: A PRAYER-INDUCING COMMENTARY ON THE GOSPEL *The Better Part* is meditative because the commentaries are drawn from the Gospel passages themselves and point back to them. They do not develop an instructional treatise on the spiritual life, nor do they focus on biblical exegesis or catechetical apologetics. Those themes are addressed only to help the magnificent figure of Christ emerge more clearly.

The four-part commentaries on each Gospel passage follow the same structure, which is based on the faculties of the human soul. Thus, each unit helps bring the whole person into contact with Christ.

- The "Christ the Lord" commentary points out how a particular passage illuminates Christ's mission and qualities as Savior, Redeemer, and Eternal King. It appeals most directly to the will, the faculty by which you make the decisions that direct your life. As you contemplate more and more the grandeur and splendor of Christ the Savior and King, your decision to follow him unconditionally grows firmer and firmer.

- The "Christ the Teacher" commentary draws out the lessons that Christ teaches by word and example, appealing more directly to the intellect. You cannot live out your desire and decision to follow Christ if you don't know the standards and criteria of thought, speech, and behavior that Christ asks of his disciples.

- The "Christ the Friend" commentary brings out the intimate and personal love of Christ's heart. Jesus doesn't want to be a distant Savior and leader; he longs to be your companion and most intimate friend, and he shows this longing over and over again in the Gospels. This commentary appeals to your heart, so that your discipleship grows in passion, intimacy, and warmth as well as determination and wisdom.[7]

- The "Christ in My Life" commentary (mostly written in the first person) consists of observations and questions in the form of prayers that help you evaluate how you should follow Christ in light of the passage you are meditating on. This is a safety net: if for some reason your reflections up to that point have stayed too abstract, this section will bring Christ's light to bear on your own life, behavior, and attitudes, provoking a fresh conversion and re-commitment to Christ. This commentary will also help ensure that your spiritual life goes beyond mere feelings and good dispositions to become truly transforming.

The quotations from saints and popes that introduce each chapter of the Gospels and each meditation unit can also spark reflection. They add spice to the commentaries by giving glimpses into the deep experience of Christ had by your older brothers and sisters in the faith.

Each unit in *The Better Part*, then, facilitates bringing your will, mind, heart, and life into contact with Christ, helping you bathe your soul in his truth and his grace. The entire series has only one aim: to help you know, love, and follow Christ more closely by encountering him more deeply and personally in prayer.

FLEXIBLE: THEMES AND VARIATIONS *The Better Part* is flexible because it can be used in so many ways—it is not a book of meditations, but a resource for personal prayer.

At the end of the book (in Appendix 1), you will find a list of Gospel passages in relation to some pivotal virtues of the spiritual life. This resource can be used in numerous ways, depending on your personal needs and preferences.

You may prefer to coordinate your meditations with the needs of your own spiritual life, in accord with your program of spiritual work. For a Christian, growth in virtue never occurs simply through one's own effort; you become more like Christ by contemplating Christ, opening your heart to his grace, loving him more, and being moved to imitate him within the circumstances of your own life. In this case, you can use Appendix 1 to find the theme you are hoping to meditate on and bookmark the units that correspond.

---

7 Sometimes this commentary includes paragraphs written in such a way that Jesus or others are speaking in the first person. This literary technique is designed to stimulate fresh encounters with familiar passages, not to revise Catholic doctrine.

You can also combine *The Better Part* with other meditation material, alternating between Gospel passages and spiritual books, or using a Gospel passage and one of its commentaries from *The Better Part* as the first point of consideration, a paragraph from another source as the second point, and so on.

The Better Part is also a good resource if you have a commitment to do a daily Gospel reflection in addition to a morning meditation.

MEDITATING WITH THE BETTER PART However you choose to arrange your meditation themes (and this is a good topic to discuss with a confessor or spiritual director), always keep in mind the difference between spiritual reading and meditation.

If you were to use *The Better Part* for spiritual reading or a daily Gospel reflection, you would simply read an entire unit or two straight through each day—a helpful and beneficial spiritual exercise.

Meditating on a unit, however, requires a different approach. In this case, each part of the unit is treated separately, like five connected rooms in an art gallery. During the Consider and Converse stages of your meditation, you spend plenty of time in one room before moving on to the next.

Start with the Gospel passage itself. You take enough time to enter into the scene with your imagination, with your mind, searching for whatever God has to say to you in that passage. You may find a word or phrase or characteristic in the Gospel passage itself that is sufficient material for consideration and conversation for the entire meditation. The next day, you begin there again, and you may find that the Holy Spirit wants you to stay with the same point and continue to savor it. This is ideal because it means that your prayer is intensely personal—direct contact between you and the Gospel, with the Holy Spirit setting the pace.

When you are ready, either in the same meditation or the next day, you move on to the first commentary. You read it and consider it calmly, inquiringly. The main point of the commentary may strike you and become the matter of further conversation and consideration, or a tangential point may pop out at you. The commentary may bring you right back into the Gospel passage, showing you something that you hadn't noticed before. Here again, your search for what Christ has to tell you proceeds at a more meditative pace than spiritual reading—there is no rush; you take your time and seek out what the Holy Spirit has to say to you.

Just one of the commentaries may occupy an entire meditation, or even two or three meditations, or on the other hand, it may take only a minute or two. Whenever you are ready, you move on to the next commentary, into the next room of the gallery, continuing to search for whatever nourishment God has ready for your soul.

If you find yourself regularly spending more than one day with the same unit, try going back to the Gospel passage each day at the start of your meditation, before moving on to the next commentary. Thus, your first point each day is the Gospel passage, then you move on to the first commentary; the next day you start again with the Gospel passage, then move right to the second commentary, and so on. God's Word really is the privileged place for your encounter with him.

Feel free to write in the margins and mark certain passages or units that speak to you in a special way. All Christians should have their favorite Gospel passages, the ones they go back to again and again to feed their souls. In fact, since *The Better Part* is built on the Gospel itself, it is a resource that can be used over and over again, through the years.

As a resource for meditation, then, *The Better Part* affords you both substantive structure (Gospel commentaries directed to your will, intellect, and heart) and flexibility. You should feel no pressure to go at any particular pace. One unit a day is more than enough material for a twenty-minute meditation done well, or even for thirty or sixty minutes. You may find yourself drawn to stay with the same unit for a few days, working through it slowly. Try your best to follow along however the Holy Spirit guides you. What matters is that your prayer life deepens and your friendship with Christ grows—not that you finish this book in record time.

SMALL-GROUP USE *The Better Part*, though primarily a resource for personal prayer, also can be adapted for use in small groups. It is more spiritual than instructional, but its Christ-centered character can make it rewarding as a change of pace from typical Bible study guides or *Catechism* studies.

A prayer group that meets each week, for instance, may use *The Better Part* throughout a liturgical season (such as Lent or Advent), or for a few weeks before a particular event (a pilgrimage, convention, or local Feast Day), or when they want to get a Christ-centered perspective on a particular aspect of the spiritual or moral life (following Appendix 1), or as the regular material for their first meeting of every month. It can also be used in this way for breakout activities during retreats or weekend conferences.

In any of these instances, the small group can read through the Gospel passage and commentaries together, a different member reading each paragraph out loud. Then the members of the group can reflect on the passage together, discussing what strikes them and what applications it has to their own lives. To facilitate this type of use, suggested questions for small-group discussion and references to the *Catechism* finish off each unit. These can be skipped when the book is being used by individuals.

Now that you understand the approach and usefulness of *The Better Part*, you can start using the meditation units (Part II) immediately. Eventually, however, you may want to take some time to read over Part I: The Fundamentals of Christian Meditation. If you feel called to go deeper in your personal prayer life, a review of Part I, with its explanation of the fundamentals of Christian prayer and meditation, could be just the kick start you need.

PART I

THE FUNDAMENTALS OF CHRISTIAN MEDITATION

GOD'S IDEA OF PRAYER

What do you picture yourself doing when you start to pray? What image, conscious or not, do you have in mind? Maybe you see yourself merely fulfilling a duty, as when you mechanically recited the Pledge of Allegiance at the start of homeroom in elementary school. Maybe you see prayer as an exercise in self-mastery and self-help, an activity (pseudo-yoga, aerobics, or weightlifting) that keeps you fit. Whatever you think you are doing when you pray affects the way in which you do it. So the more your idea of prayer matches God's, the better.

Prayer at its most basic level is conversation with God. This seems obvious, but it harbors an awesome reality. To converse with someone implies that that someone wants to pay attention to you; otherwise you have a monologue, not a conversation. The mere existence of prayer, then, implies that God is paying attention, that he is interested in spending time with you. Christian prayer is an invitation from God to the one who prays — it starts with God, not with you.

The whole Christian edifice is built on this simple but awe-inspiring reality. The *Catechism* highlights it in its very first numbers: "At every time and in every place, God draws close to man.... God never ceases to draw man to himself" (1, 27). God is always drawing close to you, and he is always drawing you closer to him. That means he is always thinking of you, just like the Good Shepherd who is always thinking of and watching over his sheep. Prayer starts here.

You are the lost and hungry sheep; God is the shepherd who knows what you desire and need and is guiding you to the lush fields and cool, refreshing waters of his Truth and Love. The shepherd sees the big picture, the whole landscape, the weather, the seasons, the dangers and the opportunities; the sheep can only focus on this little patch of grass here, and then that one over there. Prayer is the Good Shepherd, wise and loving, guiding the hungry, shortsighted, and needy sheep.

God is the real protagonist of Christian prayer. Prayer is the soul's response to God's initiative. The essence of Christian prayer is relationship. As the *Catechism* puts it: "'Great is the mystery of the faith!'... This mystery, then, requires that the faithful believe in it, that they celebrate it, and that they live from it in a vital and personal relationship with the living and true God. *This relationship is prayer*" (2558, emphasis added).

Prayer, then, is more than just a dry religious duty, more than self-centered and self-sufficient self-help techniques; Christian prayer is a friendship with

God in Christ. It's being led by the Good Shepherd to ever richer pastures in the Father's Kingdom.[1]

CHRISTIAN PRAYER: EMINENTLY CHRIST-CENTERED What matters most in prayer, then, is docility to that Good Shepherd, listening honestly, and responding honestly. God is already at work; you have only to hear and heed his voice. So how does he speak to you?

At various times in the past and in various different ways, God spoke to our ancestors through the prophets; but in our own time, the last days, he has spoken to us through his Son, the Son that he has appointed to inherit everything and through whom he made everything there is. He is the radiant light of God's glory and the perfect copy of his nature, sustaining the universe by his powerful command.... That is why all you who are holy brothers and have had the same heavenly call should *turn your minds to Jesus*, the apostle and the high priest of our religion. (Heb 1:1-3, 3:1, emphasis added)

Christian prayer consists of that "turning your minds to Jesus," the Jesus who comes to us through the revelation of the Gospels, the good news of the "boundless riches" (Eph 3:8) of Christ.

The riches of Christ are boundless because Christ is God-revealing-himself-to-man, and God is infinite. If you want to get to know someone, it is not enough to learn about him from the outside; he has to open his mind and heart to you so that you can really get to know him, his thoughts and desires, his yearnings, his way of seeing things, his concerns. Interpersonal knowledge, the knowledge of friendship, can only come through personal revelation. Christ is God-revealing-himself-to-you, offering you his friendship.

Only Christianity is so bold as to claim that in Christ we can become God's friends, because only Christianity offers a God who becomes man, a Good Shepherd who becomes a lamb in order to win the hearts of his sheep:

I shall not call you servants any more, because a servant does not know his master's business; I call you friends, because I have made known to you everything I have learnt from my Father. (Jn 15:15)

---

1. This definition of prayer—as an ongoing relationship—doesn't eliminate the need for particular times dedicated to conversing exclusively with God. There's no better way to make a relationship grow cold than by not spending quality time together. As the *Catechism* puts it, "We cannot pray 'at all times' if we do not pray at specific times, consciously willing it" (2697).

True Christian prayer, therefore, is Christ-centered prayer. Above all, it consists in contemplating and conversing with Christ, the "one Mediator" between man and God (1 Tim 2:5). In prayer you sit at the feet of the Master, listening, learning, and loving. Prayer comes before action; the active life, for a Christian, overflows from the contemplative life. Christ taught this clearly when he gently reprimanded the busy and active Martha for resenting her sister Mary's preference for the better part.[2]

CHRISTIAN PRAYER: INTENSELY PERSONAL But Christian prayer is also intensely personal. This friendship that God has struck up with you is unique because you are unique. Christ is not an abstract concept; he is a real person. Your friendship with him will be different than mine because your life experience, your personality, your problems and talents and worries and dreams are different from mine, and all those things go into a friendship.

In prayer, the Good Shepherd calls his sheep individually: "One by one he calls his own sheep and leads them out. When he has brought out his flock, he goes ahead of them, and the sheep follow because they know his voice" (Jn 10:3-4).

Prayer is Christ speaking to you in your heart, revealing himself to you in accordance with what he knows you need to discover, to know, to see. At the same time, prayer is your attentive listening to that revelation, your response to what he reveals, and the trusting, reciprocal revelation of your heart—your needs, your hopes, your desires—to him.

In this mysterious, beautiful exchange, the Holy Spirit is the bridge between Christ's heart and yours: "Now instead of the spirit of the world, we have received the Spirit that comes from God, to teach us to understand the gifts that he has given us" (1 Cor 2:12). The Holy Spirit guides you from within, into the arms of Christ, the Good Shepherd of your soul.

If you want to continue to discover and follow God's path for your life, this intensely personal prayer is a necessary element in your spiritual life. While you are here on earth, God always has more he wants to reveal to you and teach you; he has more he wants to do in your soul, making it the masterpiece that he envisioned from the moment of your creation. He also has more work he wants you to do, work that will bear eternal fruit to his glory and to your temporal and everlasting happiness. All of this, however, requires that you grow closer to him, and without a deep, personal prayer life, you simply can't.

---

2 "Martha, Martha, you worry and fret about so many things, and yet few are needed, indeed only one. It is Mary who has chosen **the better part**; it is not to be taken from her" (Lk 10:42, emphasis added).

TYPES OF PRAYER

The *Catechism* points out three basic types of personal (as distinct from liturgical) prayer: vocal, meditative, and contemplative, all of which have a place in the life of every Christian.

VOCAL PRAYER Vocal prayer consists in reciting ready-made prayers, either silently or aloud, uniting the intention of your heart to the meaning of the words. This is the kind of prayer recited together before a meal, or the prayers often used each morning to offer the day to God. The words of these prayers help you express your faith, and that conscious expression in turn reinforces and exercises your faith. All Christians should have their favorite vocal prayers, the ones that resonate best with their own experience of Christ, the ones they can go back to in moments of dryness, sickness, or difficulty.

MEDITATIVE PRAYER Meditative prayer is less formulaic. It consists in lifting the heart and mind to God through focused reflection on some truth of God's revelation. It involves the intellect, the imagination, the memory, the emotions—the whole person.

In meditation, as you turn your gaze to God's self-revelation in Christ, you are moved to respond to what you discover there, and you converse with God in the silence of your own heart, using words that flow naturally from your reflection.

Reflecting on the beauty of God's creation, for example, may move your heart to expressions of gratitude, wonder, and praise. Reflecting on the sufferings of Christ during his crucifixion may move your heart to expressions of humility, repentance, or sorrow. The essence of Christian meditation is this exchange between God and the soul, this intimate conversation that can take an infinite variety of forms.

Whatever form it takes, however, meditation puts the soul in contact with the eternal truths, with the love and goodness of God in its myriad manifestations, and thus it nourishes the soul. Just as the body needs food and water, the soul feeds on truth and love. This reality is categorically ignored by today's secularized, materialistic culture, which denies the existence of moral and spiritual truth and reduces love to mere feelings. Meditative prayer, however, only makes sense in light of this reality. Your soul, your intellect, and your will yearn for the true and the good as much as your body yearns for solid food and fresh drink. "Happy are those who hunger and thirst for what is right: they shall be satisfied" (Mt 5:6).

Meditation's loving dialogue between God and you praying in Christ opens your soul to experience the highest, most nourishing truth of all: the total, transforming, unconditional love with which God himself regards you. This experience literally feeds the soul, enlivening its own capacity for love, energizing it, and inspiring it.

Meditative prayer, then, exercises the great Christian virtues of faith, hope, and love, helping the soul that has been wounded by sin, both original and personal, to rehabilitate its capacity to discover, experience, and communicate God's own truth, goodness, and beauty.

Christian meditation differs essentially from transcendental meditation and other New Age centering techniques.[3] Christian meditation is Christ-centered, a loving dialogue between Christ and the soul that deepens your friendship with Christ. It starts with the Holy Spirit urging you to pursue a greater knowledge and love of Christ, and ends with your renewed commitment to follow and imitate Christ in the unique circumstances of your daily life.

Transcendental meditation, on the other hand, is self-centered. Instead of a dialogue with God, an opening of the soul to God, it consists primarily in calming the many passions of the soul, creating a self-induced interior tranquility and focus that overflows in certain types of feelings. The goal of transcendental meditation is to withdraw from the complexities of life in order to experience emotional tranquility; the goal of Christian meditation is to know, love, and follow Jesus Christ more completely, to discover and embrace God's will for you more and more each day.

CONTEMPLATIVE PRAYER Contemplative prayer consists of a more passive (and more sublime) experience of God. If meditation is the soul's inspired quest to discover God, contemplation is God's lifting of the soul into himself, so that it effortlessly basks in the divine light. It is the soul's silent gazing upon the grandeur of God.

---

3 Some Christian spiritualities have tried to adopt so-called centering prayer techniques from non-Christian sources. Although some of these techniques can be incorporated into the first stage of the meditation (Concentrate), they are unnecessary and can often be harmful. They frequently result in becoming ends in themselves; the one praying uses them to create certain higher emotional states, as if those states were the goal of prayer. Christian prayer is interpersonal; centering prayer is really no more than a technique for calming oneself. It originated in the context of Eastern transcendental asceticism, and these techniques are ill-suited for Christian prayer. For a more complete discussion of this issue, see the Pontifical Council for Interreligious Dialogue's document from February 3, 2003, "Jesus Christ: The Bearer of the Water of Life," available on the Vatican website, www.vatican.va.

Often meditation leads to contemplation—the line of demarcation is hazy. When you find yourself lifted into silent contemplation during your meditation, there is no need to fear. The practice of Christian meditation gradually purifies the heart and familiarizes it with the voice and the ways of God, so that little by little the soul is made more docile to the promptings of God, and God can reveal himself more and more completely.

All three types of prayer—vocal, meditative, and contemplative—put the Christian in contact with the grassy pastures and refreshing waters of God's grace. They are the sure paths along which the Good Shepherd faithfully leads his sheep.

MEDITATION VS. SPIRITUAL READING

The Better Part is not a book of meditations. Sometimes following ready-made meditations[4] is an excellent way to pray. The structure helps you stay focused, the content is sure to be healthy, and the easy access motivates you to keep up a regular prayer life. But ready-made meditations also have a disadvantage. They can become nothing more than spiritual reading.

Spiritual reading refers to reading texts—books, articles, homilies, essays—that teach you about the spiritual life; it's like taking a class from whoever wrote the book. It enlightens your conscience by helping you see yourself and the world around you from a Christian perspective. As such, it is an essential ingredient for growth as a Christian. Just as historians are always reading about history, and teachers are always informing themselves about developments in pedagogy, so Christians should constantly be refining and expanding their understanding of how to be a follower of Christ.[5]

Christian meditation also involves an effort to better understand Christ and the Christian life, and so it often yields results similar to those of spiritual reading, especially for beginners in the spiritual life. Primarily, though, meditation is a matter of the heart more than the intellect; it's like taking a leisurely walk with Christ, your friend.

The focused reflection at the core of meditation opens the soul to hear not an abstract truth about the Christian life, but a particular word that God, the

---

4 Like those published daily through the Regnum Christi website, www.regnumchristi.org.

5 Regnum Christi members' daily Gospel Reflection falls into this category of spiritual reading. It keeps you constantly in touch with Christ's criteria and example, so that throughout the day you can keep aligning your thoughts, attitudes, and actions with Christ's. It's like rebooting your computer—it clears away the interior clutter that accumulates during the day.

Good Shepherd, wishes to speak to you in the unique here and now of your life. When you tune into this word, this truth, this message from the Holy Spirit, your heart is drawn to stay with it, to consider it, to savor it. Savoring it in turn stirs your heart to express itself and give voice to your most intimate, personal yearnings, hopes, affections, or needs. In this conversation, you are actually exercising the Christian virtues of faith, hope, and love; you are exercising your friendship. In spiritual reading, you are learning, you are gaining knowledge. Both spiritual reading and meditation are useful—indeed, both are necessary for a healthy spiritual life—but it's important not to confuse them.

Although ready-made meditations have many advantages, they also have the disadvantage of easily morphing into spiritual reading. You lead a busy life with little time to prepare your daily meditation. You have committed to doing it, though, so you faithfully gather the daily meditation from the website and read it over in between errands or before speeding off to work. It keeps you in touch with spiritual things, and gives you new insights or renews old ones, but because it's a complete, self-contained meditation, you easily slip into the spiritual-reading mode: instead of using the points of reflection as springboards for focused personal reflection, attentive listening to the Holy Spirit, and intimate, heart-to-heart conversation with Christ, you simply read, understand, agree, and move on.

Spiritual reading is valuable; it will help you grow closer to Christ. The Lord is happy that you make time for him. And yet, unless you learn to go deeper, to personalize your prayer more, you will limit your growth in virtue. God wants to make you into the saint he created you to be, but that requires a more personal, heart-to-heart prayer life. He wants to give you that grace, but he needs you to give him the chance.

The Better Part is a resource designed to help your personal prayer time become more personalized, increasingly deeper, and more transforming. Instead of offering ready-made meditations, it provides a structure for meditation along with Christ-centered commentaries that are more open-ended, more flexible, more personalized than complete meditations.

THE 4-STEP STRUCTURE OF YOUR MEDITATION

AN OVERVIEW Perhaps you are already familiar with the general meditation structure recommended in *The Better Part*. Drawn from the long-lasting and fruitful traditions of Ignatian and Carmelite spirituality, it follows four steps: *Concentrate, Consider, Converse,* and *Commit.*

Sometimes a meditation flows easily, following these steps one after another without a hitch. Other times tiredness, distractions, or temptations plague you so persistently that each step demands a heroic effort. Still other times, the steps blend together and your conversation with God happens almost spontaneously. This shows that the four-step method of meditation is not an end in itself, nor is it an arbitrary concoction. Rather, this method sets out the basic elements of any heart-to-heart conversation with God, as gleaned from experience and theology. In so doing, it provides a dependable framework for your personal encounter with God in spite of the persistent and sometimes almost overwhelming obstacles to prayer that surface.

At first you may find it awkward to follow the steps. You may feel tempted to fall back into the less demanding pattern of spiritual reading, but as your prayer life deepens, this simple structure becomes second nature. When kids first learn to play basketball, they have to master the basic skills—dribbling, shooting, passing—one at a time. As they improve, they develop the ability to combine these fundamentals into a smooth, seamless whole. Eventually they are free to really play. Assimilating the structure of your meditation happens a lot like that.

MAKING PROGRESS Keep in mind that growth in the spiritual life and in prayer takes time and consistent effort. Sometimes you may feel that you are making great progress; then suddenly you seem to have a relapse. Other times you may feel that you are making no progress at all, and then unexpectedly spring forward.

This isn't because God whimsically comes and goes. Rather, he is mysteriously guiding you through a gradual purification of the selfish tendencies deeply embedded in your soul. Points of view, emotional patterns, mental landscapes—all of these, because of original and personal sin, are shot through with myriad forms of self-centeredness that clog the flow of God's grace. Thus, learning to pray better is like turning a wild, overgrown plot of rocky ground into an ordered, fragrant, beautiful garden—God supplies the sunshine, the water, and the soil, but you still have to dig and plant and prune, and then keep on digging and planting and pruning. Think of the four steps of the meditation as your gardening tools.

Understanding the reasons behind each step will help you follow them more peacefully and fruitfully. These steps can also be useful reference points as you discuss your prayer life during spiritual direction. A clear idea of these elements will make your ongoing reading about prayer more fruitful as well. Remember, every Christian should steadily strive to become an expert in prayer, since prayer is that "vital and personal relationship with the living and true God" (CCC, 2558)—the relationship which gives life itself and all of life's components their deepest, most authentic, and most satisfying meaning. Below is an explanation of each step. After the explanation you will find the full text of a real, sample meditation with all the steps identified.

STEP 1: CONCENTRATE

1. This involves drawing your attention away from the exterior activities and practical concerns that tend to monopolize your thoughts, and turning your attention to God, who is already paying full attention to you. You refresh your awareness of God's presence, which tends to be drowned out by the din of the daily grind.

2. Useful in this step are the traditional preparatory acts of faith, hope, and love, wherein you lift your heart and mind to God, tuning your attention to God's wavelength. You can use ready-made texts for your preparatory acts, compose your own, voice them spontaneously, or combine all three methods. *The Better Part* provides some sample preparatory acts. The morning prayers from your prayer book can make for good preparatory acts as well.

3. The most important part of this step is not the actual words you use. Rather, you need to remind yourself of the truths that underlie your relationship with God, reviving your most basic Christian attitudes. The goal of this step is fourfold:

    • Recall that God is truly present, listening to you, paying attention. Remember that God is all-powerful, all-wise, all-loving, and that he knows you intimately and cares for you more than you care for yourself. He deserves your praise, your attention, and your time.

    • Recall that God has something he wants to say to you. He has a word for you today. He knows what you are struggling with, in the short term and the long; he knows what the day will have in store for you; he knows the path he has marked out for your growth in happiness and holiness. He is going to work in your soul while you pray, whether you feel anything or not. Remember, your daily meditation isn't just your idea, it is a prayer commitment linked with your particular vocation in the Church, and your vocation comes from God. You know without a doubt that God has something to say to you during this time because he made the appointment.

    • Recall that you need to hear that word. You are dependent on God for everything, starting with your existence. You have failed and

sinned many times; the duties and mission you have in life are beyond your own natural capabilities; you are surrounded by morally
and spiritually corrupting influences, by a variety of temptations.
In short, you are a dependent, created being damaged by sin: you
need God's grace.

- Renew your desire to hear that word. You want to follow him. You
  believe that he is the Lord, your Savior, your Friend, and your Guide.
  You have committed your life to him; you have put your trust in
  him.

4. In this context, part of your concentration will consist in asking God for
   the grace you feel you most need, in accordance with your program of
   spiritual work. Sometimes this is called the petition or the fruit of the
   meditation. Asking God for this grace brings all those basic attitudes
   into play. At the same time, however, you leave the reins in his hands,
   knowing that he will guide you in hidden ways to the rich pastures he
   has in store for you.

5. Whether you use your favorite traditional acts of faith, hope, and love to
   achieve this concentration matters less than simply achieving it. Sometimes it is enough to call to mind your favorite verse or psalm from the
   Bible to activate all these sentiments; sometimes it's enough to remember
   the beauties of nature or one of your most powerful experiences of God.

6. As the weeks and months pass by, you may need to vary the way you
   concentrate, in order to avoid falling into a dry routine where you say
   all the right words, but in fact fail to turn your heart and mind to God.
   Without that, without concentrating on God, it will be nearly impossible for you to really enter into conversation with him and hear what he
   wants to tell you—your prayer will turn into a self-centered monologue
   or an empty, wordy shell.

7. At times these preparatory acts may launch you directly into a heart-to-
   heart conversation with the Lord, bypassing Step 2, Consider. When this
   happens, don't feel obliged to backtrack; the material of your preparatory
   acts has provided the Holy Spirit with all he needed to lift you right into
   Step 3, Converse.

8. Concentrating on God doesn't mean ignoring the realities of your life.
   Your worries and concerns and yearnings and dreams and challenges
   should all enter into your meditation. But they come into play within
   the context of your heart-to-heart conversation with the God who loves
   you. This is the difference between simply worrying and actually praying about something. When you sit down to have a cup of coffee with a

close friend, your worries and dreams don't disappear, but they fall into line behind the attention you give to your friend, and the attention your friend gives to you.

9. Related to Step 1 is your choice of time and place for your daily meditation. These factors affect your ability to Concentrate.

   • The time. Most spiritual writers agree that doing your meditation in the morning helps imbue your coming day's activities with their true Christian meaning. Your mind is fresh, so it's easier to focus. And a morning meditation can give unity and direction to your daily duties by reminding you of your life's mission (to know, love, and follow Christ) and preparing you to meet the day's unexpected (or expected) challenges. With a little effort and creativity, you can usually make room for the morning meditation, whether it's ten, fifteen, twenty minutes, or even half an hour. (If you have any doubts about the proper length of your daily meditation, you should discuss them with a confessor or spiritual director.) If the morning is simply impossible, try to find some space in your day when you know you won't be interrupted — a time when you will be able to give your best to your prayer. Use the same time slot each day as much as possible. Try not to just squeeze it in; give your best time to God.

   • The place. Where you do your meditation should be out of range of interruptions and conducive to your conversation with God. Some people prefer their church or a chapel with the Blessed Sacrament; others prefer a particular room at home. Here again creativity and practical convenience come into play. A businessman in Boston stops at a cemetery on his way to work and does his meditation walking among the tombs and monuments (during the summer) — it's the only place where he can consistently dodge interruptions. Avoid changing places frequently in a vain search for the perfect atmosphere. The place doesn't make the prayer; it is only a means to help.

   • On special days or during certain periods (e.g., vacation, Holy Week), you may find it helpful to change your normal place and time of prayer. Temporary, planned changes can keep you from falling into a dull routine.

10. If you habitually find it hard to concentrate at the start of your meditation, check on the status of your remote and proximate preparation. These terms refer to what you do outside of your meditation that affects what happens during your meditation.

- Remote preparation. You don't meditate in a vacuum. The more you live in God's presence during the rest of the day, seeking his will and finding other times here and there to pray (vocal prayers, the Rosary, examination of conscience), the easier it will be for you to turn your heart and soul to God at the start of the meditation. This is your remote preparation.
- Proximate preparation. You will also avoid a plethora of distractions if you get your meditation materials (the book you will be using, your notebook or journal for writing down thoughts) ready the night before. You can even briefly look over the passage you will be meditating on before you go to bed; this, too, primes the prayer-pump. This is your proximate preparation.

11. Jesus himself explained the step of concentrating simply and vividly: "When you pray, go to your private room and, when you have shut your door, pray to your Father who is in that secret place, and your Father who sees all that is done in secret will reward you" (Mt 6:6). The prophet Elijah discovered this truth when the Lord spoke to him on the mountain:

> Then the Lord himself went by. There came a mighty wind, so strong it tore the mountains and shattered the rocks before the Lord. But the Lord was not in the wind. After the wind came an earthquake. But the Lord was not in the earthquake. After the earthquake came a fire. But the Lord was not in the fire. And after the fire there came the sound of a gentle breeze. (1 Kgs 19:11-12)

12. Concentrate, the first step of your meditation, involves shutting the door on the storms and tumult of daily life for a time, so that you can hear the Lord's still, small voice that whispers in your heart like a gentle breeze.

STEP 2: CONSIDER

1. With life's hustle and bustle in its proper place, you are ready to listen to God's message for you today. Here you take time for focused reflection on God's words, usually as they are found in Scripture—although you can also turn to other spiritual writings, the works of the saints, Church documents, and even sacred art as texts for consideration. Gradually, with the help of your confessor or spiritual director, you will find the kind of material that helps you most, in accordance with your program of spiritual work.

2. During this stage, you slowly and thoughtfully read the text you will be meditating on. You reflect on it, you examine it, you dig into it. You read it again, searching to discover what God is saying to you through it in the here and now of your life. You exercise your whole mind: intellect, imagination, and memory. You involve your emotions, relating the passage to your own life experience.

3. This type of meditative consideration differs from study. The goal of meditation is not necessarily to learn new truths, but to give God a chance to make the truths you need most sink deeper into your mind and heart. Considering a truth involves understanding it more clearly, more deeply. But it also involves savoring it, gazing upon it, basking in it.

4. This step poses a challenge for victims of the media age. The human mind is capable of wonder, contemplation, and reflection, but when the principle source of information is mass media, these capacities can atrophy. Mass media stimulates the surface of the mind, but the constant, rapid flow of images and information militates against going deep. Meditation provides a respite from frenzied mental stimulation and gives the soul a chance to simply love and be loved in the intimacy of a spiritual embrace.

5. Just as it takes the body time to digest food and benefit from its nutrients, so the soul needs time to take in and assimilate the healing, enlightening, and strengthening truths God has revealed through Christ's gospel. Just as it takes long hours in the sun for plants to photosynthesize so they can grow and flourish, so the soul needs extended exposure to the light of Christ in order for God's grace to purify, enliven, and heal it.

6. God knows which truths you need to dwell on; part of the Consider stage is searching for them. God speaks most often in whispers, not storms, and so you have to move forward in your meditation calmly, gently, hunting for the insight God wishes to give you. This is one of the most mysterious aspects of meditation. Christ the Good Shepherd guides you toward the rich pastures and refreshing waters of his truth and grace, sometimes along an easy path and other times along a steep and difficult path. For each day when it is easy to find and savor God's word for you, there is another day when your meditation seems to entail nothing but work.

7. This exercise of seeking out where God is speaking to your soul turns Christian meditation into a quest: "Meditation is a prayerful quest engaging thought, imagination, emotion, and desire" (CCC, 2723). Usually, as you read and reflect on the subject of your meditation, you can detect where the Holy Spirit wants you to stop and consider simply by the reaction of your heart.

8. In a garden full of beautiful flowers and plants, you stay longer in front of one because you find that its beauty resonates more deeply with you. In a gallery of magnificent works of art, you are drawn to one or two of them more powerfully because they have something to say to you, in the here and now of your life, that the others don't. Likewise with meditation. If you have done your best to focus the powers of your soul on God in the Concentrate step, as you begin to Consider the material for your meditation, one or two things will catch your attention; they will jump out at you, as if they were highlighted. It may be a phrase in the actual text, or an idea that comes to your mind. That highlight is the guiding hand of the Good Shepherd. Thus the Holy Spirit gently leads you to the spiritual food your soul needs most.

9. If nothing strikes you right away, you can intensify your consideration by asking questions.
    - For instance, if you are considering a passage from the Gospel, you can enter into the scene by asking basic, journalistic questions: Who is here? What are they feeling, doing and saying? When is this event taking place? Where is it happening and what does everything look like? Why is it happening in this way? How is each person reacting? As you enter more deeply into the living Word of God, the Holy Spirit will guide your mind and heart to the point he wants you to consider. When you find it, savor it.
    - Another approach uses less imagination and more reason. You can begin to consider the material of your meditation by asking analytical questions: What strikes me about this passage? What does this mean? What does it tell me about Christ, the Church, the meaning of life? And after having looked at it in the abstract, make it personal—What does it mean for me? What is Christ saying to me in the here and now of my life? How is this truth relevant to my own struggles, my own mission and vocation, my own program of spiritual work, my own friendship with Christ, and my own journey of faith?

10. It may take almost the whole time you have set aside for meditation to discover the point God wants you to consider. This is not a cause for discouragement or frustration: during the search, the quest, you are exercising all of the Christian virtues—faith in God, hope in his goodness, love for him, humility, and trust. The more difficult the search, the more these virtues are being exercised; the Holy Spirit is giving you a vigorous spiritual workout. God knows just what you need and how to guide you; he is the Good Shepherd.

11. Sometimes you never seem to find the highlights at all. In these cases, too, God is at work. Never doubt his active presence. When the material you have set aside for consideration doesn't yield any insights worth savoring, you can feel free to turn to your favorite biblical images, your favorite vocal prayers, or your favorite verses — go back to the waters and pastures that have nourished you in the past. All mature Christians gradually discover certain truths of the gospel that can always provide food for their souls.

12. At times you may find so many highlights that you feel overwhelmed. Stay calm. Don't rush. Take one flower, one painting, one highlight at a time and exhaust it, delight in it until your heart is saturated. Only then move on to the next highlight. As long as your consideration continues to move your heart, stay with that point, like a bee extracting nectar from a blossom. Never move on just because you feel like you're supposed to. Prayer is a personal conversation, not a generic connect-the-dots operation.

STEP 3: CONVERSE

1. Precisely because Christian prayer is interpersonal, your consideration of the truths of Christ, your basking in his light, is never only passive. In an embrace, both people receive and both people give. In the embrace of prayer, you receive the truth and grace of God's revelation, and you give your personal response. As soon as the truth you are considering touches your heart, it will stir a response. This is the heart of your meditation.

2. If you are considering the wonders of God's creation, you may be moved to respond with words or sentiments of praise: How great you are, my God! How beautiful you must be if your creation is this awe-inspiring....

3. If you are considering God's mercy, you may be moved to respond with contrition, remorse, and sorrow for your sins: You are so good and generous, so patient; why, Lord, am I so slow to trust you, why am I so selfish? Forgive me, Lord; a thousand times, please forgive me; I know you have, you do, and you will, but still I ask you to forgive me; I am sorry....

4. If you are considering some of the many gifts he has given you, like your faith, your family, or the Eucharist, you may be moved to express gratitude: Thank you, Father, from the bottom of my heart; I really mean it, thank you. Thank you for giving me life, and for showing me the meaning of life, and for saving me from so many dangers, so many sins....

5. Whatever you may be considering, sooner or later, like a child in the presence of his benevolent and powerful father, you will probably find

yourself asking for good things from God: O my Lord, how I want to love as you love! How I need your grace to be patient, to see the good side of others and not just the negative. Please teach me to do your will, to be your true disciple.... This asking can also take the form of confusion and complaint, as happens so often in the Book of Psalms: Why, my God, have you forsaken me? Why do you let these things happen? Lord, I don't understand; teach me, enlighten me. Help me to go where you want me to go, because right now I don't feel like going there....

6. As your consideration gives rise to these responses, the response will naturally come to a close and give way to a new consideration, and you will find yourself turning back to the meditation material. You may look again at the same highlight you just considered, or you may move on to something else, until a new consideration sparks a new response and a new topic of conversation. This exchange—this ongoing conversation in which you reflect on God's revelation and respond in your heart, with your own words—is the essence of Christian meditation. This is usually where the soul comes into its most intimate contact with Christ through the action of the Holy Spirit. Consideration is never enough; it must stir the heart to Converse with God.

7. During your meditation, then, you may often find yourself going back and forth between Steps 2 and 3, Consider and Converse. Just because you have considered one point and conversed with Christ about it doesn't mean you can't go back and consider it again from another angle, or consider another point, and then converse about that. The conversation is two-way; you move back and forth between considering (listening) and responding, as much or as little as the Holy Spirit leads you.

8. Sometimes your response will be a torrent of words—so many that they tumble over each other as you struggle to express all that's in your heart. Other times you may find yourself simply repeating a short phrase, or even one word, and it says everything: Lord... Jesus.... Sometimes, like the famous peasant of Ars, you will simply find yourself held by God's gaze and gazing back, and words, even in the silence of your heart, will be unnecessary. Whatever its specific form, this third step of your meditation, Converse, consists in letting down the guard around your heart, so that God's word for you today penetrates, regenerates, and inflames the most secret depths of who you are.

9. In this step of the meditation, you may also feel moved to converse with the saints and angels or the Blessed Virgin Mary, speaking with them

about Christ, whom they know much better than you do, contemplating their example of fidelity to Christ, and asking for their intercession.

STEP 4: COMMIT

1. Toward the end of your meditation, it will be time for you to draw this heart-to-heart conversation to a close. There is a need to bring all the sentiments together, to wrap things up. Before you step back into life's hectic activity, you need to renew your commitment to the mission God has given you. In your prayer he has renewed his call, and now you renew your answer, accepting once again the life-project that gives meaning to your existence—that of following him, of imitating Christ by your fidelity to God's will in the big things as well as the small.

2. Usually this desire to renew your adherence to God's will flows naturally and easily out of the consideration and conversation stages. The renewal and deepening of your commitment to Christ and his Kingdom, whether or not it is accompanied by intense feelings, is actually a prayer of adoration, worship, and love: You know how weak I am, my Lord, but you also know how much I want to follow you. You have planted that desire in my heart: I am yours, Lord. Wherever I go, whatever happens, I belong to you. I never want to be separated from you. As hard as it is, I want to do your will because you are God, my Creator and Redeemer, my Father and my faithful Friend. Thy will be done in my life today, Lord; thy Kingdom come.

3. You may even find yourself responding to your considerations with acts of adoration similar to those during the Converse stage of the meditation—this is fine. It doesn't mean you have to end your meditation right then. If you have time, you can go back and continue the Consider step, or converse with other responses, like praise and gratitude. Then, at the end of the time you have set aside to meditate, you can return to this adoration, to this Commit step.[6]

4. If you can link this recommitment to the concrete tasks of your day, all the better. Most often, the daily meditation has followed themes connected to your program of spiritual work. In that case, you can recommit to following your program, or one particular point of your program, as a specific way of expressing your love for Christ. Sometimes, however, the Holy Spirit will nudge you toward a specific act of charity (i.e.,

---

8 In both the Converse and the Commit steps, then, you find the traditional types, the traditional goals of prayer: Praise, Adoration, Sorrow, Thanksgiving, and Asking—P.A.S.T.A.

visit your colleague who's in the hospital), or of self-governance (i.e., call your brother and apologize)—this, too, can give substance to your recommitment.

5. The meditation itself has glorified God and nourished your soul, regardless of any specific resolution you make in Step 4. The lifeblood of the meditation is your heart-to-heart conversation with the Lord, a conversation that puts you in contact with God and his grace, gradually transforming you into a mature Christian. You have deepened your friendship with Christ through spending this time with him. A new specific resolution may be an appropriate way to express this friendship at the end of the conversation, but often its most sincere expression is simply a renewal of your commitment to Christ and his Kingdom, to the points of spiritual and apostolic work already on your agenda, and to the everyday tasks that are his will for you.

6. This fourth step is the bridge between prayer and action. If you are working on being more courageous about sharing your faith with your coworkers, you may finish your meditation by a commitment to put forth in a natural way the Christian point of view in today's conversations around the water cooler. If God has been leading you toward being a better spouse, you may renew your commitment to Christ by promising to avoid today that particular thing that you know really bothers your wife or husband. If you have been neglecting your prayer life, you may commit to giving your best attention to your daily Rosary in the evening. The specific form your recommitment takes will depend on the overall direction of your spiritual life. It doesn't have to be anything new (although it may be); it just has to be true.

7. Finish up your meditation by renewing your commitment to Christ in your own words. Then take a few moments to write down the lights God sent you during the meditation and thank him for them. Briefly go over how the meditation went. Did you follow the steps? Did anything in particular help you? Was there anything that hindered you? This brief analysis will help you get to know better each day what kind of pray-er you are, so that you can apply this knowledge in subsequent meditations, gradually learning to pray as God created you to pray.

8. It often helps to conclude your meditation with a short vocal prayer like the Our Father, the Hail Mary, the Anima Christi, or another favorite prayer of your own. *The Better Part* provides some possibilities at the end of Part I.

Concentrate, Consider, Converse, and *Commit.* These are the four elements of a Christian meditation. The many books and manuals of prayer that enrich our Christian heritage offer numerous aids to meditation, and you should familiarize yourself with them and take advantage of them, but in the end, the methods and aids all tie in to these four steps of prayer. This tried-and-true structure will give God more room to work in your soul than he would have if you only dedicated yourself to vocal prayer and spiritual reading.

DIFFICULTIES IN PRAYER

You will always face difficulties in prayer. Just accept it. The saints all experienced it, the *Catechism* teaches it, and theology confirms it. The difficulties stem from two sources—two unique qualities of your friendship with Christ.

1. First, this friendship is mediated by faith. You can't just call Jesus on the phone, as you can with your other friends. He is always with you, but your awareness of and access to his presence passes through faith. Faith is a virtue, which means that it can be more or less developed. The less developed it is, the more effort it takes to activate your awareness of God's presence. Many modern Christians have an underdeveloped faith. They have been unwittingly contaminated by the consumer culture's veneration for quantifiable evidence ("I won't believe it unless a scientific study proves it") and its elevation of feelings over reason ("I don't feel in love anymore, so why should I stay married?")—both of which weaken faith. A scrawny faith often makes Jesus look fuzzy and seem distant, just as the sun seems weak and irrelevant when you're wearing dark glasses. Your ability to pray will suffer the consequences. Have you ever noticed how hard it is to be distracted when you watch a good movie? Effortlessly you pay perfect attention to a complex story for two hours. Contrast that with what typically happens during your fifteen minutes of meditation. What's the difference? Contact with God takes faith, "going as we do by faith and not by sight" (2 Cor 5:7). It takes the effort of "all your heart, soul, mind, and strength" (Mk 12:30) to align your fallen nature (which tends to seek fulfillment in the things of this earth) with the sublime truths that God has revealed through the teachings of the Church.

2. Your friendship with Christ is unique not only by its mediation through faith, but also because the two friends are not equals. Christ is not just your friend; he is also your Creator, your Redeemer, and your Lord; he

is all-wise and all-loving, and he's trying to lead you along the steep and narrow path of Christian maturity. So, on your part, your relationship with him requires docility. But docility demands self-denial, which rubs your concupiscence the wrong way. Remember, baptism gave you back God's grace, but it didn't take away your deep-seated tendencies to selfishness (arrogance, independence, vanity, laziness, anger, lust, greed, etc.) that you inherited from original sin. Because of them, docility chafes. Sometimes the Good Shepherd leads you where you would rather not go, or pushes you farther along when you would prefer to sit back and relax, or doesn't let you drink from a stream that looks fine to you. This divergence of wills makes prayer a constant battle.

SLOTH AND DISTRACTIONS The difficulties flowing from this need for faith and docility come in two basic varieties: sloth and distractions.

Sloth is spiritual laziness, distaste, and sluggishness in cultivating your relationship with God: I can't pray before I go to work because I need that extra few minutes of sleep; I can't go on a retreat, since the playoffs start this weekend and I really want to watch them; I know I committed to begin praying the Rosary again, but I just don't feel like it, I have so much else to do.... Anything but spend time attending to the most important thing: your "vital and personal relationship with the living and true God"(CCC, 2558)—in other words, your life of prayer. That's sloth.

In the meditation itself, sloth can tempt you in numerous ways: procrastinating (I'll do it later; I'll start meditating tomorrow), not getting your material ready ahead of time, giving in to tiredness, rushing through your preparatory acts instead of really concentrating, simply reading for most of the time instead of really engaging in the quest to consider and converse, or finishing with a vague and half-hearted commitment that really has no practical effect at all in your daily life or the pursuit of spiritual maturity. In these and many other ways, sloth slyly undermines the life of prayer.

Sloth drains energy from your spiritual life; distractions, on the other hand, steer that energy away from God. You go to Mass and sincerely want to worship God, but can't take your eyes off that family in the front pew that's making such a ruckus (or maybe you're part of that family); you pray the Rosary every day, but halfway through you realize that you have no idea which decade you're on because you're thinking about the budget presentation you have to make on Tuesday; you desperately try to spend some time every day in personal prayer, in Christian meditation, but you end up thinking about everything except God—family worries, upcoming engagements, temptations, pending bills and phone calls, job interviews, billboards, news stories.... They all violently and unremittingly claw at your attention as soon as you try to quiet your soul and attend to the Lord (more often than not, the devil has a hand in this). And sometimes when you pray, you're just plain bored. Welcome to the world of distractions.

SOLVING THE DIFFICULTIES The best defense against sloth and distractions is a good offense. Following a sound and simple meditation method like the one outlined above both flushes these temptations out of hiding—since you know clearly what you should be doing during your meditation, you catch yourself more easily as soon as you stop doing that—and also gives you a rudder and a lighthouse to navigate through their ambushes. But the method won't resolve the difficulties all by itself. You still have to steer the rudder and look to the lighthouse.

Temptations to sloth or distractions don't damage your prayer life—only giving in to temptations does that. In fact, each temptation is permitted by God because it gives you a chance for spiritual growth.

Take for example a temptation to slothfulness. The alarm clock goes off. Bleary-eyed, I wake up, and the last thing I feel like doing is getting up to pray. If I cut out my fifteen-minute meditation, I can have fifteen minutes more sleep. How sweet that sounds! But wait a minute, why did I set my alarm to get up fifteen minutes earlier than I actually need to? Because I made a commitment; I resolved to start out my day with God because he is the purpose of my life and deserves my praise and because I need his grace. A crisis of the heart has arisen: my feelings and habits of self-indulgence (egged on by the devil) tell me to hit the snooze button, roll over, and doze off again; my faith (animated by my guardian angel) tells me to turn off the alarm, throw back those cozy covers, touch my bare feet down on that cold tile floor, and keep my appointment with God.

If God wanted to, he could resolve the crisis for me: he could push me out of bed, or make the bed disappear, or give me good feelings about prayer and bad feelings about staying in bed. But he doesn't, at least not usually. Rather, he leaves it up to me, nudging my conscience perhaps, but not forcing me either way. Here is where I can exercise the virtues of faith and docility, and in exercising them, strengthen them.

Distractions work the same way. I'm in the Blessed Sacrament chapel doing my daily meditation. Someone else comes through the door and enters the silent, sacred space. He takes a seat not too far away. I can't help noticing that he's wearing brand-new tennis shoes. Are they Nikes or Reeboks? That reminds me about the marketing presentation I have to give this afternoon. My boss will be there. It's a critical account for the company.... Suddenly I realize that my mind is wandering. Up to this point, I haven't been responsible for the distraction, because I wasn't even aware of it, but now I have three options: (1) I keep thinking about the presentation. After all, a lot is hanging on it, and my meditation is a bit dry anyway. (2) I get distracted by my distraction: "There I go again. Why can't I stay focused? I always get distracted. I am such an idiotic Christian, such a hypocrite. I'm so frustrated with myself...." (3) I calmly steer my attention back to my meditation, renewing my conviction that God and his action here matter far more than fruitless worrying about my presentation (which I have already prepared anyway), and that my tendency to get distracted affords me a new opportunity to exercise my faith and docility and turn back once again to my Lord.

Will I choose 1, 2, or 3? If I choose 3, then that distraction, which the devil wants to use to distance me from God, will actually have become an instrument of God's grace, drawing me closer to him and giving him glory. God allows temptations against my communion with God in order to afford me opportunities to deepen that communion.

The more closely you try to follow the 4-step method of meditation outlined above, the more you will get to know how these ubiquitous temptations try to derail your personal prayer life in particular, and the better equipped you will be to stay on track, using them to build up the virtues of faith and docility and become the pray-er God wants you to be.

HOW DO I KNOW IF I'M PRAYING WELL? We all tend to measure our prayer by our feelings: I prayed well if I felt God's presence, if I felt an emotional thrill. That's not the way to evaluate your prayer. Your relationship with Christ is a deep friendship built on faith and love. It goes much deeper than feelings. Feelings and emotions change with the weather, with our biorhythms, with our circumstances—they are often unpredictable and always undependable. Any friendship built on feelings, therefore, is doomed to frustration and failure. Mature Christians don't seek feelings or emotional states in their prayer. If God provides good feelings too, great, but the sincere Christian is after Christ: praising him, knowing him better, discovering what he wants, and renewing and deepening the decision to imitate him and follow him in the nitty-gritty of daily life, no matter the cost. Feelings are frills, but Christ is the core.

The fruit of a healthy prayer life takes time to grow and mature. Ultimately, it shows itself by growth in virtue, as you become more like Christ. Gradually, you grow in self-governance (controlling and channeling your instincts, passions, and basic human desires), prudence (seeing clearly what ought to be done in any particular situation and doing it), love (seeing others as Christ sees them and being able to sacrifice your own preferences for their sake), fortitude (taking on challenging tasks or projects for the sake of Christ's Kingdom, and persevering through difficulties, obstacles, and opposition), and wisdom (detecting and relishing God's presence in all things and circumstances). Growth in these virtues takes place gradually, almost imperceptibly, on a day-to-day basis, just as a child slowly but surely grows into adulthood, or as plants mature in a garden. Meditation supplies much of the spiritual nutrients that cause these virtues to grow.

On any given day, then, measuring whether your meditation went well or badly is not so easy. Your meditation may have been quite pleasing to God and full of grace for your soul even when it was unpleasant and difficult from a strictly emotional perspective. An athlete may have a great practice session even though it was painful and frustrating—likewise with a daily meditation.

You'll find some helpful indicators below. The most important thing, though, is simply to keep striving to pray better. Speak about your prayer life in spiritual direction and confession, and trust that if you are sincerely doing your best, the Holy Spirit will do the rest.

My meditation went badly when I ...

- Didn't plan ahead regarding what material I would use, when and where I would meditate, making sure to turn off my cell phone, etc.
- Simply gave in to the many distractions that vied for my attention
- Let myself fall asleep
- Skipped over the first step, Concentrate, or did it sloppily; how can my prayer go well if I am not keenly aware of God's presence?
- Didn't humbly ask God to help me and to give me whatever graces I need to continue growing in my spiritual life
- Spent the whole time reading, thinking, or daydreaming; didn't stop to ask what God was saying to me and then respond from my heart
- Tried to stir up warm, fuzzy feelings and intense emotions instead of conversing heart-to-heart on the level of faith
- Didn't renew my commitment to Christ and his Kingdom at the end of the meditation
- Shortened the time I had committed to without a really important reason

My meditation went well when I ...

- Actually fulfilled the commitment I made to spend a certain amount of time in meditation every day

- Faithfully followed the methodology in spite of tiredness, distractions, dryness, or any other difficulty (or if it was impossible to follow the four-step method, did my best to give praise to God in whatever way I could throughout my meditation time)
- Stayed with the points of consideration that struck me most as long as I found material there for reflection and conversation
- Sought only to know and love Christ better, so as to be able to follow him better
- Made sure to speak to Christ from my heart about whatever I was meditating on (or whatever was most on my heart), even when it was hard to find the words
- Was completely honest in my conversation—I didn't say things to God just out of routine or because I wanted to impress him with my eloquence; I told him what was really in my heart
- Made a sincere effort to listen to what God was saying to me throughout the time of prayer, seeking applications for my own life, circumstances, needs, and challenges
- Finished the meditation more firmly convinced of God's goodness and more firmly committed to doing my best to follow him faithfully

A SAMPLE MEDITATION

The paragraphs below are adapted from a meditation directed by Father Anthony Bannon, LC, and taken with permission from www.vocation.com. Although everyone prays a little bit differently from everyone else, reading through a real meditation from start to finish can help these ideas come into focus. Comments are included in italics.

STEP 1: CONCENTRATE *I come into the place where I will be meditating. I remind myself that God is truly present, here and everywhere, that he is watching over me and listening to me, eager to spend this time together; he sees into the depths of my heart. Then I kneel or sit, make the Sign of the Cross, and address him.*

I thank you, Father, for the immense love you showed me in creating me and redeeming me, giving me this time with you, spending this time with me, intervening in my life. I know you have something to say to me today. I want to hear it; I need to hear it. I want to love you in a real way, not abstractly or in theory only. I want to love you today, and not tomorrow. I want to love you here where you have placed me and not somewhere else in my dreams. I want to love you in your Church. I want to love you in the people that you place in my path.

STEP 2: CONSIDER *First, I read the Gospel passage, then I read it again, more slowly, picturing it, paying attention to whichever words jump out at me. Maybe something strikes me right away, and I stay with that, considering it and letting it lead me into a conversation with Christ.*

Gospel Passage: Matthew 13:47-50

The Kingdom of Heaven is like a dragnet that is cast into the sea and brings in a haul of all kinds of fish. When it is full, the fishermen haul it ashore. And then sitting down they collect the good ones in baskets and throw away those that are no use. This is how it will be at the end of time. The Angels will appear and separate the wicked from the upright, to throw them into the blazing furnace where there will be weeping and grinding of teeth.

Maybe one thing that strikes you after reading the passage is a consideration like the following:

Unlike the previous parables in this chapter, which described the Kingdom as already present, this one describes the Kingdom as something still to come. Jesus speaks about the relationship between this Kingdom of God and the future life at the end of time. And Jesus seems to want to get across to us one particular message. "The Kingdom is like a dragnet that is cast into the sea and brings in a haul of all kinds of fish." The end of time is just as unexpected for us as a net that drops into the water and is pulled along behind the boat is for the fish it catches. Just as sudden as that...

STEP 3: CONVERSE *After making that reflection, you may naturally find yourself wanting to converse with Christ about it, simply and sincerely, as follows, for example:*

I know and I believe that the end of the world will come, that you will judge me and everyone. And yet, I really don't think about it very much. You thought about it a lot. You often spoke about it. Lord, you know all things; you are Wisdom itself. I thank you for this reminder that the end will come. You want me to be ready. You want me to keep the end in mind. I want to too. I don't want to live like an animal, interested only in satisfying my momentary desires. No, I want to live in the light of your truth. I believe in the power of your truth. Lord Jesus, enlighten me, guide me, never stop teaching me how you want me to live.

STEP 2 AGAIN: CONSIDER *After I have had my say and spoken what is in my heart, I turn my attention back to the Lord's word to see what else he has to say to me. I have already sought material for reflection and conversation in the passage itself, and I don't seem to find any more. So now I move on to the commentary. I read one section of the commentary, which points out something I may have overlooked. It sparks another personal reflection, so I pause and consider it—what it means, what it tells me about Christ, what it means for me, how it applies to my hopes and struggles:*

Prewritten Commentary

When it is full, the fishermen haul the net ashore. Then they do the all-important thing: they sit down and start sorting out their catch. They keep the good fish and throw away the useless ones. And Jesus said, "This is the way it is going to be at the end of time. The angels will appear and separate the wicked from the upright." At the end of time, the angels won't simply check and see how God has made us, and separate us according to the qualities that God has given us. Instead, their criteria will be our own wickedness and uprightness. In other words, we will be judged according to what we have done with those things that God has given us, whether we have used them wickedly (selfishly) or uprightly.

A personal reflection sparked by that commentary could be something like this:

PERSONAL CONSIDERATION OF THE COMMENTARY What do the angels recognize in each one of those people? They recognize which ones are members of Christ's Kingdom; they see signs of that in each person's heart, each person's character, which was formed by the choices they made throughout their lifetime.

I will be one of those fish, one of those people. Will the angels recognize in me the signs of the Kingdom that Jesus has talked about in the previous parables? Will they see in me someone who searched for the fine pearl, recognized its value and beauty, and had the good sense to sell everything else in order to possess it? Will they see me as someone who recognized the treasure in the field and sold everything else in order to buy it? When the angels find me, will they recognize in me the leaven that uplifted the people around me? Will they see in me someone who spent his whole life transforming the world around him, transforming himself as he served those around him, or will they find me no different from those I should have changed? Will they find just the flat dough of the world in my life, unrisen?

STEP 3 AGAIN: CONVERSE *At some point while you consider whatever struck you in the commentary, you may find yourself wanting to respond directly to the Lord, to say something in response to what the Holy Spirit has been saying to you through your consideration. If nothing comes spontaneously, as your time for meditation draws to its close, you will need to purposely transition into a conversation. Remember, consideration only matters insofar as it draws you into a heart-to-heart conversation with God. Your response to God that emerges out of the above consideration may look something like this:*

Lord Jesus, I thank you for speaking this parable, because so often I get too caught up with the urgent cares of today and the apparent difficulty of following you. I forget that all of this will come to an end, and that you have a bigger plan in mind.

You invite me to look at what is coming in the future life, to be ready for the dragnet. You ask me to look at heaven, which is awaiting me. Lord, I can only live as your faithful disciple, as a member of your Kingdom, with the help of your grace. I can only persevere with your help. Please never let me lose sight of the hopes and expectations that you have for me—you really do have a dream for my life; this parable reminds me that you do. The greatest thing that I can do, the greatest thing I will ever see, will be the joy on your face if you can one day say to me, "Well done, good and faithful servant." Then you will be able to receive me as you want to receive me, among the upright, and bring me into the true Kingdom of heaven.

STEP 4: COMMIT *As your meditation time comes to an end, you need to recommit yourself to Christ in light of what the Holy Spirit has been showing you through your considerations and conversation. Most importantly, you want to refocus your most basic attitudes: you are a follower of Christ, and God's will is the path of your life. You can also translate that focused attitude into a concrete commitment—for example, in accordance with your program of spiritual work, or in accordance with a particular circumstance you will be facing today. You also wrap up the meditation itself, thanking God for the graces you have received and asking forgiveness for your distractions and shortcomings. For this meditation, your recommitment may look something like this:*

Jesus, you know that I want to live as a true Christian, with my sights set on your Kingdom. Whatever you ask me today, I will do, if you give me the strength I need to do it. I know I will need your strength to be patient with my coworkers, and to give myself eagerly to this tedious project at work. If I stay faithful to your will, to my conscience, and to these normal duties of my state in life, and if I live your will with love and gratitude in my heart, then I will be ready for the last day, whenever you decide to bring it along. And don't let me hide my faith in my conversation at lunch today. Jesus, they need to know you as much as I do; make me a good messenger. Thy will be done, Lord, not mine.

Thank you, Lord, for being with me in this meditation. Thank you for the good thoughts, the good affections, and the beginnings of good resolutions that you have placed in my heart. I am sorry for the moments I have been distracted, gone off on tangents, been less attentive to your presence. Grant me in some other way any graces that I might have missed. And I also pray for each one of my brothers and sisters: I pray for each one who wants to follow you. Our Father...

SOME POSSIBLE PREPARATORY AND CONCLUDING PRAYERS

PREPARATORY PRAYERS These are provided as examples and helps. Sometimes you may need help during Step 1 of your meditation, Concentrate. These small prayers express the attitudes that you need to stir up at the start of your meditation. They can also sometimes serve as material for Consider and Converse as well.

1. *ENTERING INTO GOD'S PRESENCE*

My Lord and my God, I firmly believe that you are present here and everywhere, that you are looking upon me and listening to me, and that you see into the very depths of my soul. You are my Creator, my Redeemer, and my Father. I believe in your love for me. You never take your eyes off me. You have something to say to me today. Your love for me never grows weary. You never stop drawing close to me, and drawing me closer to you.

Lord, who am I to place myself in your presence? I am a poor creature unworthy of appearing before you, and yet amid all my misery I adore you devoutly. I ask you to forgive my many sins.

Jesus, teach me to pray. Direct my prayer, so that it may rise to your throne like fragrant incense. Let all the thoughts of my spirit and my heart's inmost sentiments be directed toward serving and praising God in a perfect way. I need to hear your Word for me today, and I long to hear it. You know how much I need you, how much I want to follow you. Grant me in this prayer the grace of knowing you better, loving you more, and becoming more like you. Grant me the grace I most need.

My loving Mother Mary, my holy guardian angel, angels and saints in heaven: intercede for me so that this prayer will help me and all the other people connected to my life.

2. TRADITIONAL ACTS OF FAITH, HOPE, AND LOVE

Act of Faith

My God, I firmly believe all that you have revealed and that the Holy Church puts before us to be believed, for you are the infallible truth, who does not deceive and cannot be deceived. I expressly believe in you, the only true God in three equal and distinct persons, the Father, Son, and Holy Spirit. And I believe in Jesus Christ, Son of God, who took flesh and died for us, and who will give to each one, according to his merits, eternal reward or punishment. I always want to live in accordance with this faith. Lord, increase my faith.

Act of Hope

My God, by virtue of your promises and the merits of Jesus Christ, our Savior, I hope to receive from your goodness eternal life and the necessary grace to merit it with the good deeds I am required and propose to do. Lord, may I be able to delight in you forever.

Act of Love

My God, I love you with all my heart and above all things, because you are infinitely good and our eternal happiness; for your sake I love my neighbor as I love myself, and I forgive the offenses I have received. Lord, grant that I will love you more and more.

Petition

My God, here present now, hear and guide my prayer, and lead me to the verdant pastures and refreshing waters of your Truth and your Love.

3. ENTERING INTO GOD'S PRESENCE THROUGH ACTS OF GRATITUDE AND HUMILITY

My Lord and my God, you are infinitely kind and merciful. I thank you with all my heart for the countless gifts you have given me, especially for creating and redeeming me, for calling me to the Catholic Faith and to my vocation, and for freeing me from so many dangers of soul and body.

You have shown me the door that leads to heaven, to being one with you forever. What am I? Mere sand. And so, why have you sought me out, why have you loved me, why have you shown me that door? Why did you become flesh and leave me your Gospel? Because you love me. I want to thank you for everything you did for me, and all that you do for me. In this prayer I want to praise and glorify you.

How I need your grace! Please guide me now. Teach me to know, love, and do your will for me. I am nothing without you; I am no one without you, but I know that with you all things are possible.

4. IN THE CONTEXT OF SEEKING GOD'S WILL

My Lord and my God, you are Love itself, and the source of all love and goodness. Out of love you created me to know you, love you, and serve you in a unique way, as no one else can. I believe that you have a plan for my life, that you have a task in your Kingdom reserved just for me. Your plan and your task are far better than any other I might choose: they will glorify you, fulfill the desires of my heart, and save those souls who are depending on my generous response.

Lord, grant me the light I need to see the next step in that plan; grant me the generosity I need to set aside my own plans in favor of yours; and grant me the strength I need to put my hands to your plough and never turn back. You know me better than I know myself, so you know that I am sinful and weak. All the more reason that I need your grace to uphold the good desires you have planted in my heart, O Lord!

Make my prayer today pleasing to you. Show me your will for me, O gentle and eternal God, and help me to say with Mary, "I am the servant of the Lord; let it be done to me according to your word," and to say with Jesus, "Let not my will be done, but yours."

5. RECALLING CHRIST'S PERSONAL LOVE FOR ME

Lord, you wished to create me. I would not exist were it not for your almighty power. You created me because you love me, and I want to love you the way you have loved me. Lord, two thousand years ago mankind walked the earth in darkness, lost by the sin of our first parents. And you, in obedience to the Father and out of love for me, decided to become flesh in the Virgin's womb. You became a man so as to suffer for me, redeem me from my sins, and open the gates of heaven for me. Thank you for your love, Jesus; thank you for being born of the Blessed Virgin. Thank you, dear Mother, for saying yes to God and allowing the Second Person of the Blessed Trinity, Jesus Christ, to become man.

Lord Jesus, you are here with me now. You came into the world to teach me. You left me the path I must take to reach you and possess you forever in the Gospel. Thank you, Jesus, for such love. You truly are almighty God. I am a poor and miserable creature; and yet you loved me and continue to love me, not only in words, but with real love: love shown in works. That is why I know that you are with me now, in my heart, watching over me. Guide my prayer, Lord, cleanse my soul of all my sins and selfishness, and fill it with your light and your love. Grant me the grace I need most, because without you, I can do nothing.

6. FROM THE CHURCH'S RICH LITURGICAL TRADITION

The Te Deum

You are God: we praise you; you are the Lord: we acclaim you; you are the eternal Father: all creation worships you. To you all angels, all the powers of heaven, Cherubim and Seraphim, sing in endless praise: Holy, holy, holy, Lord, God of power and might, heaven and earth are full of your glory. The glorious company of Apostles praises you, the noble fellowship of prophets praises you, the white-robed army of martyrs praises you. Throughout the world the holy Church acclaims you: Father, of majesty unbounded, your true and only Son, worthy of all worship, and the Holy Spirit, advocate and guide. You, Christ, are the King of glory, the eternal Son of the Father. When you became man to set us free, you did not spurn the Virgin's womb. You overcame the sting of death, and opened the Kingdom of heaven to all believers. You are seated at God's right hand in glory. We believe that you will come, and be our judge. Come then, Lord, and help your people, bought with the price of your own blood, and bring us with your saints to glory everlasting. Save your people, Lord, and bless your inheritance. Govern and uphold them now and always. Day by day we bless you. We praise your name forever. Keep us today, Lord, from all sin. Have mercy on us, Lord, have mercy. Lord, show us your love and mercy, for we put our trust in you. In you, Lord is our hope: and we shall never hope in vain. Lord, hear my prayer, and let my cry reach you.

Prefaces to the Eucharistic Prayer, Sundays in Ordinary Time I

It is truly right and just, our duty and our salvation, always and everywhere to give you thanks, Lord, holy Father, almighty and eternal God, through Christ our Lord. For through his Paschal Mystery, he accomplished the marvelous deed, by which he has freed us from the yoke of sin and death, summoning us to the glory of being now called a chosen race, a royal priesthood, a holy nation, a people for your own possession, to proclaim everywhere your mighty works, for you have called us out of darkness into your own wonderful light.

Preface to the Fourth Eucharistic Prayer

It is truly right to give you thanks, truly just to give you glory, Father, most holy, for you are the one God living and true, existing before all ages and abiding for all eternity, dwelling in unapproachable light; yet you, who alone are good, the source of life, have made all that is, so that you might fill your creatures with blessings and bring joy to many of them by the glory of your light. And so, in your presence are countless hosts of Angels, who serve you day and night and, gazing upon the glory of your face, glorify you without ceasing.

CONCLUDING PRAYERS Once you have renewed your commitment to follow Christ and expressed that in your own words and in a concrete resolution, briefly reviewed how your meditation went, and jotted down the insights God gave you (Step 4, Commit), it often helps to wrap up your meditation with a short, ready-made prayer that sums things up. St. Ignatius of Loyola used to finish with the Our Father, the Hail Mary, and the Glory Be. Here are some other options, in case you still haven't found your personal favorites. It is customary to end the meditation with the Sign of the Cross.

Prayer of Dedication

Lord Jesus,
I give you my hands to do your work.
I give you my feet to follow your way.
I give you my eyes to see as you do.
I give you my tongue to speak your words.
I give you my mind so you can think in me.
I give you my spirit so you can pray in me.
Above all, I give you my heart
So in me you can love your Father and all people.
I give you my whole self so you can grow in me,
Till it is you, Lord Jesus,
Who lives and works and prays in me. Amen.

Prayer to the Holy Spirit

Holy Spirit,
Inspire in me
What I should think,
What I should say,
What I should leave unsaid,
What I should write,

What I should do
And how I should act
To bring about the good of souls,
The fulfillment of my mission,
And the triumph of the Kingdom of Christ. Amen.

Lead Kindly Light

Lead, kindly Light, amid the encircling gloom,
Lead thou me on;
The night is dark, and I am far from home,
Lead thou me on.
Keep thou my feet; I do not ask to see
The distant scene; one step enough for me.
    I was not ever thus, nor prayed that thou
Shouldst lead me on;
I loved to choose and see my path; but now
Lead thou me on.
I loved the garish day, and, spite of fears,
Pride ruled my will: remember not past years.
    So long thy power hath blest me, sure it still
Will lead me on.
O'er moor and fen, o'er crag and torrent, till
The night is gone,
And with the morn those Angel faces smile,
Which I have loved long since, and lost awhile.

– St. J. H. Newman (1801-1890)

From St. Patrick's Breastplate

I bind unto myself today
The strong name of the Trinity:
By invocation of the same,
The Three in One and One in Three
    Christ be with me, Christ within me,
Christ behind me, Christ before me,
Christ beside me, Christ to win me,
Christ to comfort and restore me.
Christ beneath me, Christ above me,
Christ in quiet, Christ in danger,

Christ in hearts of all that love me,
Christ in mouth of friend and stranger.
    Praise to the Lord of my salvation—
Salvation is of Christ the Lord!

—Ascribed to St. Patrick of Ireland (circa A.D. 450)

Prayer of Self-Dedication to Jesus Christ

Take, Lord, and receive
all my liberty, my understanding, my whole will,
all I have and all I possess.
You gave it all to me;
To you, Lord, I return it all.
It is all yours: Do with me entirely as you will.
Give me your love and your grace:
This is enough for me. Amen.

—St. Ignatius of Loyola (1491-1556)

Prayer of St. Francis

Lord, make me an instrument of your peace.
Where there is hatred, let me sow love;
where there is injury, pardon;
where there is doubt, faith;
where there is despair, hope;
where there is darkness, light;
and where there is sadness, joy.
    O, Divine Master,
grant that I may not so much seek
to be consoled as to console;
to be understood as to understand;
to be loved as to love;
for it is in giving that we receive;
it is in pardoning that we are pardoned;
and it is in dying that we are born to eternal life. Amen.

—St. Francis of Assisi (1181-1226)

Litany of Humility

This prayer renews one's commitment to follow Christ's summary for Christian living: "Set your hearts on his kingdom first, and on his righteousness, and all these other things will be given you as well" (Mt 6:33). It should be prayed from that perspective.

Jesus, meek and humble of heart, hear me!
From the desire of being esteemed, Lord Jesus, free me!
From the desire of being loved...
From the desire of being acclaimed...
From the desire of being honored...
From the desire of being praised...
From the desire of being preferred...
From the desire of being consulted...
From the desire of being approved...
From the desire of being valued...
From the fear of being humbled, Lord Jesus, free me!
From the fear of being despised...
From the fear of being dismissed...
From the fear of being rejected...
From the fear of being defamed...
From the fear of being forgotten...
From the fear of being ridiculed...
From the fear of being wronged...
From the fear of being suspected...
From resenting that my opinion is not followed...
That others will be more loved than I, Lord Jesus, make this my prayer!
That others will be esteemed more than I...
That others will increase in the opinion of the world while I diminish...
That others will be chosen while I am set aside...
That others will be praised while I am overlooked...
That others will be preferred to me in everything...
Lord Jesus, though you were God, you humbled yourself to the extreme of dying on a cross, to set an enduring example to the shame of my arrogance and vanity. Help me to learn your example and put it into practice so that, by humbling myself in accordance with my lowliness here on earth, you can lift me up to rejoice in you forever in heaven. Amen.

–*Cardinal Merry del Val, Secretary of State under Pope St. Pius X (1865-1930)*

Mission Prayer

Lord, you have created me to do you some definite service; you have committed some work to me which you have not committed to another. I have my mission—I never may know it in this life, but I shall be told it in the next. Somehow I am necessary for your purposes, as necessary in my place as an Archangel in his—if, indeed, I fail, you can raise another, as you could make the stones children of Abraham. Yet I have a part in this great work; I am a link in a chain, a bond of connection between persons. You have not created me for naught. I shall do good, I shall do your work; I shall be an angel of peace, a preacher of truth in my own place, while not intending it, if I do but your commandments and serve you in my calling.

Therefore I will trust you. Whatever, wherever I am, I can never be thrown away. If I am in sickness, my sickness may serve you; in perplexity, my perplexity may serve you; if I am in sorrow, my sorrow may serve you. My sickness, or perplexity, or sorrow may be necessary causes of some great end, which is quite beyond me. You do nothing in vain; you may prolong my life, you may shorten it; you know what you are about; you may take away my friends, you may throw me among strangers, you may make me feel desolate, make my spirits sink, hide the future from me—still you know what you are about.

–Adapted from a reflection composed by St. J. H. Newman (1801-1890)

MORE FROM THE CHURCH'S RICH LITURGICAL TRADITION

The Gloria

Glory to God in the highest, and on earth peace to people of good will.
We praise you, we bless you, we adore you, we glorify you,
we give you thanks for your great glory,
Lord God, heavenly King, O God, almighty Father.
Lord Jesus Christ, Only Begotten Son,
Lord God, Lamb of God, Son of the Father,
you take away the sins of the world, have mercy on us;
you take away the sins of the world, receive our prayer;
you are seated at the right hand of the Father: have mercy on us.
For you alone are the Holy One, you alone are the Lord,
you alone are the Most High, Jesus Christ, with the Holy Spirit,
in the glory of God the Father. Amen.

The Apostles' Creed

I believe in God, the Father almighty, creator of heaven and earth. I believe in Jesus Christ, his only Son, our Lord, who was conceived by the power of the Holy Spirit and born of the Virgin Mary, suffered under Pontius Pilate, was crucified, died, and was buried. He descended into hell. On the third day he rose again from the dead; he ascended into heaven, and is seated at the right hand of God the Father almighty; from there he will come to judge the living and the dead. I believe in the Holy Spirit, the holy catholic Church, the communion of saints, the forgiveness of sins, the resurrection of the body, and life everlasting. Amen.

Some Possible Preparatory and Concluding Prayers

Here is some space where you can write in other prayers that you personally find helpful for wrapping up your meditation and returning to your other daily activities...

PART II

MEDITATION UNIT

The Gospel according
to St. John

THE GOSPEL OF JOHN
Chapter 1

"Moreover, you belong to God's Son: you should, therefore, be in him what members of a body are to the head. All that is in you must be grafted on to him, so that from him you may draw life and by him be ruled. True life is nowhere to be found by you except in him, who is the only source of life. Apart from him you will find naught save death and destruction. Let him be the only principle of all your actions, emotions, powers. You must live by him and for him..."

-ST. JOHN EUDES

239. AN UNWELCOME SUNRISE (JN 1:1-18)[1]

"Though he was rich, yet for our sake he became poor, so that by his poverty we might become rich." – St. Augustine

JOHN 1:1-18
In the beginning was the Word: and the Word was with God and the Word was God. He was with God in the beginning. Through him all things came to be, not one thing had its being but through him. All that came to be had life in him and that life was the light of men, a light that shines in the dark, a light that darkness could not overpower.

A man came, sent by God. His name was John. He came as a witness, as a witness to speak for the light, so that everyone might believe through him. He was not the light, only a witness to speak for the light. The Word was the true light that enlightens all men; and he was coming into the world. He was in the world that had its being through him, and the world did not know him. He came to his own domain and his own people did not accept him. But to all who did accept him he gave power to become children of God, to all who believe in the name of him who was born not out of human stock or urge of the flesh or will of man but of God himself.

---

1 Note: the unit numbering began with the Gospel of Matthew and ends with the Gospel of John.

The Word was made flesh, he lived among us, and we saw his glory, the glory that is his as the only Son of the Father, full of grace and truth. John appears as his witness. He proclaims: "This is the one of whom I said: He who comes after me ranks before me because he existed before me." Indeed, from his fullness we have, all of us, received—yes, grace in return for grace, since, though the Law was given through Moses, grace and truth have come through Jesus Christ. No one has ever seen God; it is the only Son, who is nearest to the Father"s heart, who has made him known.

CHRIST THE LORD   St. John wrote his Gospel toward the end of his long life. He addressed it primarily to those coming from a Hellenistic (pagan Greek) background, and only secondarily to his fellow Jews. But by calling Jesus the "Word of God made flesh," John wields a term shocking to both categories of readers.

For the Hellenistic Greeks, *Logos*, here translated as "Word," referred to the one unifying principle that linked together and put order in the entire cosmos. At the time when St. John was writing, Greek philosophers had developed elaborate behavioral codes that they hoped could put them in touch with this unifying force. Similarly, for the Hebrew mentality, the "Word of God" connoted God's wisdom, often personified in the Old Testament, which informs and directs all his works, including the creation and sustenance of the universe.

St. John includes both these dimensions in using the term to refer to Christ, but he corrects and elevates them by adding two additional dimensions. In showing that through the Word "all things were made," he reveals that the Hellenistic concept of Logos had missed the mark: the unity of the cosmos, its order and beauty and glory, is not drawn from some force within itself, but from a transcendent, personal, creating God. Then, in asserting that "the Word became flesh," he challenges his Jewish brethren to broaden their conception of the Messiah from a mere human king to God himself taking on human nature.

In the liturgical year, the Church offers us this tightly packed biography of our Savior on Christmas day, so that we can be justly amazed at beholding all of God's infinite power and majesty wrapped in a few strips of swaddling cloth, sleeping helplessly in his mother's arms: Jesus Christ, truly God and truly man, come gently to walk with us. Here indeed is a noble Lord, worthy of our heartfelt praise and silent adoration.

CHRIST THE TEACHER   The little cave at Bethlehem, where the Incarnation of God's Word first became visible, is a torrential fountain of Christ's doctrine. Today, however, St. John draws our attention to a less romantic, more uncomfortable lesson that we often ignore. Jesus Christ came to those who had been created in his image, and they "did not know him." He came to those who had received centuries of preparation through the Old Covenant, and they "did not accept him."

Human history is a dramatic struggle of man's attempts to discover meaning in life. It narrates the mostly unsuccessful but always passionate search for order, prosperity, and lasting happiness. You would think that when God himself decided to dwell among us to give us the answer and show us the way, we would welcome him eagerly and gladly. Such was not the case. The answer didn't fit our categories, and the way led out of our comfort zone, and therefore many turned their backs on the Savior. We are all tempted to cling to the darkness and flee the light, and St. John teaches us that overcoming this temptation can be harder than we think, though it's well worth the effort.

God will not force salvation upon us. Christ did not come to bring heaven to earth, but to lead those who would accept him from earth to heaven. Of all the world's religions, Christianity is the most respectful of human freedom—which makes perfect sense, considering that the law of Christ's Kingdom is authentic love, the perfect fulfillment of that particularly human characteristic.

CHRIST THE FRIEND *Jesus: Many people complain that I haven't made myself clear enough, that I haven't done enough to convince everyone to believe in and follow me. But they don't understand the gentle force of love that binds my Kingdom together. Have you ever turned on bright lights after being in a dark room for a long time? You know how it hurts your eyes. If I had come exactly as I am, I would have blinded you. You would have submitted, but out of fear and pain. I didn't create you for that. I created you to live in my friendship. Everything I do is to win back that friendship, which sin destroyed. So I came to meet you right where you are, right in the middle of your normal life. I came to live among you. And through my Church and my missionaries, I do the same thing in every generation all throughout the earth. My presence is bright but soft, like Christmas lights, because I know that your soul is wounded and sensitive. Trust me. Follow me. Let me guide you. I am here for that.*

CHRIST IN MY LIFE All that exists has come from you. Help me grasp this truth, Lord. You, who call me by my name, who have gone to heaven to prepare a place for me, who suffered on the cross to redeem me from sin, who come to me humbly and quietly in the Eucharist—you are the very same One who created and sustains every molecule, every sub-atomic particle, every galaxy, every activity of this vast, beautiful, incomprehensible universe...

It is a terrible thought: you came to give us the fullness of life that every heart longs for, but not every heart is willing to accept it. Lord Jesus, I too resist the inklings of your grace too often. Help me to be strong in doing what is right and resisting temptation. Help me to follow you, to be your messenger to everyone in my life...

You are so gentle with me, Lord. You always forgive; you always nudge; you always wait with infinite patience. Thank you. Make me more like you. I want to be your light and your goodness to everyone around me. I want to attract them to you, however far away they may be, as the star of Bethlehem attracted the wise men. Jesus, meek and humble of heart, make my heart more like yours...

Questions for
SMALL-GROUP DISCUSSION

1. What struck you most in this passage? What did you notice that you hadn't noticed before?

2. The fact of the Incarnation radically altered the course of history. What facts have most radically altered the course of your personal history? What should be influencing most your personal history right now?

3. Why do you think so many people refuse to welcome Christ into their lives, even when they hear about his love and know others who have welcomed him?

4. Christ has come to meet us in very human ways, through family, friends, priests, and other members of the Church. How can we be better channels for bringing him to others?

Cf. Catechism of the Catholic Church, 525-534 on the Christmas mystery; the mysteries of Jesus' infancy and the mysteries of his hidden life; 456-463 on why Jesus came to earth in the Incarnation; 897-913 on the mission of lay people in the Church

240. A GENEROUS KING (JN 1:19-28)

"God's providence of mercy, having determined to save in the last days the world which was perishing, foreordained the salvation of all nations in Christ." – Pope St. Leo the Great

JOHN 1:19-28

This is how John appeared as a witness. When the Jews sent priests and Levites from Jerusalem to ask him, "Who are you?" he not only declared, but he declared quite openly, "I am not the Christ." "Well then," they asked, "are you Elijah?" "I am not," he said. "Are you the Prophet?" He answered, "No." So they said to him, "Who are you? We must take back an answer to those who sent us. What have you to say about yourself?" So John said, "I am, as Isaiah prophesied: a voice that cries in the wilderness: Make a straight way for the Lord." Now these men had been sent by the Pharisees, and they put this further question to him, "Why are you baptising if you are not the Christ, and not Elijah, and not the prophet?" John replied, "I baptise with water; but there stands among you — unknown to you — the one who is coming after me; and I am not fit to undo his sandal-strap." This happened at Bethany, on the far side of the Jordan, where John was baptising.

CHRIST THE LORD John the Evangelist (the writer of this Gospel) had to counteract a misconception that lingered for a long time among the early Christian communities. For more than a hundred years after Christ's resurrection, pockets of John the Baptist's disciples continued to claim and preach that the Baptist himself was the true Messiah. Correcting this mistake is one of the minor motifs of John's Gospel. In this first chapter, the Gospel writer makes abundantly clear that John is not the Messiah. The inquirers query him point blank. They ask him if he is the Messiah, and he says no; they ask him if he is the Prophet promised long ago by Moses (and often identified with the promised Messiah), and he says no; they ask him if he is Elijah (who was supposed to come again to announce the Messiah's arrival, but whom some thought would be the Messiah), and again John denies it, lest they misunderstand. Jesus Christ is the Messiah, the Prophet greater than any prophet, the One who came to set all things right — he alone, and no one else. John had clear and distinct ideas about Jesus. Do we?

The bickering about John the Baptist's identity may seem like an anachronistic squabble, but if it were, the Holy Spirit would not have included it in the Gospels. In fact, Christ's disciples fall into the same kind of bickering all the time. We are always taking sides and arguing among ourselves about which preacher or bishop or religious order or pious group is better than another. How happy this makes the devil! The mature Christian knows that there is one Lord whom we all are meant to serve, and if we hang our hat on anything else, it's due to our own pride, vanity, or narrow-mindedness.

CHRIST THE TEACHER The "priests and Levites" had charge of Jerusalem's Temple worship. John came from a family of priests, so it was only natural for them to come and find out why he — one of their own coterie — was acting so abnormally and making such a stir among the people. The Pharisees were members of the ruling body of Israel, the Sanhedrin. The Sanhedrin took charge of reining in false prophets, so they sent a delegation to investigate this new rabble-rouser. Both groups who questioned John listened to his message only through the filter of their personal agendas, and both groups missed the point. Their own preconceived notions impeded their acceptance of God's word spoken through John.

How often we fall into the same trap! We take refuge in our own exaggerated sense of self-sufficiency and sit in judgment over the Church's teaching. In many ways, we are trained to do this. Humility, simplicity, faith—these essential Christian virtues are in scant supply at most institutes of higher learning; we prefer to make truth conform to our own wishes rather than adjust our lives to the demands of truth. God "never ceases to draw man to himself," as the Catechism says (#27), but man (and that includes all of us) tends to resist the tug. From now on, let's not.

CHRIST THE FRIEND Generous kings hoard neither their wealth nor their privileges; they multiply and distribute their royal abundance, extending their friendship to all who will welcome it. Christ is a generous King, offering every man and woman his friendship and renewing the offer each day. He sent John the Baptist to announce his arrival, generously giving him a role in building up the Kingdom. In the same way, he has entrusted the defense and expansion of his Kingdom to the Church and therefore to each of us as members of the Church. Just as he gave John the honor and responsibility to announce his coming, so he gives us the chance to spread his reign. Ever since our baptism we have been members of his royal court, and from the moment of our confirmation, we accepted our appointment as ambassadors of the Eternal King. We have nothing to fear, because our natural powers did not earn this honor (it was a gift of grace), and our natural powers alone will not win success (Christ's grace is at work in and through us). He has involved us so intimately in his plan (in fact, we are his plan) because he wants our friendship, and friends share their most important occupations. His consists in rescuing his lost sheep.

CHRIST IN MY LIFE I want to be a true Christian, Lord. I want to follow you. Anyone who is trying to follow you and spread your Kingdom is my ally, not my adversary—even if they use methods I may not prefer or emphasize different aspects of your message than I do. I want to be an agent of unity and charity in your family of believers. Teach me to curb my tongue, and to open my heart as wide as you have opened yours…

How can I take away my filter of subjective prejudices and half-baked ideas in order to hear your voice loud and clear? How can I wipe away the film of preconceived opinions that are clouding my mental vision without my realizing it? I can't. I need your grace to come and cleanse my heart and my mind. You can do it, Lord. You can cut through the grime. Give me a new heart and a new mind, full of your light and your love...

St. John the Baptist, pray for me. I, too, have been given a role in Christ's Kingdom, just as you were. I am glad to have something to do that can please him and deepen our friendship. With your prayers, protect and guide me as I strive to fulfill my life's mission. With your example, help me to see God's providential hand in all the events and people that swirl around me, so that I may always be faithful to whatever he asks of me...

Questions for
SMALL-GROUP DISCUSSION

1. What struck you most in this passage? What did you notice that you hadn't noticed before?

2. Christ's persona and mission are inexhaustible sources of study and meditation. What should we be doing to understand him more deeply each day?

3. What are some influences around us that encourage intellectual pride—that tendency to require everyone, even the Church, to measure up to one's personal standards, trusting more in one's own understanding than in the revealed truth of Jesus Christ—and how can we counteract them?

4. What are some of the factors that keep Christians from engaging fully in their mission to spread the Kingdom of Christ, and what can we do this week to help overcome them?

Cf. Catechism of the Catholic Church, 523 on the role of John the Baptist; 554-555 for Jesus' own revelation of his glory; 1267-1270 on our responsibility to participate in the mission of the Church due to our baptism

241. THE FIRST STEP (JN 1:29-34)

"Today the Holy Spirit floats over the waters in the form of a dove, so that by this sign it might be known that the world's universal shipwreck has ceased, as the dove had announced to Noah that the world's flood had subsided." – St. Peter Chrysologus

JOHN 1:29-34

The next day, seeing Jesus coming towards him, John said, "Look, there is the lamb of God that takes away the sin of the world. This is the one I spoke of when I said: A man is coming after me who ranks before me because he existed before me. I did not know him myself, and yet it was to reveal him to Israel that I came baptising with water." John also declared, "I saw the Spirit coming down on him from heaven like a dove and resting on him. I did not know him myself, but he who sent me to baptise with water had said to me, 'The man on whom you see the Spirit come down and rest is the one who is going to baptise with the Holy Spirit.' Yes, I have seen and I am the witness that he is the Chosen One of God."

CHRIST THE LORD John the Baptist's favorite title for Jesus is "the Lamb of God." Clearly it also became one of John the Evangelist's favorite titles, since he used it twenty-nine times in the Book of Revelation. It brings together three images that would have been familiar to the Jews of that time, and by being applied to Christ, it indicates that in him those images find their full meaning.

God required the Jews to sacrifice a lamb twice a day to expiate the sins of the people (cf. Ex 29:39). Thus the lamb symbolized the price to be paid for sin. The primary holy day of the Jews was (and remains) the Passover. In the Passover ceremony, each family sacrifices and eats a lamb to recall their liberation from Egypt in the days of Moses. On that night, God killed all the firstborn children and animals of the Egyptians, but spared those of the Hebrews. In order to indicate which households the angel of death was to skip over, God commanded the Hebrews to kill a lamb and mark their doorposts with its blood. Thus the Passover lamb signified God's merciful and saving love. Finally, the Messiah announced by the prophets was described as a lamb who went silently to the slaughter, to take the sins of his people upon himself and wipe them away.

John proclaims: "Behold the Lamb of God," and we turn our eyes to Christ, the real lamb of God, the Incarnation of God's desire and power to free us from the slavery of selfishness, vanity, lust, and greed, and to lead us to the promised land of joyful friendship with him. So apt is this title that the Church repeats it every time Mass is celebrated: "Lamb of God, you take away the sins of the world, have mercy on us."

CHRIST THE TEACHER John tells his disciples about Jesus. Some of the future Apostles had originally been John's disciples. They were there with him on the banks of the Jordan, helping him baptize, when he first pointed out who the Master was. They heard his testimony about Jesus, and it sparked their interest, and so they went to meet the Lord for themselves.

Jesus chooses to use the testimony of those who believe in him to draw others into his friendship. If John had kept quiet about what God had shown him, his disciples might never have found the Lord. Likewise, Christ is counting on us to introduce him to others.

This takes humility. John was not looking for his own glory, but for God's. His own popularity and success didn't go to his head. His mission mattered more. In our efforts to build Christ's Kingdom, we can hardly choose a better model than John, who teaches us never to work merely for our own satisfaction or for the esteem of our peers. Our goal is Christ and our path is his will—and in the end, nothing else matters.

CHRIST THE FRIEND John saw "Jesus coming towards him."

Jesus: How much I love to do this. I never force my way into anyone's life, but I come toward everyone. I want to attract their attention because I want their friendship and happiness. I am always taking the first step. Isn't that what happened with you and me? Don't you remember? I caught your attention. Even before that, I had been coming toward you in many ways. It's like when you are in love, and you go out of your way to run into the person you love, just to get a glimpse of them, just hoping that they will stop and talk to you. I love you like that. I even come right up to your heart and knock, hoping you will let me in. I always have more to give you, more to teach you, more for us to do. My love never runs out of words, attention, encouragement, projects—my love never runs out, period. Keep welcoming me; keep looking out for me. I am still coming toward you, and I will never stop coming toward you.

CHRIST IN MY LIFE You are the Savior of all people. You are the light of the world. You are the Lamb of God. I don't want these words to become meaningless phrases in my heart. Keep my faith fresh, Lord. Just because I sometimes get tired or fall into routine, that doesn't mean that you have changed. You are still God, still the Lord, still the Teacher. Open my eyes to see all the wonders of your love...

I think of all the people in my life: family, friends, colleagues, acquaintances.... You have a mission for each one of them. You are calling each one of them to be saints. And I can either help them discover and fulfill that mission or hinder them. I want to help them. I want to encourage them in whatever way I can to hear and heed your call in their life. With the zeal of your heart, set my heart on fire...

Thank you for coming into my life, Lord. Before you came I was like an unlit candle. Jesus, never let me be separated from you. O Lord, what would I do without my faith in you? How vulnerable I would be to the lies and destructive seductions all around me! Keep me faithful to your will, Lord, and make me an instrument of your peace...

Questions for
SMALL-GROUP DISCUSSION

1. What struck you most in this passage? What did you notice that you hadn't noticed before?

2. At Mass, when we pray "Lamb of God, you take away the sins of the world, have mercy on us," what should be on our hearts and minds? Why do you think the Church puts the title "Lamb of God" on our lips right before we receive Holy Communion?

3. What most often inhibits our taking advantage of opportunities to speak about Christ and the Church to others who need God? What can we do to overcome this?

4. How can we pay closer attention to God, so as not to miss the times when he "comes towards us"?

Cf. Catechism of the Catholic Church, 608 on "The Lamb of God"; 863-865 and 897-913 on the role of the laity in the mission of the Church; 27 and 30 on God taking the initiative in our friendship with him

242. WANTING THE RIGHT THING (JN 1:35-42)

"If, then, you seek to know what path to follow, take Christ because he is the way."
– St. Thomas Aquinas

JOHN 1:35-42

On the following day as John stood there again with two of his disciples, Jesus passed, and John stared hard at him and said, "Look, there is the lamb of God." Hearing this, the two disciples followed Jesus. Jesus turned round, saw them following and said, "What do you want?" They answered, "Rabbi,"—which means Teacher—"where do you live?" "Come and see," he replied; so they went and saw where he lived, and stayed with him the rest of that day. It was about the tenth hour. One of these two who became followers of Jesus after hearing what John had said was Andrew, the brother of Simon Peter. Early next morning, Andrew met his brother and said to him, "We have found the Messiah"—which means the Christ—and he took Simon to Jesus. Jesus looked hard at him and said, "You are Simon son of John; you are to be called Cephas"—meaning Rock.

CHRIST THE LORD In these few verses St. John gives us three key titles of Christ, each of which should stir our hearts to gratitude, praise, and adoration.

First, John reemphasizes that Jesus is the "Lamb of God," a title worth reflecting on again and again. The lamb appeared over and over in the Jewish scriptures and in their traditions. The central allusion, however, was to the Passover, when the Israelites sprinkled the blood of the Passover lamb on the lintels of their doors (cf. Ex 12). The lamb had been sacrificed in order to save the Israelites, so that Moses would be able to lead them out of slavery. Christ was to be slain as well—on the cross of Calvary—and his blood was to be sprinkled on the lips of his faithful when they receive Holy Communion. In this way, Christians would be saved from the slavery of sin and led into the freedom of eternal life, the unquenchable abundance of heaven, by Jesus Christ, the Lamb of God. Christ is not only Lord; he is also Savior.

Second, Jesus is called "the Messiah," or "the Anointed One" (the Greek word for this gives us the title "Christ"). This title referred to the promised successor to the throne of David, whom God had anointed king of his Chosen People. Under David's kingship Israel had become a world power, reaching its peak of greatness and influence. God had promised that the line of David would never entirely fail, and he promised that a son of David would ascend to the throne to reinstate a new and even greater golden age for Israel. This Messiah (kings were "anointed" as a sign of their being chosen and strengthened by God for their divine mission on his behalf) would save Israel from all her sufferings and oppression, from all the misery that her sin had heaped upon her.

It is to save us, to rescue us from our own ignorance, weakness, and confusion that Jesus came. In relation to mankind, God's glory consists in the human race reaching its full potential, in all people discovering the joy of a life lived in communion with God. Christ is the bearer of this glory, the King who comes to establish the sovereignty of God—with the peace and the fullness it entails—in every human heart.

CHRIST THE TEACHER Third, St. John points out that the two disciples called Jesus "Rabbi," which means "teacher" or "master." Rabbis were popular Jewish leaders, not by position or birth, but by their knowledge of the things of God and their ability to teach and pass on that knowledge. In Matthew 19 and John 13, Christ makes an explicit and exclusive claim to this title, affirming that he is the definitive teacher of the things of God and demanding the absolute allegiance of his followers.

Even in this passage, we detect the unprecedented authority Jesus claims when he renames Simon. In the Jewish scriptural tradition, only God gave new names to people, and he only did so when he gave them a prominent role in his plan of salvation and connected them in a special way to his covenantal promise. Christ's exercise of such authority during his first meeting with Simon certainly would have given these disciples a hint that this Galilean was no average rabbi. (It also is one of the many indications in the Gospels that the preeminent role of Peter, and thus of the Papacy, was instituted and intended by Christ himself, and not merely an invention of the early Church.) Christ is Lord and Savior, but he is also the Master, a Teacher unlike any other. To follow him and learn from him should be our greatest joy.

Although Christ's titles bespeak his greatness, his behavior in this first encounter with John and Andrew shows his simplicity and humility. He walks by the place where they and John the Baptist are baptizing. He simply walks by. He makes no grand entrance, employs no intimidating tactics. When John and Andrew finally decide to go after him, he turns around to welcome them. He makes no demands, gives no orders, and passes no judgment. Rather, he engages them in a conversation and issues an invitation to come and spend time with him. This is how Jesus works. This is how he calls us, gently, unexpectedly, personally. The era of flashing fire on the mountaintop is over; the era of good-hearted friendship and intimate companionship with the eternal God has begun.

CHRIST THE FRIEND This is Jesus' first encounter with his first disciples. It is the beginning of the second half of human history—an important occasion. Surely the evangelist is describing every detail with care, most especially the very first words that Jesus speaks in this Gospel. He asks his future Apostles a simple question: "What do you want?" (What do you seek? What are you hoping for?) It is still one of Christ's favorite questions. Jesus already knows the deepest desires of every heart, but many people never take the time to reflect on their own deepest desires. Jesus poses the question in order to spur that kind of reflection. Unless we take time to examine ourselves and our lives, we can easily end up looking for meaning and happiness in the wrong places, mindlessly latching onto every passing fancy and popular guru, bouncing from fashion to fad, never drinking of the living water that only he can give.

Jesus: My first two disciples gave the right answer to this question. They asked where I was staying. What did they want? They only wanted to come and stay with me. That is how you answered the question too. How it pleases me to find humble, thirsting hearts—what a feast I have in store for them! What do you want? What are you seeking? If you want the right thing, everything else will fall into place. If you don't, nothing you do will give rest to your soul.

CHRIST IN MY LIFE Where do you live, Lord? I want to find you and stay with you. You are the creator of the mountains, the ocean, the clouds, and the stars. You are the wisdom that gives order to the universe. You are the spark of light that gives man a knowing mind and a loving heart. You are the source and goal of all things. And you have come to live in my heart. You are mine, and I am yours. Let me stay with you...

I need a Teacher, Lord, and I choose to sit at your feet and listen to you. Sometimes I find myself yearning so much to understand things—to have true wisdom—that I am almost in pain. You made me with a need for truth. You are the Truth. Speak to my heart, Lord. Send your Spirit to teach and guide me. Never take your eyes off of me...

What do I want? I want so many things! I want happiness, Lord. I want happiness for myself and for those around me. Fulfillment, meaning, satisfaction. I want my life to bear the fruit you created it to bear. I want to look into your eyes and see you smile on the day you call me home to eternity, and I want to hear you say, "Well done, good and faithful servant..."

Questions for
SMALL-GROUP DISCUSSION

1. What struck you most in this passage? What did you notice that you hadn't noticed before?

2. Jesus' first words in the Gospel of John are: "What do you want?" What would the voice of popular culture say in response to that question?

3. Why did Jesus wait until the two disciples came after him? Why didn't he go after them first?

4. Every one of the disciples who comes to Jesus in this first chapter of John's Gospel does so at the invitation of an intermediary. When was the last time you invited someone to come and meet Jesus? What happened? Why don't we invite people more often?

Cf. Catechism of the Catholic Church, 602, 613, 1137 on the meaning of the title "Lamb of God"; 436-440 on the meaning of the title "Messiah"; 512-521 on the life of Christ as a definitive "teaching" of the things of God

243. YOU WILL SEE GREAT THINGS (JN 1:43-51)

"We have been granted by the good Lord the privilege of sharing in that greatest, most divine, chief of all names, so that, honored with the name of Christ, we are called Christians." – St. Gregory of Nyssa

JOHN 1:43-51

The next day, after Jesus had decided to leave for Galilee, he met Philip and said, "Follow me." Philip came from the same town, Bethsaida, as Andrew and Peter. Philip found Nathanael and said to him, "We have found the one Moses wrote about in the Law, the one about whom the prophets wrote: he is Jesus son of Joseph, from Nazareth." "From Nazareth?" said Nathanael, "Can anything good come from that place?" "Come and see," replied Philip. When Jesus saw Nathanael coming he said of him, "There is an Israelite who deserves the name, incapable of deceit." "How do you know me?" said Nathanael "Before Philip came to call you," said Jesus "I saw you under the fig tree." Nathanael answered, "Rabbi, you are the Son of God, you are the King of Israel." Jesus replied, "You believe that just because I said: I saw you under the fig tree. You will see greater things than that." And then he added "I tell you most solemnly, you will see heaven laid open and, above the Son of Man, the angels of God ascending and descending."

CHRIST THE LORD Jesus issues bold commands. He says to Philip, "Follow me." Imagine the look in his eyes as he gazed at Philip and said those words. Imagine how much force and love and vibrant life must have been in that look. It was no generic, philosophical observation. It was a penetrating, life-changing encounter.

This is the heart and soul of Christianity. Not its creed, not its ceremonies, not even the Bible, but the person of Christ the Lord, looking into the eyes of every man and woman, and inviting them to follow him. If he is the Lord, then he is to be followed; he is to be obeyed—not because after much study and reflection we have concluded that he is worthy of our standards, but because he is the Lord. Our hearts were made to know, love, and follow him, which is why his call stirred Philip so radically, and which is why we always know when he's asking something of us. His call to our hearts often takes place in the most unglamorous ways, because he's not trying to impress us (he's from Nazareth, after all—the boondocks of Palestine); he simply wants to lead us; he wants to befriend us.

CHRIST THE TEACHER Jesus' first actions in his ministry consist in gathering around himself a group of followers—not dramatic speeches, or dozens of miracles, or clashes with his enemies. No, first he wants to shape the nucleus of his Church. Right from the beginning, this is his priority. These men will become his Apostles. For the next three years, he will spend the vast majority of his time—almost all his time, in fact—with them. He will teach them with his words and example. He will let them get to know him, reveal his thoughts and desires to them, train them for their mission in his Kingdom, and gradually reveal to them what that mission is.

Christ's Kingdom is the rule of his love and wisdom in the hearts of his followers. It is the family of those who believe in him; it is the Church, militant, suffering, and triumphant. And just as the foundation of the Church occurred through his one-on-one attention to and formation of his Apostles, who would go and do the same in other places, multiplying themselves in others just as Christ had multiplied himself in them, so the growth of the Church throughout the centuries has taken place in the same way. And if we want to help the Church grow in our day, we will follow the same methodology. We will gather around the successors to the Apostles, the Pope and the bishops, by studying and obeying the teachings of the Church, in order to come to know Christ and to love him. We will spend time with him in prayer and the sacraments. And then we, like other Christs, like new apostles, will invite those around us to come and follow the Lord.

CHRIST THE FRIEND *Jesus: When I told Nathaniel that I had seen him under the fig tree, I was referring to a moment of spiritual crisis and enlightenment that he had had a few months earlier. It was something that occurred as he was meditating and reflecting in the shadow of a fig tree. Only he and God knew about it. It was a moment of preparation that I sent him, readying him for this encounter with me. When I mentioned it, he knew immediately that he was to come and be my follower.*

You have had many moments like his under the fig tree: those times, brief or long, of intimate spiritual sensitivity, of spiritual struggle, of interior growth and discovery. I have been with you for each of them. They are my action in your soul. I am always thinking of you and working in your heart—I can't help it, because my love draws me to you every moment of the day and night. I want you to have the confidence in me that Nathaniel had. I want you to follow me more closely, because it pains me more than I can describe to see you looking for satisfaction in places where you can never find it—comfort and pleasure, your own achievements and success, outdoing others. Come and follow me more closely, and you will see heaven laid open, and even greater things...

CHRIST IN MY LIFE I have heard you say to me what you said to Philip, "Follow me." I have heard it so many times! Never let me stop being amazed that you, the creator of all things, came into my life, looked me in the eye, smiled, and invited me to be your royal companion, your collaborator, and your ambassador. I want to be generous with you, Lord; I want to be your worthy disciple...

How I love your Church! Bless the Pope, Lord, and bless all your bishops and priests. Keep your Church united around you. Calm the erosive winds of infidelity and disobedience. And give me, I beg you, the courage, confidence, and humility to take up my mission within the Church and carry it out. Blessed be your name throughout the earth...

Thank you for stirring my heart so many times. I don't want to live on the surface of life, giggling and bantering and chatting and skipping along aimlessly. I don't want to throw myself into the latest distractions laid out on the smorgasbord of popular culture, without a thought for the purpose for which you created me. I want to enjoy the good things of this world profoundly, as you created me to. Grant me wisdom, Lord...

Questions for
SMALL-GROUP DISCUSSION

1. What struck you most in this passage? What did you notice that you hadn't noticed before?

2. Why do you think Jesus didn't give Philip any reasons to follow him—why did he just say, "Follow me"? Why didn't Philip argue in response to Nathaniel's objection to following Christ—why did he simply say, "Come and see"?

3. Why do you think Jesus chose to reach out to the world through his Church? Why not just go directly to each soul without any intermediaries?

4. Who did in your life what Philip did in Nathaniel's life, inviting you to "come and see" the Lord?

Cf. Catechism of the Catholic Church, 874-896 on the hierarchical structure of the Church; 1533 and 1962 on holiness and the gospel as the vocation of all the disciples of Christ; 897-913 on the laity's mission in the Church and the world; 914-933 on the different manifestations of the mission of consecrated persons in the Church and the world

THE GOSPEL OF JOHN
Chapter 2

"At rest on the heights of virtue, rich beyond measure with divine gifts, she who surpassed all others in grace lavishly pours out streams of graces on thirsty souls. She bestows healing for bodies and souls, powerful to save men from both spiritual and corporal death. What man ever went away from her sick or sad or without heavenly light to guide him? Who has not returned home glad and rejoicing having obtained what he prayed for from Mary, the Mother of our Lord?"

– ST. AMEDEUS OF LAUSANNE

244. GLORY DAWNS (JN 2:1-12)

"By her maternal charity, Mary cares for the brethren of her Son who still wander through this world in the midst of dangers and difficulties until they are led to the happiness of their heavenly home." – Second Vatican Council, Lumen Gentium 61

JOHN 2:1-12

Three days later there was a wedding at Cana in Galilee. The mother of Jesus was there, and Jesus and his disciples had also been invited. When they ran out of wine, since the wine provided for the wedding was all finished, the mother of Jesus said to him, "They have no wine." Jesus said "Woman, why turn to me? My hour has not come yet." His mother said to the servants, "Do whatever he tells you." There were six stone water jars standing there, meant for the ablutions that are customary among the Jews: each could hold twenty or thirty gallons. Jesus said to the servants, "Fill the jars with water," and they filled them to the brim. "Draw some out now" he told them "and take it to the steward." They did this; the steward tasted the water, and it had turned into wine. Having no idea where it came from—only the servants who had drawn the water knew—the steward called the bridegroom and said, "People generally serve the best wine first, and keep the cheaper sort till the guests have had plenty to drink; but you have kept the best wine till now." This was the first of the signs given by Jesus: it was given at Cana in Galilee. He let his glory be seen, and his disciples believed in him. After this he went down to Capernaum with his mother and the brothers, but they stayed there only a few days.

CHRIST THE LORD Mary knew how to treat the Lord: there was a crisis, and she went to him for a solution. The vast majority of Jews living in Palestine were poor. Wedding feasts and religious festivals were their sole respite from a life of hard labor and simple survival. In fact, wedding feasts often lasted for days at a time (they took the place of our honeymoons, which didn't exist in first-century Israel), and the entire town participated. To run out of wine in the middle of it would not only deflate the festive atmosphere, but it would also deeply shame the newlyweds and their families, turning what should be the most joyous days of their lives into an embarrassment. Attentive to the needs of those around her, Mary saw the crisis coming, and she knew just what to do. Even when the words of Jesus' answer seemed like a rebuff, she knew that he would come through. Jesus will never reject the humble appeal of faith—he is a Lord who "came not to be served but to serve" (Mt 20:28), and he's hoping that we will have as much confidence in him as his mother did.

We shouldn't overlook the power Jesus shows in this miracle. It was the "first of his signs," and by it he "let his glory be seen," to the benefit of his disciples, whose faith it deepened. Picture what happened. Pretend you are one of the servants. You fill up six huge stone kegs with water (no easy task when you have to go back and forth to the well). Then this young rabbi from the neighboring town tells you to draw some out (some of the water, remember—you know it's water, because you put it in there yourself) and bring it to the steward in charge of testing the wine before serving it. Imagine how dumbfounded you would be by such an order. But you do it. And you're carrying the water over to the steward, glancing nervously back over your shoulder at Mary and Jesus, who motion for you to keep going. You hand the gourd to the boss, looking down, maybe even closing your eyes in anticipation of his wrathful rebuke. And then, all of a sudden, he smacks his lips and hums with pleasure.... Jesus turned a hundred gallons of water into excellent wine, effortlessly. This is our Lord.

CHRIST THE TEACHER Jesus treated his mother with love and respect. He sees her not only as God's chosen instrument, but also as the woman who brought him into the world, took care of him when he was a helpless infant, and taught him to speak, to pray, to work, and to live. Both Jesus and Mary were free from sin, but that made them more human, not less. And so the natural, incomparable bond that forms between a mother and her son was deeper, purer, and more binding in their case than in any other case in human history. Since baptism has brought us into Christ's family, our love and respect for Mary should echo Christ's.

On the other hand, no one knows Jesus better than his mother. She bore him in her womb, nursed him at her breast, and raised him from childhood to manhood. Thirty of his thirty-three years on earth were spent in almost constant contact with her. When he begins his public ministry, she fades into the background but remains faithful: when he was in agony on the cross, she was there beside him. When she says something about him, therefore, we should take it to heart (just as he took to heart her hint that he should do something about the wine crisis), and in this passage she gives us an unambiguous lesson about how to relate to Jesus.

The Bible is inspired, so it is no coincidence that Mary's last biblical words say everything that needs to be said: "Do whatever he tells you." If we followed that one piece of advice, heeding Christ's every order and suggestion (those in the Scriptures, those of his Church, and those in our conscience), the water of our normal, everyday activities would quickly be turned into the wine of supernatural joy and fruitfulness. We would no longer be mere men and women; we would be saints.

CHRIST THE FRIEND *Jesus: I brought my disciples to a wedding feast. Think about that for a moment. Do you think it is something that happened by chance? Not at all. Too often people think of me as a stern taskmaster, distant and removed from the healthy joys and activities of the human experience. But I was the one who invented those joys and activities!*

I came to earth not just to teach you theology and not to douse your zest for life, but to bring everything about life back to its fullness, back to its complete and rightly ordered fruition. I know much better than anyone else that it is part of human nature to celebrate, to enjoy the good things of creation, like marriage and wine. But only I can teach you how to do so in a balanced, healthy way, in a way that will deepen your joy and not cheapen it. Stay close to me, seek to know me better, and I will show you how to experience more fully the life I have given you.

CHRIST IN MY LIFE Lord, I am so used to this miracle—too used to it. I have heard about it so many times. But when I stop to really reflect on what you did, I am amazed. Why do I live on the mundane surface of things so much? Why can't I keep in mind the wonders of your love, the gift of your presence, the assurance of your wisdom? You are all mine, Lord, and I am all yours. Keep me closer to your heart...

If I don't seek out and fulfill your will, whose will is left? Mine is ignorant and narrow-minded. No one else has your wisdom, love, and fidelity. I want to know your will, your teaching, and your criteria. I want to learn to hear your voice. I want to live out all the normal responsibilities of my life as you would have me live them out, because I know that if I do, you will make my life bear abundant fruit...

I don't want to be one of those sad, cold, self-righteously pious, proper people. I want to be a saint, the saint you created me to be. The true saints, the ones your Church encourages me to look at, are so full of life that wherever they go they cause a revolution. Fill me with life, Lord, with your life, with true life. Make my words and my glance glow with the warmth of your love. Teach me to do your will...

Questions for
SMALL-GROUP DISCUSSION

1. What struck you most in this passage? What did you notice that you hadn't noticed before?

2. What characterized the relationship between Jesus and Mary? How would you venture to describe it?

3. If "Do whatever he tells you" is the motto of Christian culture, what would you define as the motto of popular culture?

4. What has helped you carry on your social life with the joy, spontaneity, and self-dominion that a Christian ought to have, without falling into excesses or superficiality?

Cf. Catechism of the Catholic Church, 487-507 on Mary's role in the Kingdom; 2288-2291 on respect for health and temperance

245. SPRING CLEANING (JN 2:13-25)

"He is the center of history and of the world; he is the one who knows us and who loves us; he is the companion and friend of our life." – St. Paul VI

JOHN 2:13-25

Just before the Jewish Passover Jesus went up to Jerusalem, and in the Temple he found people selling cattle and sheep and pigeons, and the money changers sitting at their counters there. Making a whip out of some cord, he drove them all out of the Temple, cattle and sheep as well, scattered the money changers' coins, knocked their tables over and said to the pigeon-sellers, "Take all this out of here and stop turning my Father's house into a market." Then his disciples remembered the words of scripture: Zeal for your house will devour me.

The Jews intervened and said, "What sign can you show us to justify what you have done?" Jesus answered, "Destroy this sanctuary, and in three days I will raise it up." The Jews replied, "It has taken forty-six years to build this sanctuary: are you going to raise it up in three days?" But he was speaking of the sanctuary that was his body, and when Jesus rose from the dead, his disciples remembered that he had said this, and they believed the scripture and the words he had said. During his stay in Jerusalem for the Passover many believed in his name when they saw the signs that he gave, but Jesus knew them all and did not trust himself to them; he never needed evidence about any man; he could tell what a man had in him.

CHRIST THE LORD In the chronology of John's Gospel, this event takes place at the beginning of Jesus' public ministry. John's point of view, however, rightly interprets it in light of Christ's entire life. Here Jesus is already speaking of his Resurrection. Thus we see how clearly Jesus understood his mission from the very start.

Christ is the ultimate defender of mankind's authentic relationship with God, and therefore he cleanses the Temple (an architectural symbol of that relationship) of everything that detracts from true faith and heartfelt worship. The officials in charge of the Temple take umbrage at this flouting of their authority, and Christ responds by explaining, albeit indirectly, his own identity and his reason for coming to earth. He calls himself the Temple (the word Jesus used, "sanctuary," was the inner part of the Temple, the most important part), because as true God and true man, he is the paradigmatic meeting place of the divine and the human. This meeting place, this communion between God and man, will be rejected at first (at the crucifixion), but he will assure us that in the end it will take root and endure (from the Resurrection into the age of the Church).

God had revealed himself directly to only one ancient nation, the nation of Israel. He had instructed them to build a Temple, a place of worship and communion between the one true God and his Chosen People. Solomon's Temple had housed the altars of sacrifice as well as the Ark of the Covenant itself, the box containing the tablets of the Ten Commandments. No holier place existed on earth—until the coming of Christ. Now, in the aftermath of Christ's coming, the presence of God has spread throughout the globe; every

Christian heart is a sanctuary of the Holy Spirit, and every Catholic Tabernacle contains the living presence of the very author of the new and everlasting Covenant. Christ would later say that he was "greater than Solomon," for as magnificent as Solomon's Temple was (it was considered one of the wonders of the ancient world), it only foreshadowed the true Temple, the one that human hands could never destroy.

CHRIST THE TEACHER Few times in the Gospels do we see Christ act or speak out in anger, and when he does, it is always to condemn hypocrisy. By all appearances, the Temple officials were directing their fellow Jews in proper rituals of worship. In actual fact, however, they were adulterating that worship.

God had given his people the Temple to be a house of prayer and worship. The buying, selling, and money changing that went on in the Temple area had long been happening there. When pilgrims came to worship, they had to offer victims to the priests, who would sacrifice them to Yahweh on their behalf. Strict rules governed the qualifications of the victims — not just any animal would do. Therefore, businesses cropped up that specialized in making the right beasts easily available. Likewise, pilgrims came from all over the civilized world and brought money of various mintages. These had to be weighed, valued, and exchanged in order to be used for purchasing the sacrificial victims. Gradually, greed had infiltrated even these sacred services — the money changers demanded exorbitant fees and the vendors overcharged.

In this way, what was meant to be heartfelt service to God became a path to worldly success. The Temple officials were by all appearances exemplarily religious, but actually they were greedy merchants. This contradiction between appearances and reality is hypocrisy. The frightening thing is how easily we fall into it; we are experts at finding ways to project ourselves as exemplary Catholics, while on the inside we still seek the kingdom of "me" rather than the Kingdom of Christ.

CHRIST THE FRIEND St. John tells us that the Lord knew human nature well; he "could tell what a man had in him."

Jesus: This should comfort you: I know the contradictions that disturb your mind and heart, the temptations that beset you, the streak of falls and failures that mark your path of discipleship. None of that surprises me. In fact, I came because of them. If you hadn't needed someone to save you, to redeem you, to renew your weary and dying soul, why would I have had to come? You don't need to make yourself perfect before you can have confidence in me. Your trust can be vast, joy-filled, and unrestrained right now, if only you will be honest and open. I came because I want your friendship — but I want your friendship, the one that comes from your heart, not from your masks. Approach me in prayer—just as you are!

CHRIST IN MY LIFE Lord, only through my friendship with you can I live in communion with God. You are the one Mediator, Lord—the one true Temple. I believe in you, and I have put all my hopes in you. I want to know, love, and follow you more each day, because in you I will become what I long to be: rich in virtue and wisdom, free from selfishness and sin, strong in love and purified from greed, lust, envy, and arrogance...

I wish you would come and cleanse the money-grubbing, pleasure-grabbing tendencies out of my heart once and for all. You know that I want to be patient, generous, and wise. So why am I so often impatient, selfish, and foolish? My only comfort is that you know me through and through, and even so, you chose me. No task is too great for you, not even bringing light and order to my dark and disordered soul...

I want my life to be fully at the service of what is good, true, and right—of your Kingdom. I want to give myself to you. I believe in you, Lord. All the energy and vitality you have given me, I put back in your hands. The tasks you have given me to do, I do for love of you. I am a temple dedicated entirely to your glory and your goodness, because all I have I have received from you...

Questions for
SMALL-GROUP DISCUSSION

1. What struck you most in this passage? What did you notice that you hadn't noticed before?
2. What are some of the hypocrisies that easily creep into our lives as Catholics today?
3. What has helped you most in making your friendship with Christ more heartfelt and personal, and less superficial and mechanical?
4. As Christians, we consider our bodies to be temples of the Holy Spirit. How should that affect the way we treat our bodies? What does popular culture think of the human body, and how does that affect how popular culture encourages us to treat our bodies?

Cf. Catechism of the Catholic Church, 583-586 on Jesus and the Temple; 2468 and 2505 on hypocrisy; 2559-2564 on praying from the heart

"Sin which destroyed the divine life within us demands a satisfaction, an expiation without which it would be impossible for divine life to be restored to us. Being a mere creature, man cannot give this satisfaction for an offense of infinite malice, and, on the other hand, divinity can neither suffer nor expiate. How is this problem to be solved? The Incarnation gives us the answer. Consider the babe of Bethlehem. He is the Word-made-Flesh. The Word asks of us a human nature to find in it wherewith to suffer, to expiate, to merit, to heap graces upon us. It is through the flesh that man turns away from God; it is in becoming flesh that God delivers man. The flesh that the Word of God takes upon himself, is to become the instrument of salvation for all men."

– BLESSED COLUMBA MARMION

246. NIGHT LINES (JN 3:1-15)

"Eternal Trinity, you are like a deep sea, in which the more I seek, the more I find; and the more I find, the more I seek you." – St. Catherine of Siena

JOHN 3:1-15
There was one of the Pharisees called Nicodemus, a leading Jew, who came to Jesus by night and said, "Rabbi, we know that you are a teacher who comes from God; for no one could perform the signs that you do unless God were with him." Jesus answered: "I tell you most solemnly, unless a man is born from above, he cannot see the kingdom of God." Nicodemus said, "How can a grown man be born? Can he go back into his mother's womb and be born again?" Jesus replied: "I tell you most solemnly, unless a man is born through water and the Spirit, he cannot enter the kingdom of God: what is born of the flesh is flesh; what is born of the Spirit is spirit. Do not be surprised when I say: You must be born from above. The wind blows wherever it pleases; you hear its sound, but you cannot tell where it comes from or where it is going. That is how it is with all who are born of the Spirit." "How can that be possible?" asked Nicodemus. "You, a teacher in Israel, and you do not know these things!" replied Jesus. "I tell you most

solemnly, we speak only about what we know and witness only to what we have seen and yet you people reject our evidence. If you do not believe me when I speak about things in this world, how are you going to believe me when I speak to you about heavenly things? No one has gone up to heaven except the one who came down from heaven, the Son of Man who is in heaven; and the Son of Man must be lifted up as Moses lifted up the serpent in the desert, so that everyone who believes may have eternal life in him."

CHRIST THE LORD Christ's mission is universal. He was sent so that everyone who believes in him may receive eternal life. Nicodemus was a leader of the Jewish nation. He would have known the Old Testament prophecies about the promised Messiah not only restoring the Kingdom of Israel, but also being a "light for the nations." God had entrusted Israel with a universal mission to be the firstborn son of all the nations, a priestly people that would channel God's blessings to all the other peoples of the world. Therefore, when Christ spoke of himself as the one sent to save the world, Nicodemus would have recognized the Messianic claim. All that remained was for him to accept it. We know from later passages that eventually he did accept it and became a secret disciple.

Nicodemus needed a large dose of faith to believe and live in accord with Christ's claim. After all, at the time Jesus appeared to be nothing more than a rough-and-ready rabbi from Galilee. For us, it should be much easier. Christ's prediction that he would be raised up like Moses' bronze serpent has come true. (When the Israelites were wandering in the desert, they were plagued by an infestation of poisonous serpents. To cure them, God had Moses make a bronze image of a serpent on a stick and hold it up; everyone who looked upon the image was saved.) In every corner of the globe, the crucifix looks down upon mankind, and the entire world looks up at it. These looks of love fill thousands of churches, chapels, and classrooms, millions of living rooms and bedrooms. Christians are fingering their crucifix necklaces on subways and airplanes, in hospitals and army camps. Other fingers are touching it on innumerable rosaries, stirring lips and hearts to constant prayer. Truly, the universality of Christ's claim has been verified by the unconquerable universality of his Church.

CHRIST THE TEACHER Nicodemus was a member of Israel's ruling body, the Sanhedrin. He had come to speak with Jesus in secret, to find out the truth about this controversial rabbi from Galilee. In their conversation, Jesus wins over his heart, so much so that, as we know from other passages, Nicodemus became an undercover disciple.

The Lord knew how to speak to the poor. He knew how to clothe the mysteries of God in language accessible to the humblest of workers, but he also knew how to reach out to those who were educated, sophisticated, and in charge. The gospel breaks through all boundaries of race, class, and rank. Christ's wisdom is universal, just as his Church is Catholic (catholic means "universal"). No other message or body of doctrine is more worth studying through and through than the science of Christ. It is the fullness of truth, because Christ himself is Truth. It never stops satisfying every kind of thirst the soul can have, like a fountain that everyone in the city can go back to again and again and always be refreshed.

That the Church's saints, religious, bishops, cardinals, and popes have come and still come from every race, class, and rank continuously shows that it is carrying Christ's unflagging, universal torch, a torch that every Christian should also carry.

CHRIST THE FRIEND Nicodemus was like so many of us. He was only able to take small, hesitant steps toward the Lord. Why? He hadn't understood the depths of God's love. He thought the Messiah was only coming to put the finishing touches on what had already been done throughout salvation history, when Christ's true mission was the complete renewal of the human spirit. This is still his mission; this is still his dream for every human heart.

His Spirit comes not only to heal our wounds but to give us an entirely new birth, an entirely new life—not just once, but continually, until we are ready for heaven. It takes faith and trust to accept Christ's agenda. At times, like Nicodemus we are tempted to stop at whatever point we have already reached, clinging to the well-known comfort of our well-known world. But Jesus has more to give us, more to show us, more for us to do. He has more life for us to grow into. He has spoken to us of earthly things, and maybe we have learned his lessons well; now he wishes to speak to us of heavenly things.

CHRIST IN MY LIFE Thank you for the gift of faith, Lord. You are the Savior of the world. You created this world, and when our sin cut it off from your friendship, you came down to live among us so you could win that friendship back. Make me like that. Make me generous. Make me eager to do good for my neighbor, to spread the soothing balm of goodness and understanding in this world that is so full of bitterness…

Your words are nourishment for my soul and for every soul. The world is full of so many words, Lord. We are drowning in them. Yet that doesn't take away the value of your wisdom. Today, your Church still speaks in your name to the rich and poor, the educated and uneducated, the young and old. Give me a share of your wisdom too, so that I can plant seeds of faith with the words that come from my mouth...

I have known you for a long time, Lord, and you have given me so much. Yet, I feel as if I still need much more. How can it be that as I grow older, I feel a heightened need for your enlightenment and guidance? I want to be born yet again, to experience the freedom of mature virtue, the fruitfulness of flourishing love. With the knowledge of your heart, Lord, make my heart wise...

Questions for
SMALL-GROUP DISCUSSION

1. What struck you most in this passage? What did you notice that you hadn't noticed before?

2. How should our being born again from above through baptism affect our daily living?

3. In the context of our lives, what would constitute a generous response to God's generous offer of salvation in his only Son? In other words, for us right now, what does "believing in Jesus" really entail?

4. When popular culture mentions God, what characteristics does it usually highlight?

Cf. Catechism of the Catholic Church, 599-618 on the meaning of Christ's death on the cross; 2567, 30, 142, and 1-3 on God's unceasing invitation of love to all mankind

247. GOD'S GAME PLAN (JN 3:16-21)

"How precious must man be in the eyes of the Creator, if he gained so great a Redeemer, and if God 'gave his only Son' in order that man 'should not perish but have eternal life.'" – St. John Paul II

JOHN 3:16-21
"Yes, God loved the world so much that he gave his only Son, so that everyone who believes in him may not be lost but may have eternal life. For God sent his Son into the world not to condemn the world, but so that through him the world might be saved. No one who believes in him will be condemned; but whoever refuses to believe is condemned already, because he has refused to believe in the name of God's only Son. On these grounds is sentence pronounced: that though the light has come into the

world men have shown they prefer darkness to the light because their deeds were evil. And indeed, everybody who does wrong hates the light and avoids it, for fear his actions should be exposed; but the man who lives by the truth comes out into the light, so that it may be plainly seen that what he does is done in God."

CHRIST THE LORD You never really know someone until you know what's in their heart—what motivates them, what they're looking for, why they do what they do. In this conversation with Nicodemus, Jesus lays bare the heart of God.

The history of salvation, from the fall of Adam and Eve until the final judgment, revolves around the coming of Jesus Christ, the Savior, the Son of God. Why did he come? Because the Father sent him. Why did the Father send him? Because he "loved the world so much." He simply couldn't bear to see us perish in our sins; he longed to share with us his everlasting life. God cares. And Jesus Christ is the definitive proof that he cares. He cares so much that he is willing to sacrifice his only Son to atone for the sins that have separated man from God, the source of all good things. We need look no further to find the very core of the gospel: "God loved the world so much that he gave his only Son, so that everyone who believes in him may not be lost but may have eternal life." No hidden agenda, no selfish undertones—pure generosity. This is the heart of God, of the Lord who longs for our friendship.

Only when a Christian internalizes this fundamental and overarching motive of God does Christian discipleship really begin to mature. This is Christ's revolution. That disinterested, self-forgetful love that has the power to overcome all evil and renew every human heart and the human race as a whole. The rules and rituals of Christianity are not its core, but its leaves. Joy, the kind of joy that none of life's contrarieties can diminish, as the lives of countless saints from every walk of life so powerfully attest to, is its flower. But its root is God's love, and its fruit is God's love lived out in the humdrum routine of daily life by the followers of Christ.

CHRIST THE TEACHER With these few sentences, Jesus lifts the veil of heaven and gives us a brief glimpse into the life of God himself.

The conversation between Father, Son, and Holy Spirit that led to the Incarnation and the salvation of sinful mankind was one of love. Love spoke to Love, and Love answered, and Love himself came to earth to teach us love. God is a relationship of eternal love between the Three Divine Persons.

Theologians reflecting on the Trinity see its image in the human family. The love of husband and wife in an embrace of complete and mutual self-giving yield a child. It is love that brings them together and love that brings new life. Similarly, but in an even more marvelous way, the Father and the Son look upon each other with such love that the love itself is another Person, another source of love, the Holy Spirit.

CHRIST THE FRIEND Jesus has proven his love by coming to earth "for our sake and for our salvation." He invites us to believe, so that we might not perish but have eternal life. He did not come for his own sake, but for ours. This is the epitome of friendship. "No one has greater love than this, to lay down one's life for one's friends" (Jn 15:13). But in his conversation with Nicodemus, Jesus once again points out that we remain free to accept or reject his offer of friendship, his offer of salvation. He makes it starkly clear: "Whoever does not believe in him has already been condemned." Salvation depends on God and on us; God has done his part, now we must do ours.

Nicodemus: I remember the tone of the Lord's voice that night. We were talking quietly, almost alone. Only one of his young disciples was there with us. We were sitting outside near a fire on a hillside under the stars. How could I forget this, my first conversation with the Master? His voice resonated with the very love of which he spoke. His eyes glimmered in the firelight with eager enthusiasm. I knew even then that it was the enthusiasm that had been at the origin of his mission to earth. As he spoke of those who believed in him, he grew joyful and glad. Then his words trembled with sadness and disappointment when he spoke of those who did not believe. How could I not be convinced by his wisdom, brighter and hotter than the fire between us? It was a risk for me to come to him that night, but I am ever grateful that I took it.

CHRIST IN MY LIFE I am so glad to be loved, Lord, and yet I am so slow to love. My heart is so inconstant. If I like someone, I treat them the way you would have me treat them, but if they rub me the wrong way, I bristle and gripe. Teach me to be a mature Christian. Teach me to love in word and deed, in thought and action. Teach me to love everyone the way you love...

I praise you, Father all-powerful, Christ, Lord and Savior, Holy Spirit of love. You have revealed yourself to me, and you have drawn me to share in your life and your love. Stay near to me, God. You have created me in your image and you have given life to this world because of your love. In your goodness make me an instrument of your mercy...

Lead me, Lord, to the pinnacle of love. I don't ask to be taken to new places or given new tasks. I ask you to unveil your beauty here where I live and work, where you have placed me. I ask you to infuse me with your love in the tasks you have already given me to do. I believe in you, Lord. Thy will be done...

Questions for
SMALL-GROUP DISCUSSION

1. What struck you most in this passage? What did you notice that you hadn't noticed before?

2. As Christians, how can we cultivate our relationship with a God who is a Trinity, not just with a generic God? How does our Trinitarian God differ from the gods of other religions?

3. When life and faith present us with difficult questions, where does popular culture encourage us to look for answers? How can we be more like Nicodemus in those moments, bringing our problems to Christ, and how can we encourage those around us to be more like Nicodemus?

4. If a non-believing friend of yours asked you, "If God is so loving, why does he let bad things happen to good people?" how would you respond?

Cf. Catechism of the Catholic Church, 238-260 on the Trinity; 50-67 on God's plan of "loving goodness"; 144-152 on what it means to "believe"

248. GREAT AND LITTLE (JN 3:22-36)

"He was to be manifested visibly, so that the world would see him and be saved." – St. Hippolytus

JOHN 3:22-36

After this, Jesus went with his disciples into the Judaean countryside and stayed with them there and baptised. At the same time John was baptising at Aenon near Salim, where there was plenty of water, and people were going there to be baptised. This was before John had been put in prison. Now some of John's disciples had opened a discussion with a Jew about purification, so they went to John and said, "Rabbi, the man who was with you on the far side of the Jordan, the man to whom you bore witness, is baptising now; and everyone is going to him." John replied: "A man can lay claim only to what is given him from heaven. You yourselves can bear me out: I said: I myself am not the Christ; I am the one who has been sent in front of him. The bride is only for the bridegroom; and yet the bridegroom's friend, who stands there and listens, is glad when he hears the bridegroom's voice. This same joy I feel, and now it is complete. He must grow greater, I must grow smaller. He who comes from above is above all others; he who is born of the earth is earthly himself and speaks in an earthly way. He who comes from heaven bears witness to the things he has seen and heard, even if his testimony is not accepted; though all who do accept his testimony are attesting the truthfulness of God, since he whom God has sent speaks God's own words: God gives him the Spirit without reserve. The Father loves the Son and has entrusted everything to him. Anyone who believes in the Son has eternal life, but anyone who refuses to believe in the Son will never see life: the anger of God stays on him."

CHRIST THE LORD Jesus is everything. First, John tells us, he is the bridegroom. This is an image taken from the Old Testament, which often referred to Israel as God's chosen bride. Imagine God calling himself a bridegroom. How passionately he must love each human soul, the whole human family! This is not the language of a cold architect or a distant watchmaker.

Second, he is the one who "comes from above... who comes from heaven... he... speaks God's own words." Only Jesus can speak definitively about the things of God. The fullness of God's own self-revelation is found in him. In this especially, Christianity differs from the rest of the world's religions: Christ is God himself come to reveal to man—in language man can understand—the truths that are beyond his natural knowledge. Therein lies the unique authority of the Catholic Church, the preserver and loudspeaker of God's self-revelation.

Third, he has "the Spirit without reserve." Those who consider Jesus to be just another guru among many, and who measure his teachings against the reams of merely human wisdom that history has churned out through the centuries are making a terrible mistake.

Finally, "The Father loves the Son and has entrusted everything to him." Jesus and God the Father are a perfect unity.

Could John have been any clearer in bearing witness to the full divine identity of Jesus Christ, the rabbi from Nazareth? Even those of us who already believe in him should never tire of savoring the fullness of his glory, letting it nourish our minds and hearts. The better we know the Lord, the fuller our lives will be.

CHRIST THE TEACHER In John the Baptist, Jesus gives us an icon of humility.

Every Christian has the same mission, basically, as John the Baptist. We are called to bear witness to Christ, to help people understand who he really is, and to bring them into the circle of his disciples. Essential to this mission is the virtue of humility, summed up perfectly by John in his greatest phrase: "He must grow greater, I must grow smaller." Our mission in life is to know, love, and follow Christ ourselves and to make him known, loved, and followed by as many others as possible. In this we will find our fulfillment, because we were made to love, and love is self-giving—giving of ourselves for the good of the beloved—not self-aggrandizing. In this we will also find our joy, as John the Baptist did: "This same joy I feel, and now it is complete" (Jn 3:29).

Jesus is the center of the universe. He is the focal point of history. We are simply his friends, his ambassadors, and his assistants. He loves us as passionately as a bridegroom loves his bride, but we cannot experience that love unless we first truly realize that we are not at the center of things, that we don't strictly deserve his love—rather, it is freely given to us. Just as Mary became the Mother of God because she saw herself as "the handmaid of the Lord" (Lk 1:38), and just as John the Baptist could experience the joy of Christ only because he freely ceded his own glory to Christ, just so, life for us will only click into place when we learn to look beyond the mirror.

CHRIST THE FRIEND *Jesus: How faithful a friend and messenger John the Baptist was for me! Look at him now, as his disciples come back, rankled from conversations in which they were complaining about John's diminishing and my rising popularity. But John was not fazed by their comments. He sought nothing for himself. He, the greatest of all prophets, had more to be proud of than any of his disciples, and yet he graciously accepts a lower status. If only all my followers would learn from him! The body of my Church is always being lacerated by divisions, rivalries, envy, and even intrigue. This above all is what keeps many more of my beloved souls from believing in me. They look at those who claim to believe already, see them posturing and backbiting just like everyone else, and turn away.*

Am I not enough for your soul? Is my friendship not enough to give you joy as it gave joy to John? Why do you seek approval from others when I have already given you my whole heart? Stay a while with me. Let me in, so I can conquer your heart.

CHRIST IN MY LIFE Lord, all throughout these first chapters of John's Gospel, the constantly recurring theme is that many refuse to believe in you. Today is no different. Those whom you came to save refuse to believe in you. Move their hearts, Lord! Why did you give me the gift of faith and not them? I understand very little of these mysteries. Teach me, Lord, to do your will and build your Kingdom...

You are meek and humble of heart. John was meek, gladly fading into the background once his part had been played. And I? I am full of a burning desire for recognition, praise, and influence. Purify my heart, Lord. How can

I conquer souls for your Kingdom by using the enemies' weapons? Jesus, meek and humble of heart, make my heart more like yours...

I want to love you, and I want to show you my love in every detail of this day. I want to give myself to the mission you have entrusted to me. I am limited—I have limited time and resources, but your love is unlimited. Pour your love into my heart so that it can overflow in how I do my work today, all for the glory of your name and the triumph of your Kingdom...

Questions for
SMALL-GROUP DISCUSSION

1. What struck you most in this passage? What did you notice that you hadn't noticed before?

2. Why do you think it is so easy even for Christians to divide up into factions? What can we do to avoid this kind of thing?

3. If an agnostic friend came up to you and asked how you would define humility and why it was important, what would you tell them?

4. What are some ways in which we can exercise and grow in the virtue of humility?

Cf. Catechism of the Catholic Church, 456-460 on why the Son of God became man; 461-463 on the meaning of Christ's Incarnation; 464-469 on how it is possible for Jesus to be both human and divine at the same time

"In your spiritual ascent and your search for a closer union with God, you must allow yourself no rest, no slipping back. You must go forward till you have obtained the object of your desires. Follow the example of mountain climbers. If your desires turn aside after objects that pass below, you will lose yourself in byways and your mind will be drawn in all directions. Your progress will be uncertain. You will not reach your goal. And you will not find rest after your labors. But if your heart and mind, led by love and desire, withdraw from the distractions of the world, you will grow strong. Your recollection will deepen the higher you rise on the wings of knowledge and desire. Little by little as you abandon baser things to rest in the one true and unchangeable Good, you will dwell there, held fast by the bonds of love."

–ST. ALBERT THE GREAT

249. QUENCHING CHRIST'S THIRST (JN 4:1-30)

"To show that he was not different from us, he undertook hard work, he went hungry and thirsty, he took rest and sleep, he did not shirk suffering, he revealed the Resurrection." – St. Hippolytus

JOHN 4:1-30
When Jesus heard that the Pharisees had found out that he was making and baptising more disciples than John—though in fact it was his disciples who baptised, not Jesus himself—he left Judaea and went back to Galilee. This meant that he had to cross Samaria. On the way he came to the Samaritan town called Sychar, near the land that Jacob gave to his son Joseph. Jacob's well is there and Jesus, tired by the journey, sat straight down by the well. It was about the sixth hour. When a Samaritan woman came to draw water, Jesus said to her, "Give me a drink." His disciples had gone into the town to buy food. The Samaritan woman said to him, "What? You are a Jew and you ask me, a Samaritan, for a drink?"—Jews, in fact, do not associate with Samaritans. Jesus replied: "If you only knew what God is offering and who it is that is saying to you: Give me a drink, you would have been

the one to ask, and he would have given you living water." "You have no bucket, sir," she answered, "and the well is deep: how could you get this living water? Are you a greater man than our father Jacob who gave us this well and drank from it himself with his sons and his cattle?" Jesus replied: "Whoever drinks this water will get thirsty again; but anyone who drinks the water that I shall give will never be thirsty again: the water that I shall give will turn into a spring inside him, welling up to eternal life."

"Sir," said the woman, "give me some of that water, so that I may never get thirsty and never have to come here again to draw water." "Go and call your husband," said Jesus to her, "and come back here." The woman answered, "I have no husband." He said to her, "You are right to say, 'I have no husband'; for although you have had five, the one you have now is not your husband. You spoke the truth there." "I see you are a prophet, sir," said the woman. "Our fathers worshipped on this mountain, while you say that Jerusalem is the place where one ought to worship." Jesus said: "Believe me, woman, the hour is coming when you will worship the Father neither on this mountain nor in Jerusalem. You worship what you do not know; we worship what we do know: for salvation comes from the Jews. But the hour will come—in fact it is here already—when true worshippers will worship the Father in spirit and truth: that is the kind of worshipper the Father wants. God is spirit, and those who worship must worship in spirit and truth." The woman said to him, "I know that Messiah—that is, Christ—is coming; and when he comes he will tell us everything." "I who am speaking to you," said Jesus, "I am he." At this point his disciples returned, and were surprised to find him speaking to a woman, though none of them asked, "What do you want from her?" or, "Why are you talking to her?" The woman put down her water jar and hurried back to the town to tell the people. "Come and see a man who has told me everything I ever did; I wonder if he is the Christ?" This brought people out of the town and they started walking towards him.

CHRIST THE LORD Passing through Samaria was not the only route from Judea to Galilee, but Jesus chose that route. He knew the bigger picture. He is always attentive to our needs, just as he was attentive to the needs of this woman and her countrymen. He never uses his knowledge and power to oppress and abuse, but only to amplify his love.

Christ is the Savior of the World, the Messiah, the long-awaited King, greater even than Jacob, inheritor of the Promise and father of the Twelve Tribes of Israel, so he tells this divorcee. He graces the Samaritan woman with one of the richest descriptions of himself and his work that appear in all the

Scriptures. Why? Why tell so much to someone so insignificant? Because to him, she wasn't insignificant at all. He wanted to be known by her, to give her hope, to save her. Ours is a Lord who wishes to shower us with his love, to fill us with the "living waters" of "the Spirit and truth," and to "tell us everything." This is the God in whom we believe; this is the Lord we serve.

CHRIST THE TEACHER Jesus was tired after his journey. He sat down by the well, thirsty, hungry, worn out. He was so thirsty that he skirted all social protocol and asked a Samaritan woman to give him a drink. But his tiredness doesn't hold back his love. He had come to rescue the lost sheep—this was his mission. The Samaritan woman came to the well at noon, the hottest hour of the day. The other women of the village would have come in the cooler hours of early morning and evening. This one was obviously avoiding contact with her peers. Jesus certainly notices this, seeing in her eyes the anxiety that comes from an unstable life, but he also sees a spark of sincerity—her rocky path through life had worn down any façade of self-righteousness or self-delusion. She was a woman in search of answers and direction, though she had perhaps given up on finding them. Jesus sees all this in her eyes, and he can't contain the love that overflows in his heart. He sees a soul in need, and he can't help reaching out. This is why he came.

Jesus became one of us on purpose with a mission in mind. Because of our sin, we could no longer raise ourselves up to friendship with God; so God comes down to meet us. In the Incarnation of Christ and the Church (which is the extension of that Incarnation throughout history) God continues to come down to meet us. He addresses us, he walks with us, he humbles himself so much that he even needs us to give him a drink: "Whatever you did for one of the least brothers of mine you did for me" (Mt 25:40). When the Samaritan woman encountered this God who was man, she was so transported with joy and so eager to spread the news that she forgot to bring back her water jar, the very reason she came to the well in the first place. Christ is the kind of friend who can make a real difference in our lives, one who can put things in perspective—if we let him.

CHRIST THE FRIEND *The Samaritan woman: I knew something was different about that man as soon as I came up to the well. He looked at me in a way that men didn't usually look at me. I met his eyes for just a second, and then I looked away. But I wanted to look again. I had seen in his glance something that I had only dreamed about before: he knew me completely—he knew exactly what kind of person I was. Yet it didn't bother him; in fact, it was as if he was glad to see me—not because he wanted* anything from me, but because he seemed to want something for me, as if he were pure kindness. So when I looked away, because that was the proper thing to do, I was just dying to look at him again, to see that kindness in his eyes, to drink it in.

But then I thought, no, it's only my imagination. And then he spoke to me. He asked me for a drink. And that was the beginning of a conversation that changed my life. I didn't understand everything he told me, but I understood that he knew me – he knew me through and through and he still cared about me, he was interested in me. For him, I was important, not just because I could give him something, but just… well, just because. In his eyes, I mattered. Even then I knew that what he said about being the Messiah was true. How else could I explain the change that was already happening in my heart? It was as if a door had opened in my life where before there had only been a thick, dark, high wall protecting my broken heart. He freed me. I had to tell the others in the town. I knew he was the Savior, and I just had to tell everyone. I knew that as soon as they met him they, too, would realize it. And they did! Before that day I was just surviving; after that encounter with his words, his glance, his presence – from then on I began to live.

CHRIST IN MY LIFE Jesus, tell me everything. Tell me about myself and the meaning of my life; tell me about your love and your wisdom and your plan for my life. Lord, give me your living water – how thirsty I am! I have tasted your gifts; I know at least a little bit about what you are offering. I want to know more. I want to live closer to you. I want to lead others to your heart, just as you led me…

I believe in you, Lord, and in your eagerness to save souls who are stuck in sin and darkness. And I believe that you can save them, just as you turned this woman's life around – just as you have turned my life around. Thank you for guiding me. Thank you for not giving up on me. Thank you for giving me a mission in life…

What does it mean, Lord, to worship in "Spirit and truth"? You want it; you came to make it possible. To worship is to acknowledge your greatness, majesty, and goodness. You want me to do so not only in external ceremonies but in my heart, in my attitudes, in my choices. You want me to live as you would have me live, Lord, trusting in you, seeking your will always. Teach me to do so, because this is what you desire…

Questions for
SMALL-GROUP DISCUSSION

1. What struck you most in this passage? What did you notice that you hadn't noticed before?

2. Would you say that your community of believers has come to believe in Christ with as much conviction as the Samaritan woman, who told the whole town about Christ? If not, what is holding you back?

3. In your Christian journey so far, what moment or experience has been most similar to the experience of this Samaritan woman?

4. The Samaritan woman was looking forward to the coming of the Messiah to get answers to life's questions. Where does popular culture encourage us to seek those answers?

Cf. Catechism of the Catholic Church, 2560-2562, 2652 on the encounter at Jacob's well as an image of prayer; 436-440 on the meaning of the title "Messiah"

250. FOOD FOR LIFE (JN 4:31-42)

"The best way to become a saint is to plunge ourselves in the will of God, as a stone is immersed in the water. We must allow ourselves to be tossed like a ball here and there according to his good pleasure." – St. Clement Hofbauer

JOHN 4:31-42

Meanwhile, the disciples were urging him, "Rabbi, do have something to eat; but he said, "I have food to eat that you do not know about." So the disciples asked one another, "Has someone been bringing him food?" But Jesus said: "My food is to do the will of the one who sent me, and to complete his work. Have you not got a saying: Four months and then the harvest? Well, I tell you: Look around you, look at the fields; already they are white, ready for harvest! Already the reaper is being paid his wages, already he is bringing in the grain for eternal life, and thus sower and reaper rejoice together. For here the proverb holds good: one sows, another reaps; I sent you to reap a harvest you had not worked for. Others worked for it; and you have come into the rewards of their trouble." Many Samaritans of that town had believed in him on the strength of the woman's testimony when she said, "He told me all I have ever done," so, when the Samaritans came up to him, they begged him to stay with them. He stayed for two days, and when he spoke to them many more came to believe; and they said to the woman, "Now we no longer believe because of what you told us; we have heard him ourselves and we know that he really is the savior of the world."

CHRIST THE LORD The Samaritans recognized Jesus as the "Savior of the world." The Samaritans were descended from Jews who had intermarried with non-Jews and abandoned the Jewish faith when the Kingdom of Israel was splitting up. They didn't get along well with the Jews. Jesus' stop here in Samaria, their generous response, and the phrase "Savior of the world," therefore, all come together to point to the universality of Jesus' mission. He has come to reestablish communion between God and all mankind. He has come to plug all lost hearts back into the source of true happiness: the love, truth, and mercy of God.

Jesus is consumed with longing to fulfill this mission. His hunger, which St. John just mentioned a few verses ago, has vanished because he has been doing what he is passionate about: saving souls. And he wants his disciples to share the joy by dedicating themselves to the same mission. He paints a picture of it for them, likening the spiritual harvest of bringing sinful and estranged people back into communion with God to the physical harvest of wheat. When a crop is ready for harvest, the farmers work eagerly and enthusiastically to gather it in; when a crop fails and the harvest is meager, the farmers are grieved—they wish they had more work. Jesus shows his disciples that the world is full of men and women like these Samaritans who are searching for the truth, whom God has prepared to hear the message of truth. The leaders of Jerusalem were indignant at Christ's claims to be the Messiah, but the outcast Samaritans drink it all in. Seeing such a huge harvest ready to be gathered in should fill Christ's disciples with a keen desire to roll up their sleeves and get to work. The Lord came to conquer hearts—the hearts of all men.

CHRIST THE TEACHER Whenever we encounter great individuals, we want to know what makes them tick. We want to discover the source of their greatness, so we can tap into it. St. John knows what makes Jesus tick. John is "the beloved disciple," who reclined next to Jesus during the Last Supper, leaning against him and listening to the beatings of his heart. As he finishes narrating this fascinating scene of Jesus' encounter with the Samaritan woman, he makes clear what Jesus is all about, what is in his heart. In so doing, he teaches us the key to being Christ's disciples: "My food is to do the will of the one who sent me, and to complete his work." Christ is a man consumed by his mission. Only that mission matters. To fulfill the Father's will, to complete the mission (the "work")—this is Christ's passionate desire. It pushes him on; it fills him with purpose and energy.... It is his food.

When we were baptized, we also were anointed in the name and the Spirit of Christ. When we were confirmed, we were anointed again and sent out as ambassadors of Christ and of his Church to gather in the abundant harvest of souls like the Samaritan woman, who are looking for Jesus and just need someone to point him out. As Christians, we are other Christs, continuing his saving mission in the world, and our food, too, should be none other than God's will.

CHRIST THE FRIEND Jesus explains that sometimes those who plant and those who harvest celebrate together. Other times, however, those who plant may never see the harvest, and those who gather may not have labored in the planting. In this way, he gives courage and comfort to those who have decided to accept his offer of friendship and work with him to build the Kingdom; he prepares them for two possible scenarios as they try to gather the harvest.

Jesus: At times you will see success and results right away; your efforts to build my Kingdom will yield abundant fruit quickly and easily. In those times, you must not give in to the temptation that will surely come, that of thinking that your talents and efforts alone have brought in the crop. I was the one who prepared those people to find me and hear my call through your voice. Rejoice then, but remember that the soil had been fertilized, tilled, and planted by other hands, and that I was the one who made the seeds grow. Other times I will ask you to do the fertilizing, tilling, and planting, and you may never see the results. Are you ready for that? I ask that of you because I know you love me, and I want to purify your love. If you persevere even when you don't see results, you will have to exercise that love, and you will no longer be working for the praise and recognition of others, but solely for me and my Kingdom. Then, as your love grows, you will begin to experience true joy and true freedom. I will be able to fill your soul with my wisdom and love, because it will have been emptied a little bit more of the vanity and pride that clogs the flow of my grace.

CHRIST IN MY LIFE I believe that you are the Savior of the world, Lord. And I believe that the world needs a Savior. We are all thirsty for the living water of your Spirit. I am thirsty, Lord. Increase my faith. Deepen my conviction. What does it really mean for me to say that I believe you are the Savior of the world? It made a difference in the lives of these Samaritans. Help it make a bigger difference in my life, Lord...

You lived wholly for the mission your Father had given you. I, too, have a mission. You have given me life and faith and relationships and responsibilities. You have made me a member of your Church, the extension of your Incarnation. How I long for my life to be focused and ordered, as yours was! Teach me to make your will the compass of my life, the quest of my heart, my anchor and my guiding star...

I want to build your Kingdom. I want to put my talents at the service of the men and women you love so much, the ones you came to save. But you know that my motives are not pure. So much selfishness is still mixed in. Purify me, Lord. Remind me that you are the Lord of the harvest and I am only one worker among many. Help me to find all my satisfaction in loving you by doing your will...

Questions for
SMALL-GROUP DISCUSSION

1. What struck you most in this passage? What did you notice that you hadn't noticed before?

2. All Christians are called to have one constant and burning desire in life — one "food" — to discover and fulfill the mission God has in mind for them. What other desires tend to seep into our lives and drain us of its force?

3. What more can we do to gather in the harvest that God has prepared around us?

4. What things tend to make us hesitant to bring others closer to Christ and how can we overcome them?

Cf. Catechism of the Catholic Church, 606-618 on the centrality of obedience to the Father's will in Christ's life and mission; 904-913 on the mission of the laity to exercise Christ's priestly and kingly offices in the world

---

251. A JOURNEY IN FAITH (JN 4:43-54)

"What is it that made the holy apostles and martyrs undergo fierce struggles and terrible agonies, if not faith, and above all faith in the Resurrection?" – Pope Benedict XIV

JOHN 4:43-54

When the two days were over Jesus left for Galilee. He himself had declared that there is no respect for a prophet in his own country, but on his arrival the Galileans received him well, having seen all that he had done at Jerusalem during the festival which they too had attended. He went again to Cana in Galilee, where he had changed the water into wine. Now there was a court official there whose son was ill at Capernaum and, hearing that Jesus had arrived in Galilee from Judaea, he went and asked him to come and cure his son as he was at the point of death. Jesus said, "So you will not believe unless you see signs and portents!" "Sir," answered the official "come down before my child dies." "Go home," said Jesus, "your son will live." The man believed what Jesus had said and started on his way; and while he was still on the journey back his servants met him with the news that his boy was alive. He asked them when the boy had begun to recover. "The fever left him yesterday," they said, "at the seventh hour." The father realised that this was exactly the time when Jesus had said, "Your son will live"; and he and all his household believed. This was the second sign given by Jesus, on his return from Judaea to Galilee.

CHRIST THE LORD Few passages show the sheer power of Jesus as eloquently as this miracle. In response to the courtier's request, Jesus simply tells him to go home, his son will live. And it happens exactly as Christ said it would. He spoke just one word, sickness and death fled, and life was restored. The effortlessness of the miracle is reminiscent of the Creation narrative in Genesis, where God simply says the word, "Let there be," and the infinite variety of existing things come into being out of nothing. This divine power continues to work in the Church today. When an ordained priest pronounces, in the person of Christ, the words of consecration, "This is my body... this is the cup of my blood," the bread is immediately transformed into Christ's body and the wine into his blood – just as easily and gently as Christ's word restored health to the courtier's son. When the priest pronounces the words of absolution in the confessional, "I absolve you from your sins in the name of the Father..." a moral healing, as real and as miraculous as the healing of the courtier's son, really takes place.

We easily take Christ's Lordship for granted. He is so gentle and patient with us that we can lose the sense of wonder that should accompany our journey of faith. Is it so small a thing to create a daffodil out of nothing, to bring solar systems and galaxies into existence where a moment before there was only nothingness, not even empty space? Is it so small a thing to transform bread and wine into Christ, the Son of God made man, and to do so in such a way that Christ himself becomes the nourishment of Christians? To recover and to nurture a healthy sense of wonder at who the Lord is and all that he does is pleasing to God and good for the soul. Children are full of wonder, and our Lord promised that unless we become like children, we will not enter into his Kingdom (Mk 10:15).

CHRIST THE TEACHER The court official is a paradigm of how difficult it can be to follow Christ, and how rewarding it is to persevere in the midst of such difficulties.

He is a high-ranking courtier in the royal palace of King Herod. And yet, with all his influence and wealth, he is helpless in the face of his son's illness. As he looks at his son, feverish and wasting away, he acutely feels this helplessness.

He feels for the first time how trifling the honors and powers of high society really are—they can do nothing to help him in the things that really matter. He hears that Jesus, the wonder-working rabbi from Nazareth, is back in Capernaum. The thought occurs: maybe he should go and ask Jesus to heal his son. But it would mean humbling himself in front of a simple carpenter. It would mean ridicule and talking behind his back from his colleagues at court, who mock the simple faith of the common people. It would mean admitting that this working-class, uneducated rabbi is God's chosen one when all the sophisticated Jewish leaders were calling him an imposter and a rabble-rouser. To go to Jesus would mean losing his carefully cultivated reputation, and maybe even compromise his chances at promotion. It is a high price to pay, he thinks. But then he looks at his son, and his father's heart yearns and cries out. No, he thinks again, it is a small price to pay for the life of my son.

And so the fashionable courtier makes the twenty-mile trip from Capernaum to Cana, humbles himself, and begs Jesus to come and heal his child. Jesus looks at him and seems to decline the request. He seems to reproach the courtier, and those around him, for needing to see signs and miracles in order to believe in him. Something in Jesus' voice and look invites the courtier to insist, however, and he does. This insistence shows that he already believes, that he has already relocated his trust. No longer does he rely on his own strength and position; now he has put all his confidence, all his hope, in Jesus. And Jesus answers his prayer. Then, without seeing the result, but taking Jesus at his word, the court official "believed what Jesus had said and started on his way."

CHRIST THE FRIEND The tragedy of his son's illness detached the courtier's heart from the vain promises of the world and impelled him to seek out Christ. As a result, he and all his family were brought into the saving realm of grace. Such is the unchanging pattern of growth in Christ. Whenever we admit the limits of our own resources and turn to Jesus for help, we give God's grace room to work.

Jesus: I performed this miracle for the courtier and his family, but I also did it for you. The miracle showed them how much I cared about them. Once they realized that, their lives blossomed. I care for you as much as I cared for them. I know you as fully as I knew them. I want you to believe in me, and I want you to believe that whatever I ask of you, I ask because I love you. If you believe in me more each day, your life will blossom more each day. I have so much I want to show you and teach you. Follow me; listen to me. I know you are still sick with selfish tendencies. Do you believe I can heal you? Ask me. Trust me. Let me walk with you.

CHRIST IN MY LIFE Lord, I praise you for your glory. All the wonders of this world, from the smallest buttercup to the farthest star, sing of your goodness. I am surrounded by gifts of your love. Why don't I think of this more often, Lord? Guide my thoughts to you. Help me to see your love at work in all things. Thank you for coming to earth to show us your face. Hallowed be thy name...

I am so often torn between following your path of trust and humility and gliding along the wide road of doing what everybody else is doing. Why do I care so much about what others think and say? Why is it so hard for me to do what I know you are asking and inviting me to do? You know, Lord; you know how weak I am. But what does my weakness matter when I have you all to myself to be my strength...

I know you and I believe in you. But what about all the courtiers in the world today who don't know you? Their lives are full of suffering, and they don't know where to go to find relief, meaning, and strength. Draw them to yourself, as you drew this court official. Move their hearts, and make me your ambassador. I will tell them of you...

Questions for
SMALL-GROUP DISCUSSION

1. What struck you most in this passage? What did you notice that you hadn't noticed before?

2. Which personal occurrences have taught you the most about or given you the most intense experience of God's goodness?

3. Why do you think Jesus didn't offer to go to the courtier's home to cure his son, as he did other times in the Gospels?

4. How do you think life in the court official's family might have changed after this encounter with Christ?

Cf. Catechism of the Catholic Church, 150-152 on what it means to believe in Christ; 153-165 on the characteristics of faith; 547-550 on the signs of the Kingdom of God

THE GOSPEL OF JOHN
Chapter 5

"Suppose you want to fill some sort of bag, and you know the bulk of what you will be given, you stretch the bag or the sack or the skin or whatever it is. You know how big the object that you want to put in and you see that the bag is narrow so you increase its capacity by stretching it. In the same way by delaying the fulfillment of desire God stretches it, by making us desire he expands the soul, and by this expansion he increases its capacity."

– ST. AUGUSTINE

252. STIRRING THINGS UP (JN 5:1-18)
"Whether I receive good or ill, I return thanks equally to God, who taught me always to trust him unreservedly." – St. Patrick

JOHN 5:1-18
Some time after this there was a Jewish festival, and Jesus went up to Jerusalem. Now at the Sheep Pool in Jerusalem there is a building, called Bethzatha in Hebrew, consisting of five porticos; and under these were crowds of sick people—blind, lame, paralysed—waiting for the water to move; for at intervals the angel of the Lord came down into the pool, and the water was disturbed, and the first person to enter the water after this disturbance was cured of any ailment he suffered from. One man there had an illness which had lasted thirty-eight years, and when Jesus saw him lying there and knew he had been in this condition for a long time, he said, "Do you want to be well again?" "Sir," replied the sick man, "I have no one to put me into the pool when the water is disturbed; and while I am still on the way, someone else gets there before me." Jesus said, "Get up, pick up your sleeping-mat and walk." The man was cured at once, and he picked up his mat and walked away.

Now that day happened to be the sabbath, so the Jews said to the man who had been cured, "It is the sabbath; you are not allowed to carry your sleeping-mat." He replied, "But the man who cured me told me, 'Pick up your mat and walk.'" They asked, "Who is the man who said to you, 'Pick up your mat and walk?'" The man had no idea who it was, since Jesus had disappeared into the crowd that filled the place. After a while Jesus met him in the Temple and said, "Now you are well again, be sure not to sin any more, or something worse may happen to you." The man went back and told the Jews that it was Jesus who had cured him. It was because he did things like this on the sabbath that the Jews began to persecute Jesus. His answer to them was, "My Father goes on working, and so do I." But that only made the Jews even more intent on killing him, because, not content with breaking the sabbath, he spoke of God as his own Father, and so made himself God's equal.

CHRIST THE LORD Jesus is back in Jerusalem, where the Jewish leaders continue to resist his teaching and ignore his signs. St. John gives no explanation for why these leaders refused to believe in Jesus, but he explains clearly what they refused to believe: "It was because he did things like this on the Sabbath that the Jews began to persecute Jesus.... He [Jesus] spoke of God as his own Father, and so made himself God's equal."

The complicated tangle of laws restricting the kind of work that could be done on the Sabbath was the Jewish leaders' pride and joy. It had become so complex and convoluted over the years that normal people had no hope of complying in every detail. Only the Pharisees, an important faction in the Sanhedrin, Israel's ruling body, kept faithful to all the restrictions, and this gave them moral and spiritual ascendancy over the populous. When Jesus returns to the pristine spirit of the Sabbath law, performing deeds that reveal God's goodness and give reason to praise him (that was the primary purpose for keeping the Sabbath holy, so that it would be a day dedicated to thanking and praising God), he threatens the Pharisees' ascendancy. Jesus, then, became an enemy to the status quo and to the leaders who had the power and influence therein. When the leaders challenge him, he uses the opportunity to reveal his identity as the Son of God. His comment about the Father who goes on working during the Sabbath refers to God's omnipotence that sustains the universe at all times—the rivers continue to flow, the sun continues to shine, and the crops continue to grow whether or not it's the Sabbath. God's love has no time limits, and Jesus' every word and action is a revelation and manifestation of God's love, so he, too, continues to work, Sabbath or no.

Jesus' Sabbath miracles manifest and validate his claim to be the divine Messiah. The Pharisees and other Jewish leaders recognized the claim but rejected its validity. They preferred being petty princes in their own little kingdoms to becoming disciples of the true King whose rule brings everlasting life. Today many people still reject Christ's claim. We who have chosen—by the light of his grace—to become his disciples should constantly renew our commitment. It's always possible to start clinging to the status quo so tightly that we end up missing the miracles he wants to send us.

CHRIST THE TEACHER Jesus asks this lame man a strange question, "Do you want to be well again?" How could the man not want to be well again? After thirty-eight years, his hope may have shriveled. Jesus stirs it up. Christ will never act in our lives unless we hope. Hope is the virtue of desiring the right things, confident in God's willingness and ability to give them. Hope can be cultivated. We have a responsibility to consciously steer our desires for happiness and fulfillment toward Christ and God's will. Do we want to leave behind our selfishness and learn to love? Do we really want to? Jesus has to ask this question first, because he will never force his way into our lives. We must want to be his followers, because all his followers are his friends, and friendship can't be forced.

Then he tells the man to get up. For almost forty years, the man had been unable to get up. He was lame. But Jesus asks him to get up all the same. When he makes the effort, simply because Jesus told him to, the miracle kicks into action. It is true that in the spiritual life we are helpless. Without God's grace we will never be made whole, never be forgiven, never achieve the spiritual maturity we were made for and that we long for. And yet, God's grace always requires our cooperation. We must obey, we must follow, we must trust—sometimes beyond the high-visibility range of our reason. We must respond to God's invitation in whatever little ways he may ask us in order for him to do wonderful, amazing things in and through us.

CHRIST THE FRIEND This man had been ill for thirty-eight years. It seems from Jesus' later comment when they meet in the Temple that his own sins had been the cause of his illness. It was an illness that made him an invalid, helpless and incapable of contributing to the society around him. And to top it all off, he was a lonely man. He didn't have any friend or family member who could help him down to the pool after the stirring of the waters. And then one day a young rabbi comes up to him. He squats down beside him, looks into his eyes, and asks him if he wants to be cured. Jesus is always taking the initiative in our lives. He knows what we need more than we do. He knows how much we have suffered and how our sins have damaged our souls. He comes to heal and renew us.

The sick man: Of course I wanted to be cured. That's why I was still waiting at the pool. It seemed an odd question to me. So I looked up at this man. I looked into his eyes as I told him that I wasn't fast enough to make it to the healing waters. What I said didn't seem to matter. He looked at me intently, but gently. I don't know how else to describe it. And then he seemed to smile, and there was a fire in his eyes. And he told me to get up, pick up my sleeping mat, and walk. I thought to myself, "Doesn't he see that I can't get up, that I can't carry anything, let alone my sleeping mat? I can't even walk! Doesn't he see me?" For thirty-eight years I had been lame, unable to do any of those things, and this man was telling me to stand up. It was a crazy thing to say. But his eyes weren't crazy. He just kept looking at me intently. I was going to tell him what a crazy idea it was, but his eyes wouldn't let me. Somehow, the fire in his eyes kindled one in my own, and all of a sudden I knew that I just had to do what he was telling me. But how could I? I had to try. Even as part of me objected—it was such an absurd thing that he was saying—I couldn't help but start to hope. And he kept looking at me and, well, I don't know how it happened, but I just started to get up, and all of a sudden I could. And then I picked up my mat. And I started walking. After thirty-eight years! I turned to thank him—but he was gone.

CHRIST IN MY LIFE Why didn't the leaders of Jerusalem believe in you? They saw your miracles, but even that couldn't pry their hearts away from their own self-centeredness. It seems so unreasonable. And yet, can I say that my faith is robust and confident? Am I not like those leaders, unable to free myself from my own self-centeredness, in spite of all you have done for me? Teach me, Lord, to do your will. Increase my faith...

Many times, the little things you ask me to do seem impossible. How can I be patient and kind to people who irritate me, who are ungrateful? How can I overcome the repugnance I feel sometimes in the face of my responsibilities? How can I simply trust you when so many things go wrong and nothing seems to work? Lord, I believe in you. If you tell me to get up and walk, I will. Thy will be done...

I want to be as generous as you are, Lord. You saw this man, knew his suffering, and came to his rescue. You have made me your ambassador; you want me to do the same for everyone around me. You want me to keep my eyes open for opportunities to serve, help, and do good. You want me to make that my obsession, as it was yours. Give me your grace, Lord, so that I, too, can "go on working"...

Questions for
SMALL-GROUP DISCUSSION

1. What struck you most in this passage? What did you notice that you hadn't noticed before?

2. Why do you think so many of the leaders of Jerusalem refused to believe in Jesus, even in the face of miracles?

3. What would you say is the most common reason that people today, in your community, refuse to believe in Jesus?

4. What are some things we can do to stir up and keep healthy the right desires in our hearts?

Cf. Catechism of the Catholic Church, 27-30 on the natural human desire for God; 65-67 on Christ as the definitive revelation of God; 172-175 on the oneness of our faith in Christ

253. AIMING AT GOD'S WILL (JN 5:19-30)

"There is one most priceless pearl: the knowledge of the Savior, the mystery of his Passion, the secret of his Resurrection." – St. Jerome

JOHN 5:19-30

To this accusation Jesus replied: "I tell you most solemnly, the Son can do nothing by himself; he can do only what he sees the Father doing: and whatever the Father does the Son does too. For the Father loves the Son and shows him everything he does himself, and he will show him even greater things than these, works that will astonish you. Thus, as the Father raises the dead and gives them life, so the Son gives life to anyone he chooses; for the Father judges no one; he has entrusted all judgement to the Son, so that all may honour the Son as they honour the Father. Whoever refuses honour to the Son refuses honour to the Father who sent him. I tell you most solemnly, whoever listens to my words, and believes in the one who sent me, has eternal life; without being brought to judgement he has passed from death to life. I tell you most solemnly, the hour will come—in fact it is here already—when the dead will hear the voice of the Son of God, and all who hear it will live. For the Father, who is the source of life, has made the Son the source of life; and, because he is the Son of Man, has appointed him supreme judge. Do not be surprised at this, for the hour is coming when the dead will leave their graves at the sound of his voice: those who did good will rise again to life; and those who did evil, to condemnation.

I can do nothing by myself; I can only judge as I am told to judge, and my judging is just, because my aim is to do not my own will, but the will of him who sent me."

CHRIST THE LORD Prior to this discourse, the Jewish leaders Jesus is speaking with had recognized Jesus' claim to be one with God the Father. That made them mad, and it confirmed their determination to do away with Jesus. This was the perfect opportunity, then, for Christ to clarify himself. Now was the time to explain that he wasn't saying he was one with God, but that he was just closer to God than other people, and so he had some special insights into the meaning of life. That would have put him on the same level as other rabbis and relieved the tension.

But Jesus doesn't do that. In fact, he amplifies and reiterates his claim to be one with the Father. Jesus is God made man. He is the one true God come to dwell among his people to save and instruct them, to give them life. Jesus is God, and he will exercise the divine prerogative of judging men and awarding eternal life or condemning to eternal death. This is his mission. The Word of God became incarnate in order to redeem sinners and bring them eternal life. And since there is only one God, anyone who believes in the true God will also believe in Jesus because he and the Father are one.

The Lord is so much more than a great philosopher, a mighty king, or a flashy leader. Jesus, the same Jesus who comes to us each day in Holy Communion, who forgives our sins through the priest in the confessional, and who waits patiently for us in the Tabernacle—this same Jesus is God, creator of all things, redeemer of all people, omniscient, omnipotent, all-loving, all-good. It is too much for us to understand. He knows that. And so he gives us once again the clue to living in accordance with these overwhelming truths. "My aim is to do not my own will, but the will of him who sent me," he explains. If the Father's will was the Lord's rule of life, the same should be true of his faithful subjects.

CHRIST THE TEACHER The eternal life that Jesus came to win for us doesn't begin in heaven; it begins on earth. Life in Christ is life in communion with God, and life in communion with God is what we were made for. It's where our happiness and fulfillment lie. It begins in this life and continues for all eternity, as we profess every Sunday: "We look for the resurrection of the dead and the life of the world to come."

Through the centuries, Christians have clashed over how this life is to be obtained. Some have claimed that faith alone brings the soul into friendship with Christ; others have claimed that good deeds will do it. But the Church's teaching has always been clear: friendship with Christ and the eternal life that comes with it require both faith and good works. In fact, although we can distinguish conceptually these two sides of the Christian life, in the reality of daily living there simply is no separation between them. This is because the human person is a unity of spirit and matter. Consequently, whatever one truly believes and commits to (in one's mind and will) necessarily manifests in actions. What we care about automatically affects the choices we make and the actions we perform. This is why Jesus can say in the same discourse, "Whoever listens to my words, and believes in the one who sent me, has eternal life," and then a few lines later, "Those who did good will rise again to life; and those who did evil, to condemnation."

Only by God's grace can we receive eternal life. But God's grace comes only to those who believe in Jesus. And to believe in Jesus is to live as Jesus would have us live. The life he gives us renews the whole person—mind, heart, and behavior. This fundamental truth explains why so many people who would like to believe in Christ can't seem to make the act of faith. They know instinctively that to say to Christ, "I believe in you" means saying at the same time, "I will follow you." But if they follow Christ, they have to leave their selfish ways behind. Here is the core of the spiritual battle. Only when a person comes to see that friendship with Christ offers more fulfillment than an atomized, self-centered existence will they be able to believe and follow the Lord.

CHRIST THE FRIEND Jesus only wants one thing—for us to have life. Death was the consequence of original sin and continues to be the consequence of all sins. Spiritual death ensues from sin because sin is rebellion against God, a willful separation of oneself from communion, from friendship with God. But since God alone is the source of all life, separation from him means separation from life, from the fullness of that meaningful and fruitful life that he created us to experience. And if friendship with God is not reestablished while one's earthly, biological life lasts, the separation from God will endure in an eternal "condemnation." But those who believe and trust in Jesus regain communion and friendship with God, and so they can be reborn to a meaningful and fruitful life here on earth. And if they stay faithful to their friendship with God until the end of their earthly sojourn, they will "rise again to life" at the end of history, and they will enjoy that friendship for all eternity.

Jesus: When I look at you and think of you, which I am always doing, I picture you living the life I created you to live. I know that now you still struggle and suffer, but this is only a passing stage. You are still recovering from sin. You are still in rehabilitation, and that always hurts. Keep going. Keep seeking my will. Keep getting up every time you fall. I am right at your side. I am leading you to a life that will fill you with more joy and wisdom and love than you can possibly imagine. I am the life, and I want you to spend forever with me.

CHRIST IN MY LIFE When I try to understand you, Lord, I am blinded by the immensity of your mystery. And yet I know that you came to earth and walked among men and that you continue to stay with me now in your Church and through your sacraments, precisely because you didn't want to keep your distance. You want me to know you. Little by little, Lord, reveal yourself to me. Open my eyes; I want to see your glory...

I know that you want to give me eternal life. You want to give me what I yearn for, passionately, in the very core of my being. You created me for that. But you can only give it to me if I am willing to follow you, if I am willing to seek and fulfill your will, no matter what. I want to, Lord. I want to spend my days doing good for those around me, just as you did, helping others to find life in you, now and for all eternity...

Thank you for becoming my Savior. Thank you for renewing my life. Sometimes I forget that I need you. But right now, I know that without your grace my life would have no meaning, like a lamp that's unplugged. Jesus, fill me with your life and make me a channel through which your life can flow into others and renew them too. Nothing matters more. Come, Lord Jesus, be my Savior...

Questions for
SMALL-GROUP DISCUSSION

1. What struck you most in this passage? What did you notice that you hadn't noticed before?

2. Why do you think Jesus so emphasizes his union with the Father in this discourse?

3. How would you explain to an inquiring, non-believing acquaintance the relationship between faith and good deeds in the pursuit of salvation? How would you explain the Christian idea of "eternal life"?

4. Some people criticize Christians for being too focused on the afterlife. How would you respond to such a criticism?

Cf. Catechism of the Catholic Church, 1811 on how to persevere in friendship with Christ; 1739-1742 on the relationship between grace and freedom; 1021-1022 on judgment and reward according to faith and works; 1038-1041 on the last judgment; 2006-2011 on the relationship between salvation, merit, and good deeds

254. EASY TO PLEASE (JN 5:31-47)

"... This love for Christ must ever be the chiefest and most agreeable result of a knowledge of Holy Scripture." – Pope Benedict XV

JOHN 5:31-47

"Were I to testify on my own behalf, my testimony would not be valid; but there is another witness who can speak on my behalf, and I know that his testimony is valid. You sent messengers to John, and he gave his testimony to the truth: not that I depend on human testimony; no, it is for your salvation that I speak of this. John was a lamp alight and shining and for a time you were content to enjoy the light that he gave. But my testimony is greater than John's: the works my Father has given me to carry out, these same works of mine testify that the Father has sent me. Besides, the Father who sent me bears witness to me himself. You have never heard his voice, you have never seen his shape, and his word finds no home in you because you do not believe in the one he has sent. You study the scriptures, believing that in them you have eternal life; now these same scriptures testify to me, and yet you refuse to come to me for life! As for human approval, this means nothing to me. Besides, I know you too well: you have no love of God in you. I have come in the name of my Father and you refuse to accept me; if someone else comes in his own name you will accept him. How can you believe, since you look to one another for approval and are not concerned with the approval that comes from the one God? Do not imagine that I am going to accuse you before the Father: you place your hopes on Moses, and Moses will be your accuser. If you really believed him you would believe me too, since it was I that he was writing about; but if you refuse to believe what he wrote, how can you believe what I say?"

CHRIST THE LORD Jesus makes no effort to overpower his antagonists. He reaches out to them using their own language, their own form of argumentation. The Jewish scribes and Pharisees and other leaders in Jerusalem at that time were scholars. They dedicated themselves to study and memorize the Scriptures and the many commentaries and interpretations of them that had accumulated through the centuries. This was an important work for these leaders because the Scriptures were the record of the special revelation that God had given to them and to no other nation. It was a rigorous work, too—copies of the text had to be handwritten; no printing press was around to help supply everyone with personal libraries.

Part of this rabbinic intellectual culture included a legal system in which at least two witnesses were required to affect a verdict, and the accused person was not permitted to witness in his own defense. Jesus graciously admits and accepts these criteria as he defends his own claims to be the divine Messiah. He points to three witnesses that all of his interlocutors should recognize: John the Baptist, whom everyone agreed was a prophet, and who had explicitly declared Christ to be the Messiah; the Father, whose divine power is evident in Christ's miracles; and the Scriptures themselves, which record the revelation that was directed in its every detail toward the coming of Jesus Christ.

Jesus seeks to conquer hearts and minds—to rescue them from the darkness of self-absorption and lead them into the light of truth—but he does so by coming into our lives and speaking our language, reaching out to us in ways we will understand. This has always been, still is, and ever will be the way of the Lord.

CHRIST THE TEACHER Jesus' case is already complete and incontrovertible because of his three witnesses, but he goes even one step further, hoping to win over these reluctant rabbis. He tells them exactly why they find it difficult to accept his message: "... You have no love of God in you... you look to one another for approval and are not concerned with the approval that comes from the one God." The Pharisees and scribes who rejected Jesus did so because they had let themselves be carried away by their own successes. In their zeal for perfection, they had begun to pay too much attention to being more respected and popular than the other guy. This kind of religiosity was attractive to them because it provided a standard of success that was within their own, natural reach: if they only have to be better than their neighbor, they have no need of God's assistance in order to be successful. If they had been seeking the kind of success God wanted, however, they would have had to admit their sins and failings and come to depend on God's help. But depending on God was an uncomfortable thing because it meant that God would get the glory; it was much more satisfying, in the short term, to achieve success by their own efforts and claim all the glory for themselves.

The Gospel writers spent so much time describing Jesus' clashes with these self-righteous and self-seeking antagonists because the Holy Spirit knows that we are just like them. Why are we not yet the saints that God wants us to be? Why has God's grace not yet yielded the over-abundant harvest of spiritual fruit that he promises us? Because the love of God in our hearts is still not pure, we still seek our satisfaction too much in being thought well of by our neighbors, in beating our competitors, and in achieving great things by our own power. Even in the apostolate, our self-giving and love for the Church is often tainted with a vain thirst for success and a jealous desire to appear more pious than others. Inasmuch as we still seek glory for ourselves, we handcuff the transforming power of God in our lives.

CHRIST THE FRIEND Jesus is a faithful friend. Once again he publicly praises John the Baptist, who had dedicated his life to serving Christ and bearing him witness. Jesus never forgets deeds done to please him and build up his Kingdom. He is interested in everything we do because he loves us more than the most loving parent, more than the most faithful spouse. He appreciates every effort we make in his name, for his sake. How much confidence this should give us! Even if no one ever knows or sees our sacrifices, our small acts of self-denial and self-giving, Jesus is gathering them up like beautiful flowers and enjoying each one of them. Each one weaves the patchwork of our life. How much freedom this truth can give to our souls! We no longer have to scratch and fight our way to the honors platform in order to win prizes that perish and recognition that withers. In Christ, we can flourish without fear. *Jesus: My love is enough for you. Live in the light of my love. Live for loving me. Seek my approval in all you do; I am so easy to please, and no whims or selfishness or bad moods cloud my appreciation. I lived and died and rose for you. I want to give you the kind of peace and joy that doesn't wear away. All you need is my love.*

CHRIST IN MY LIFE I believe in you, Lord, but I know so many people who don't believe in you. They are still looking for meaning in awards and money and reputation. They are stuck on that thankless merry-go-round. Thank you for taking me off that and putting me on the path of life. Forgive me for my ingratitude, for the times I resent your demands. Make me your disciple, your spokesperson, to bring many others to your friendship...

I know that you are always speaking to me, arranging all the events and encounters of my day in order to draw me closer to you. You love me that much. I know it, Lord, and yet I am still a bad listener. Teach me to find you, to see you, to hear your voice in all the happenings of my busy life. Teach me to detect your will and do it, gladly, eagerly, simply because I love you...

Sometimes I am afraid that I am not doing enough for you, Lord. But that's because I keep thinking that I need to earn your love the way I have had to earn the love of others. But you are not like that. You already love me, and nothing I do can increase or decrease that love. Cast out my fears and fill me with the courage and energy that comes from knowing I am loved unconditionally and infinitely by you...

Questions for
SMALL-GROUP DISCUSSION

1. What struck you most in this passage? What did you notice that you hadn't noticed before?

2. The people Jesus was addressing knew the Scriptures backwards and forwards, and yet they couldn't recognize that Jesus was the fulfillment of all the prophecies they knew so well. How can we avoid falling into this kind of subjective understanding of God's revelation?

3. Which elements of popular culture encourage us to seek the approval of other people instead of God's approval? How can we avoid this?

4. In what ways have you discovered God coming and speaking to your heart in a language you understand particularly well, just as he came and spoke to the Jewish leaders using arguments that they were experts in?

Cf. Catechism of the Catholic Church, 80-83 on Sacred Scripture; 84-95 on the proper way to interpret Sacred Scripture; 101-104 on Christ as the center of Sacred Scripture; 109-119 on the levels of meaning in Sacred Scripture and criteria for interpreting it; 2123-2128 on reasons behind disbelief; 1459 on the consequences of sin for our spiritual lives

THE GOSPEL OF JOHN
Chapter 6

❋

"It was his will that his gifts should remain among us; it was his will that the souls which he had redeemed by his precious blood should continue to be sanctified by sharing the pattern of his own passion. For this reason he appointed his faithful disciples the first priests of his Church and enjoined them never to cease to perform the mysteries of eternal life. These mysteries must be celebrated by every priest in every church in the world until Christ comes again from heaven, so that we priests, together with the congregation of the faithful, may have the example of Christ's passion daily before our eyes, hold it in our hands, and even receive it in our mouths and in our hearts and so keep undimmed the memory of our redemption."

– ST. GAUDENTIUS OF BRESCIA

255. FEEDING THE HUNGRY (JN 6:1-15)

"This is the food which sustains and nourishes us on our journey through life, until we depart from this world and are united with Christ." – St. Gaudentius of Brescia

JOHN 6:1-15

Some time after this, Jesus went off to the other side of the Sea of Galilee—or of Tiberias—and a large crowd followed him, impressed by the signs he gave by curing the sick. Jesus climbed the hillside, and sat down there with his disciples. It was shortly before the Jewish feast of Passover. Looking up, Jesus saw the crowds approaching and said to Philip, "Where can we buy some bread for these people to eat?" He only said this to test Philip; he himself knew exactly what he was going to do. Philip answered, "Two hundred denarii would only buy enough to give them a small piece each." One of his disciples, Andrew, Simon Peter's brother, said, "There is a small boy here with five barley loaves and two fish; but what is that between so many?" Jesus said to them, "Make the people sit down." There was plenty of grass there, and as many as five thousand men sat down. Then Jesus took the loaves, gave thanks, and gave them out to all who were sitting ready; he then did the same with the fish, giving out as much as was wanted. When they had eaten enough he said to the disciples, "Pick up the pieces left over, so that nothing gets wasted." So they picked them up, and filled twelve hampers with scraps left over from the meal of five barley loaves. The people, seeing this sign that he had given, said, "This really is the prophet who is to come into the world." Jesus, who could see they were about to come and take him by force and make him king, escaped back to the hills by himself.

CHRIST THE LORD Before dying, Moses promised that some day God would send another leader to the people of Israel, someone as great as himself, who had been the greatest and humblest of God's servants. This figure was referred to as "the prophet": "I will raise up a prophet like yourself for them from their own brothers; I will put my words into his mouth and he shall tell them all I command him. The man who does not listen to my words that he speaks in my name, shall be held answerable to me for it" (Dt 18:18-19). Through the centuries, the Jewish people had come to identify this figure with the promised Messiah, the one who would liberate their nation from oppression and usher in a new golden age, similar to the one they had enjoyed under King David.

The magnitude of the miracle Jesus performs by multiplying the loaves and fishes, added to the many other miracles that he had already done, convinces the crowds that he is indeed the promised Savior, the one whom God had sent into the world to finish the job of salvation that had begun with Moses and the Exodus. They recognized him, but they did not listen to him. He showed by his miracles that he was God's chosen one, but with his words he spoke of a new kind of Kingdom, an everlasting Kingdom that was within men's hearts, not in political platforms. The crowds refused to understand this, and so Christ refused to let them make him their King.

CHRIST THE TEACHER Five loaves and two fish cannot feed a crowd of five thousand men (plus at least as many women and children). It is impossible. Not even a year's salary (the equivalent of two hundred denarii) could buy enough for such a feast, as Philip nervously points out. And yet, when the Apostles hand over their paltry resources to the Lord, they become more than enough to do the job.

The same goes for every Christian apostle. Whose natural talents and wisdom are sufficient to defeat the forces of evil that hold the world in tow? Whose innate strength is sufficient to put an end to the selfishness, lust, and greed that rage within the human heart? How can the meager resources of a single parish or diocese suffice to do battle with media moguls, corrupt politicians, international banking cartels, and other agents of the culture of death? We only have five loaves and two fish; by ourselves we can do nothing. Only if we put all we have into Christ's hands, trusting in him and not ourselves, can we hope to make a real difference for the good of the Kingdom—in our hearts and in society at large. Every small act of charity adds to the Church's much-needed reservoir of grace and strength. What we could never achieve on our own, we can immeasurably surpass with God. As Jesus himself put it, "For God everything is possible" (Mt 19:26).

CHRIST THE FRIEND Friends look out for each other. "Looking up," Jesus saw that the crowd following him didn't have any food; that he remedied the situation demonstrates his desire for our friendship. He wants to be our partner in life, our companion; our confidant. He is looking out for us, always keeping his eyes open for an opportunity to feed our hungry hearts with his beauty and truth. He wants to supply for our needs; it is his greatest joy. As he puts it later in this same Gospel, "I have come so that they may have life, and have it to the full." Those are the words of a friend we can count on.

Philip: How could I ever forget that day? None of us wanted to bother with the needs of that huge crowd of people. We were exhausted and just wanted to get away and relax. I was especially exhausted. Maybe that's why he teased me a bit and tested me with the question about where we could buy some bread for that huge mass of hungry people; he knew I would be exasperated. But our tiredness didn't impede us from learning the lesson he wanted to teach. In fact, it helped. He wanted us to learn what love is. He looked out at those people, who had sacrificed their own comfort in order to come and be with him, and he saw how hungry they were. He couldn't hold back his yearning to feed them. He was always like that. He was always looking for ways to fill our starving minds and hearts with his abundant truth and wisdom. He was totally for us. Actually, most of the time I felt as if he was totally for me. He knew me so well; he always knew exactly what I needed, and he always took the first step to give it to me.

CHRIST IN MY LIFE I know that you are most interested in what happens inside me, in my heart and in my mind. You care about what I think about, pay attention to, and decide to do. You want to be King of my heart because you know exactly what my heart needs in order to experience the satisfaction and meaning that it longs for. Lord Jesus, Savior of all people, make your Kingdom come in my mind and heart...

So often I let myself be carried away by nervousness, stress, worry, and fear. How I need you to increase my faith, Lord! You are God; you are omnipotent! All I need to do each day is put my five loaves and two fish into your wise and powerful hands, and you will make my life a fountain of light and hope and goodness. Teach me to trust in you, to rejoice in you, to fear only whatever could separate me from you...

Your heart never tires of giving. You are a furnace of love that never grows cold. When you look at me, you think only of all that you want to do for me. Why am I not more like you, Lord? What is keeping me from loving others with that kind of energy, constancy, and creativity? I give you my meager five loaves and two fish. Lord Jesus, show me how to follow you more closely, teach me to love as you love, giving myself to others as you give yourself to me...

Questions for
SMALL-GROUP DISCUSSION

1. What struck you most in this passage? What did you notice that you hadn't noticed before?

2. What are the differences between the benefits that we could expect from a prosperous worldly kingdom and the benefits we should hope for from God's Kingdom?

3. In what ways are we often tempted to hoard our few loaves, instead of giving them to Christ so he can multiply them?

4. How can we tell if we are really counting on Christ to give our lives mean-ing—as he wants us to—instead of depending on our own efforts?

Cf. Catechism of the Catholic Church, 27-30 on God as the only source of true happiness; 430-440 on Christ as the fulfillment of God's plan of salvation, begun in the Old Testament; 2816-2821 on the meaning of the "Kingdom"

256. WORKING FOR BREAD THAT LASTS (JN 6:16-35)

"... In the same way we call Christ our bread, because he is the food of those who are members of his body." – St. Cyprian

JOHN 6:16-35

That evening the disciples went down to the shore of the lake and got into a boat to make for Capernaum on the other side of the lake. It was getting dark by now and Jesus had still not rejoined them. The wind was strong, and the sea was getting rough. They had rowed three or four miles when they saw Jesus walking on the lake and coming towards the boat. This frightened them, but he said, "It is I. Do not be afraid." They were for taking him into the boat, but in no time it reached the shore at the place they were making for.

Next day, the crowd that had stayed on the other side saw that only one boat had been there, and that Jesus had not got into the boat with his disciples, but that the disciples had set off by themselves. Other boats, however, had put in from Tiberias, near the place where the bread had been eaten. When the people saw that neither Jesus nor his disciples were there, they got into those boats and crossed to Capernaum to look for Jesus. When they found him on the other side, they said to him, "Rabbi, when did you come here?" Jesus answered: "I tell you most solemnly, you are not looking for me because you have seen the signs but because you had all the bread you wanted to eat. Do not work for food that cannot last, but work for food that endures to eternal life, the kind of food the Son of Man is offering you, for on him the Father, God himself, has set his seal." Then they said to him, "What must we do if we are to do the works that God wants?" Jesus gave them this answer, "This is working for God: you must believe in the one he has sent." So they said, "What sign will you give to show us that we should believe in you? What work will you do? Our fathers had manna to eat in the desert; as scripture says: He gave them bread from heaven to eat." Jesus answered: "I tell you most solemnly, it was not Moses who gave you bread from heaven, it is my Father who gives you the bread from heaven, the true bread; for the bread of God is that which comes down from heaven and gives life to the world." "Sir," they said "give us that bread always." Jesus answered: "I am the bread of life. He who comes to me will never be hungry; he who believes in me will never thirst."

CHRIST THE LORD Jesus is not flattered by the adulation of the crowds. He is acutely aware that his mission is not to bring people a paradise on earth (which is what they want—"You are… looking for me… because you had all the bread you wanted to eat"), but to bring them "bread from heaven," the truth and freedom of living in communion with God. He will not accept their allegiance unless they accept his message; he will not compromise his undertaking to enjoy an ego trip. Christ is a Leader entirely focused on his mission, not on himself. If we are to be faithful to him, we need to follow in those footsteps.

CHRIST THE TEACHER The Jewish rabbis had long predicted that the Prophet who would come to carry on Moses' work of salvation would prove himself through a miracle similar to that of the manna, the bread which God miraculously sent his people each morning during their forty years of wandering through the desert—bread "from heaven" as they called it, meaning from the sky. Such a sign is what the people are asking for here. Christ responds by explaining that the miraculous bread they are talking about—the promised Messianic sign—is much more than an abundance of bread that will feed the body; it is bread that actually comes from heaven (not just from the sky) and imbues the world with divine life. The people's eager response, "Give us that bread always," shows that they have understood the elevated nature of this new manna, and they desire it.

Through that conversation, and through the miracle of the multiplication of loaves that took place the previous day, Jesus has prepared them for this crucial moment, the first announcement of the Sacrament of the Eucharist, the living sacrifice of and communion with Christ's own body and blood which will inundate the world with his very life. He had been looking forward to telling them. Now the time had come. We can imagine the moment in which he speaks the next phrase, how he paused to search their faces, looking into their eyes, hoping that they would respond with faith and trust, but knowing that many of them would not. Finally, as they gaze on him with keen anticipation, he speaks: "I am the bread of life. He who comes to me will never be hungry; he who believes in me will never thirst." He spoke those tremendous, mysterious words and then stood looking intently into their faces, eagerly hoping for a trusting response of childlike faith. What went through their minds? What goes through our minds?

CHRIST THE FRIEND Jesus knows the deepest yearnings of our hearts; he knows what we hunger for, what we thirst for: happiness, meaning, and fulfillment. He knows it, because he made us to desire lasting joy and satisfaction. When we achieve that, we are achieving the purpose for which he created us. But he also knows that we cannot do it alone. Ever since original sin separated us from friendship with God, our most fundamental desire has been frustrated. That's why he came to earth; that's why he established his Church; that's why he constantly embraces us through the sacraments, especially the Eucharist. In Christ, the human heart feasts on the abundance of life for which it was made; without Christ, it slowly starves.

Jesus: Your heart is restless, I know. That's good. You want more out of your life; I do too. I am what you're looking for. Know me better; listen to me; trust me more. Why do you keep trying to be a saint on your own? Your efforts can do nothing alone. I am not asking you to go off and become perfect and then come back to me so I can let you into my Kingdom. My Kingdom is not something you get into by submitting a résumé, as if you were applying for a job. My Kingdom is my family. You don't have to earn my love; I love you already. You only have to trust me, lean on me, and follow me. Why else would I give my own life to be your food? Be at peace. I am with you.

CHRIST IN MY LIFE Thank you for caring more about my salvation than your reputation, Lord. Thank you for staying faithful to your mission. Thank you for refusing to flatter the crowds and insisting on teaching the truth. O Lord, you have made me your ambassador, so give me that same burning desire to build your Kingdom. Cleanse my desires, purify my heart, and teach me to seek your will above all things...

I believe that you are truly present in the Eucharist. I believe that you want to give me your own life, to enable me to share in your divine nature, to bring me into your family. I want to eat this bread, Lord. I want to eat it worthily, to receive you with faith, hope, and love, not just out of routine, not just because everyone else does it. O Lord, stir up in my mind a deep awareness of your gift in the Eucharist...

Okay, Lord, I admit it once again: I cannot follow you by relying only on my own strength. I need your grace. You want it that way. You created me to need you, so that I would be drawn by my own inner yearnings to live in a communion of knowledge and love with you. Be my strength, Lord; be my light, my food, my joy, my all...

Questions for
SMALL-GROUP DISCUSSION

1. What struck you most in this passage? What did you notice that you hadn't noticed before?

2. Where do you think Christ gets the strength to stay "on task" (i.e., doing his Father's will) even when it means giving up his popularity among the crowds?

3. How can we appreciate more Christ's great gift of the Eucharist, both individually and as a community?

4. If Jesus Christ really is the bread of life, we who know this should be eager to take advantage of every opportunity to bring others closer to him. In what ways should this eagerness manifest itself? What opportunities do we tend to squander?

Cf. Catechism of the Catholic Church, 1382-1405 on the benefits of devotion to the Eucharist; 1333-1338 on the meaning of "bread" in the Eucharist, and the Catholic interpretation of John 6

257. BELIEVING OR COMPLAINING (JN 6:36-51)

"He gave himself to be our food; unhappy is the one who is unaware of so great a gift."
– St. Cajetan

JOHN 6:36-51

"But, as I have told you, you can see me and still you do not believe. All that the Father gives me will come to me, and whoever comes to me I shall not turn him away; because I have come from heaven, not to do my own will, but to do the will of the one who sent me. Now the will of him who sent me is that I should lose nothing of all that he has given to me, and that I should raise it up on the last day. Yes, it is my Father's will that whoever sees the Son and believes in him shall have eternal life, and that I shall raise him up on the last day." Meanwhile the Jews were complaining to each other about him, because he had said, "I am the bread that came down from heaven." "Surely this is Jesus son of Joseph," they said. "We know his father and mother. How can he now say, 'I have come down from heaven?'" Jesus said in reply, "Stop complaining to each other. No one can come to me unless he is drawn by the Father who sent me, and I will raise him up at the last day. It is written in the prophets: They will all be taught by God, and to hear the teaching of the Father, and learn from it, is to come to me. Not that anybody has seen the Father, except the one who comes from God: he has seen the Father. I tell you most solemnly, everybody who believes has eternal life. I am the bread of life. Your fathers ate the manna in the desert and they are dead; but this is the bread that comes down from heaven, so that a man may eat it and not die. I am the living bread which has come down from heaven. Anyone who eats this bread will live for ever; and the bread that I shall give is my flesh, for the life of the world."

CHRIST THE LORD Jesus is no ordinary leader. He is not even the greatest king among all kings. He is absolutely unique. When he speaks of God, he speaks of "my Father," whom he alone has "seen," who sent him, whose will Jesus fulfills perfectly. To hear Christ, to know him, and to follow him means to hear, know, and follow God himself. That is why "whoever believes" in him "has eternal life." To believe in Christ is to give one's life to him, to entrust oneself to his care—and when we do that, he faithfully leads us to his Father's house.

Through the centuries, many have continued to "complain" about Jesus, contending that he is only a man, only a great teacher, or only a great religious leader: "We know his father and mother. . . ." Only when we allow ourselves to be drawn by the love of God, when we give in to God as he tugs at our hearts ("No one can come to me unless he is drawn by the Father"), only then can we see beyond the confines of our limited understanding; only then does Jesus of Nazareth become for us Jesus the Christ, Christ the Lord.

CHRIST THE TEACHER Christ packs three momentous lessons into this discourse. First, he points out the mystery of faith, that no one can believe in him "unless he is drawn by the Father." Faith in Jesus Christ supplies us with life's only dependable fuel, and yet, faith in Christ is God's gift. For this reason, we need to pray ceaselessly for an increase of faith, both for ourselves and for those who have yet to believe.

Second, faith in Christ leads to "eternal life." Later in the Gospel, Jesus tells us that eternal life consists in knowing "you, the only true God, and Jesus Christ whom you have sent" (Jn 17:3). In biblical language, "knowing" implies deep interpersonal intimacy, the kind of relationship that we all yearn for. That we can have this with God himself, who is more lovable, more beautiful than any other person is or ever could be, is the Good News of Jesus Christ.

Third, Jesus himself is the "bread" of this eternal life, its source and sustenance. Without bread, without food, physical life perishes; without Jesus, without his "flesh for the life of the world" in the Eucharist, our life of intimate communion with God will perish. It's that simple—and it's that crucial. Eleven times in this discourse Jesus speaks of himself as the bread of life; you'd think we would get the message. But if someone were to measure our real devotion to the Eucharist—our active and prayerful involvement in Mass, our recollection in receiving Communion, the frequency and sincerity of our visits to the Tabernacle—would they conclude that this Sacrament is, in actual fact, our bread of life?

CHRIST THE FRIEND Those who believe in Jesus will have "eternal life"; they will "not die" but "will live forever"; those who come to him will be "raised on the last day." How odd for Jesus to be thinking of that even before he himself has been raised! And yet, it is why he came; it is the goal of all his sufferings and efforts. He wants to bring each of us into the everlasting Kingdom of light and joy, and he never lets that goal drift into the background. Friendship with Christ is not a temporary fix, a psychological gimmick to make our little trip through life a bit livelier. When Jesus Christ extends his hand in friendship (which he never stops doing), he means to walk with us in time and in eternity—if we're willing.

Jesus: So many people still think of me as a harsh taskmaster. They think of Christianity as a list of dos and don'ts (mostly don'ts). But my desire, the Father's desire, is to give everyone the fullness of life that they yearn for. Everything I taught and did, everything my Church teaches and does, is directed to that goal. You know this. You believe it. Let my love seep more and more into your heart; let the hope I bring overflow in the enthusiasm of your glance and the simple joy of your smile. You know the truth about what is in store for those who believe in me. Always remember it and think about it. When sadness or discouragement creep up on you, turn back to me and my promises, and I will renew your peace, your joy, your confidence, and your enthusiasm.

CHRIST IN MY LIFE I don't want to complain anymore, Lord. I want to listen to you, to believe in you, to let myself be drawn to you. O Lord, I feel so contradictory! My selfishness, my resistance to believing without understanding completely, my tendency to make everything and everyone bow down to my own standards and ideas—all of this holds me back. Free me from myself, Lord; teach me to do your will...

I don't know how I'm supposed to remember all that you have taught me, Lord. The supply of your wisdom is too deep and too rich for me to keep it all in my mind. And yet, I want to live wholly engaged by your gospel, wholly enthralled by your message. Take my life in your hands, Lord. Guide my thoughts, desires, and decisions, so that I live entirely docile to your inspirations and your will...

You keep talking about raising up on the last day those who believe in you. It was on your mind. Why is it not more on my mind? Increase my faith, Lord. Teach me to see the world as you see it, to want the true and lasting good of my neighbor (and my family, and my colleagues) as much as you do. With the burning love of your heart, inflame my heart...

Questions for
SMALL-GROUP DISCUSSION

1. What struck you most in this passage? What did you notice that you hadn't noticed before?

2. Why do you think so many people consider Jesus Christ to be just one more great (or not so great) historical personage, when the Gospels make it so clear that he claimed to be the one and only Son of God and Messiah?

3. What evidence is there in our daily lives that we conceive of the Eucharist as necessary food for our spiritual life, as Christ conceives of it? What evidence should there be?

4. How would you describe your relationship with Christ? Is it more like an antidote to personal problems, or is it an adventure of friendship, one of mutual self-revelation and discovery?

Cf. Catechism of the Catholic Church, 55, 161-165 on faith and eternal life; 166-175 on the nature of faith; 1337-1344 on the institution of the Eucharist

258. EATING RIGHT (JN 6:52-59)

"This sacrament is operative to produce both love and union with Christ. The greatest showing of love is to give oneself as food." – St. Albert the Great

JOHN 6:52-59
Then the Jews started arguing with one another: "How can this man give us his flesh to eat?" they said. Jesus replied: "I tell you most solemnly, if you do not eat the flesh of the Son of Man and drink his blood, you will not have life in you. Anyone who does eat my flesh and drink my blood has eternal life, and I shall raise him up on the last day. For my flesh is real food and my blood is real drink. He who eats my flesh and drinks my blood lives in me and I live in him. As I, who am sent by the living Father, myself draw life from the Father, so whoever eats me will draw life from me. This is the bread come down from heaven; not like the bread our ancestors ate: they are dead, but anyone who eats this bread will live for ever." He taught this doctrine at Capernaum, in the synagogue.

CHRIST THE LORD History is replete with kings and emperors who put up with no opposition. If the subjects of Ivan the Terrible had ever been caught "arguing with one another" about the veracity or wisdom of one of his declarations, they would have met with a quick and speedy death. But Jesus leaves each one free to accept or reject him, to trust him or abandon him. Our Lord is all-powerful, but he refuses to abuse his power; he called the Jews to believe in him and follow him—just as he calls each one of us—but he never forces us. His is a Kingdom of justice, but also one of love.

Jesus describes himself as being sent from the Father, as sharing the very life of the Father. Christ is a man, and he is God. These are remarkable claims. But they don't stop there. He claims that he will give his own flesh as our food, so that we might enter into that divine life as well. We will remain men and women, but we will have the life of God within us. Jesus claims a Lordship unlike any ever claimed before or since. He is Master both of earth and of heaven; he is the Lord of both human and divine life. No wonder his claims caused his listeners to argue amongst themselves; it is no ordinary thing to believe in such a Lord.

CHRIST THE TEACHER Great teachers know that "repetition is the mother of learning," as the old saying goes. If they deem a certain lesson more important than others, they will repeat it over and over again, in different ways perhaps, until the students pick it up. In this discourse, responding to his audience's understandable difficulty in grasping how it will be possible for all of them to "eat his flesh," Jesus clarifies what he means.

This was the perfect opportunity for Christ to say, "Wait a minute, what I really meant was that my body and blood will just be symbolized by bread and wine. Of course I didn't mean that bread and wine really would become my body and blood. Don't be foolish!" The strange thing is he doesn't say that. He does not water down his claim, as if eating his flesh were just a metaphor for believing in his doctrine; on the contrary, he reiterates the importance of really eating his flesh and drinking his blood. Seven times throughout his speech he repeats that his flesh is to be eaten and his blood to be drunk by those who wish to have eternal life. Seven times. None of his listeners concluded that he was speaking with poetic imagery; they all understood him to mean what he said. Many of them did not accept it, and they abandoned him. Those who stayed were rewarded much later, when at the Last Supper Jesus showed how this strange saying was to play out: through the Sacrament of the Eucharist—his flesh made into our food, his blood made into our drink, so as to flood this dying world with the eternal life of God.

CHRIST THE FRIEND Love gives itself; it shares itself completely. Christ loves to the extreme: he gives us his own life. He shares with us his own divine existence—"Whoever eats me will draw life from me." This is the meaning of the Eucharist, which the Church calls the "source and summit" of Christian life. It is the sacrament of love par excellence, because there Love makes himself available 24/7. We will never be able to comprehend exactly how it happens, but we know that it does happen, and we know why: so that we will "live forever." In the face of such love, the only appropriate response is to humbly accept this precious gift, relish it, and give our own love in return.

Jesus: When your friends go away, you often give them a gift or a keepsake to remember you by; when I returned to heaven, I left you my very self to remember me by. When you are separated from friends for extended periods, you occasionally make yourself present to them through letters and calls and e-mails; while I am reigning in heaven, I stay with you all the time in the Tabernacle. You may think that my love is kind of generic, because the Eucharist is so simple and ordinary, and because everyone gets the same kind of host. But that's not how it is at all. I am fully present in every host. And each one of you receives me personally from the hands of the priest—one-on-one. And don't forget that I am God, so nothing limits my love—not time, not space, not tiredness, not bad moods, nothing: I love you as if you alone were loveable. When I come to you in Holy Communion, and when I wait for you in the Tabernacle, all my thought and all my desire is focused on you. I know it's hard for you to understand this, but it's true. Think about me waiting for you there in the Tabernacle, interceding for you, offering myself for you at every moment... for you. You never have to doubt my love again.

CHRIST IN MY LIFE Thank you for creating me free and respecting my freedom. Because you made me free, I can love, and in loving, I come to resemble you and enter into your friendship. O Lord, purify my heart. Help me to choose more often, more definitively, and more passionately to give myself to those you have put under my care. I want to love with all the force of my freedom, just as you do...

Bread is such a simple food, Lord. It's so normal, so basic. And that's how you come to me. O Lord, open my eyes so that I will see you as you truly are in this mysterious sacrament. And open my eyes so that I will see you as you truly are, present and active in the normal, basic activities and events of my life. You came to walk with me and accompany me through life. I don't want to walk alone anymore...

I want to be like the Eucharist. I want my life to nourish the hearts and souls of those around me. I want to pour out all my energy, all my talent, and all my love for the sake of your Kingdom, bringing others closer to you and closer to the happiness you created them to enjoy. How can I give myself more? How can I be more like you? Teach me to do your will, Lord, and to seek first your Kingdom...

Questions for
SMALL-GROUP DISCUSSION

1. What struck you most in this passage? What did you notice that you hadn't noticed before?

2. Why do you think so many of his listeners don't accept Christ at his word? How do you think Christ reacts when we take time to visit him in the Eucharist, to go there and thank him—to pour out our troubles to him and ask for his help?

3. If Christ himself, his entire being and life, is truly present in the Eucharist and reserved in the Tabernacles of all our Catholic Churches, why do you think so few people spend significant time with him there?

4. If an unbelieving but inquiring acquaintance asked you about the difference between receiving communion in the Catholic Church and receiving it in other Christian churches, what would you tell them?

Cf. Catechism of the Catholic Church, 1324-1327 on the Eucharist as the source and summit of ecclesial life; 1373-1381 on the real presence of Christ in the Eucharist; 1382-1401 on the nature and benefits of Holy Communion; 1345-1390 on the Mass

259. FREE TO STAY OR GO (JN 6:60-71)

"Do not, my child, approach Jesus Christ with the hope of bending his will to yours: what I desire is that you yield yourself to him and that he receive you, so that he, your Savior, may do with you and in you whatever he pleases." – St. Cajetan

JOHN 6:60-71

After hearing it, many of his followers said, "This is intolerable language. How could anyone accept it?" Jesus was aware that his followers were complaining about it and said, "Does this upset you? What if you should see the Son of Man ascend to where he was before? It is the spirit that gives life, the flesh has nothing to offer. The words I have spoken to you are spirit and they are life. But there are some of you who do not believe." For Jesus knew from the outset those who did not believe, and who it was that would betray him. He went on, "This is why I told you that no one could come to me unless the Father allows him." After this, many of his disciples left him and stopped going with him. Then Jesus said to the Twelve, "What about you, do you want to go away too?" Simon Peter answered, "Lord, who shall we go to? You have the message of eternal life, and we believe; we know that you are the Holy One of God." Jesus replied, "Have I not chosen you, you Twelve? Yet one of you is a devil." He meant Judas son of Simon Iscariot, since this was the man, one of the Twelve, who was going to betray him.

CHRIST THE LORD Why do many disciples leave Christ, while the Twelve stay with him? The question touches one of the great mysteries of our faith: human freedom. Somehow, in the depths of the human heart, God leaves us free to accept or reject the gift of faith. It always begins with God ("no one could come to me unless the Father allows him"), but the choice to stay or "leave" remains with each individual: "Do you want to go away too?" Jesus Christ is the Lord of life and history, but he refuses to impose his rule on hearts that want to "stop going with him" and return to their former way of life. God has given us the gift of life, but he leaves us free to administer it as we wish. In the Kingdom of Christ, there are no misanthropes.

CHRIST THE TEACHER For the Christian, difficulties are opportunities. In the face of this "intolerable language," Christ turns to his closest followers and invites them to make an explicit act of faith, to believe in him not because it makes perfect sense to do so, but simply because of who he is. He elicits their trust by assuring them that his words are "spirit and life," but not by removing all obstacles from their understanding. (By saying, "It is the spirit which gives life, not the flesh," he is not reneging on his assertion that his flesh is real food, just explaining how it can be living food.) For those who reassert their faith in him, trusting in him more than in their own understanding, this crisis becomes a milestone. Likewise, when we face moments of crisis, when the demands of faith outstrip the powers of understanding, we can either lean on ourselves and fall, or lean harder than ever on Christ and rise to the heights of love.

CHRIST THE FRIEND Try to imagine how Jesus spoke the words, "Do you want to go away too?" Try to picture his expression as he looked into the faces of his chosen Twelve. He cared deeply about them; he had handpicked them to be his closest companions. He had given them his heart, and now, as other followers gave up on him, he looked to them with a tinge of sadness, perhaps even with apprehension. Would they too abandon him? How near God draws to us in Jesus Christ! He humbles himself—he makes himself weak, almost powerless, in the face of our freedom. He doesn't want mindless robots or heartless slaves; he wants friends, forever.

CHRIST IN MY LIFE You know that I don't understand everything you ask of me—I don't understand the half of it, I am afraid. But you also know that I trust in you. You have the words of eternal life, and no one else does. I know I don't. I am counting on you, Lord, on your example and your teaching. I want to be like you and follow you in all of my relationships and responsibilities. Never let me be separated from you...

Many people react to your Church's teaching just the way these listeners did that day in Capernaum—since it makes them uncomfortable and it doesn't fit into their expectations, they reject it. I am tempted to do the same thing sometimes; the vocation you have given me isn't easy or smooth; I often get flustered. But I know that you love me, and I never want to go back to living with you just on the sidelines...

You can count on me, Lord. I don't promise that I will never fall or fail, because I know that I am weak and full of selfishness. But I promise that I will always turn to you for help, take your hand, and get up again. It's so simple, really. Only you have the words of eternal life. So what else is there for me to do except listen to you, follow you, and do whatever you ask of me? Teach me to do your will...

Questions for
SMALL-GROUP DISCUSSION

1. What struck you most in this passage? What did you notice that you hadn't noticed before?

2. How can we become more aware of our gift of freedom and use it more responsibly?

3. Why do you think Jesus chose to leave us his body and blood under the form of bread and wine?

4. It wounds Christ's heart when people reject him. By exercising our faith, especially in a solid and deep Eucharistic devotion, we can, in a sense, make up for those rejections. In what specific ways can we thus console the heart of Christ in our present circumstances?

Cf. Catechism of the Catholic Church, 396, 1738-1742 on the reality and mystery of human freedom; 153-165 on the importance and nature of faith

THE GOSPEL OF JOHN
Chapter 7

"Happy the soul to whom it is given to attain this life with Christ, to cleave with all one's heart to him whose beauty all the heavenly hosts behold forever; whose love inflames our love; whose contemplation is our refreshment; whose graciousness is our delight; whose gentleness fills us to overflowing; whose remembrance gives sweet light; whose fragrance revives the dead; whose glorious vision will be the happiness of all the citizens of that heavenly Jerusalem. For he is the brightness of the eternal glory, the splendor of eternal light, the mirror without spot."

– ST. CLARE OF ASSISI

260. FOCUSING ON THE MISSION (JN 7:1-19)

"What food, what honey could be sweeter than to learn of God's providence, to enter into his shrine and look into the mind of the creator, to listen to the Lord's words at which the wise of this world laugh, but which really are full of spiritual teaching?" – St. Jerome

JOHN 7:1-19
After this Jesus stayed in Galilee; he could not stay in Judaea, because the Jews were out to kill him. As the Jewish feast of Tabernacles drew near, his brothers said to him, "Why not leave this place and go to Judaea, and let your disciples see the works you are doing; if a man wants to be known he does not do things in secret; since you are doing all this, you should let the whole world see." Not even his brothers, in fact, had faith in him. Jesus answered, "The right time for me has not come yet, but any time is the right time for you. The world cannot hate you, but it does hate me, because I give evidence that its ways are evil. Go up to the festival yourselves: I am not going to this festival, because for me the time is not ripe yet." Having said that, he stayed behind in Galilee. However, after his brothers had left for the festival, he went up as well, but quite privately, without drawing attention to himself. At the festival the Jews were on the look-out for him: "Where is he?" they said. People stood in groups whispering about him. Some said, "He is a good man"; others, "No, he is leading the people

astray." Yet no one spoke about him openly, for fear of the Jews. When the festival was half over, Jesus went to the Temple and began to teach. The Jews were astonished and said, "How did he learn to read? He has not been taught." Jesus answered them: "My teaching is not from myself: it comes from the one who sent me; and if anyone is prepared to do his will, he will know whether my teaching is from God or whether my doctrine is my own. When a man's doctrine is his own he is hoping to get honor for himself; but when he is working for the honor of one who sent him, then he is sincere and by no means an impostor. Did not Moses give you the Law? And yet not one of you keeps the Law!"

CHRIST THE LORD Jesus is a man with a mission. In this passage, he shows this focus on the mission in two ways. First, he explains to his relatives who were going to Jerusalem for the annual, weeklong celebration commemorating Israel's entrance into the Promised Land why he won't be going with them. (This was the Feast of Tabernacles, which coincided with the autumn harvest. It was called the Feast of Tabernacles because the residents and pilgrims who participated in it would erect huts or tents [the word tabernacle means, literally, tent] to live in during the festival as a way of recalling the years during which the Israelites wandered in the desert after being liberated from Egypt and before entering the Promised Land.) At this point in his ministry, Jesus has already traveled throughout Galilee, curing the sick, casting out demons, performing miracles, and preaching to huge crowds of Jewish and Gentile followers. His relatives think that it's time for him to make the same kind of showing in Jerusalem—if he really wants to become famous, he will have to make a name for himself with the educated and sophisticated leaders of the big city. But Jesus doesn't travel with the family caravan. Instead, he waits until the midpoint of the eight-day festival, when the huge crowds of pilgrims are already gathered, when the festival is well underway, when the preparations, the small talk, and the mutual catching up of friends and relatives is over, and everyone's attention is focused on the activities in the Temple. Jesus chose carefully the "right time" to go up to the festival. He took his mission seriously, and he marshaled all his intelligence, prudence, and strategic judgment in order to bring it to completion.

Second, he explains once again that he is not seeking honor and recognition for himself but is carrying out the will of the Father who sent him. This explains why he doesn't raise an army and stage a violent takeover of the city—which he easily could have done, judging by the crowds' reaction to his preaching. This also explains why he continues to teach and argue and explain instead of just forcing his will on the antagonistic Jewish leaders. His mission at this point is merely to deliver a message—the Father's message.

Jesus is a man with a mission, and when we were baptized and confirmed, we became his accomplices in fulfilling that mission. We should be as focused and determined and energetic in carrying it out as he was.

CHRIST THE TEACHER Two key lessons come out in this speech. First, Jesus explains to his relatives that since his job is to expose the self-seeking ways of the world and invite men to repent, he will constantly experience opposition and resistance. People don't like to be told that they are selfish, and they will often show their animosity to that message by persecuting the messenger. This was true for Jesus, and it is true for his followers. If we are faithfully bearing witness to Christ and his message, we too will incur resentment and opposition. All Christians who are true to their vocation to be other Christs can say with Jesus that the world "does hate me, because I give evidence that its ways are evil." Opposition is part of the Christian's daily bread.

Second, Jesus reveals the prerequisite for understanding his doctrine: "... If anyone is prepared to do his [the Father's] will, he will know whether my teaching is from God or whether my doctrine is my own..." The disposition of our will determines our capacity to recognize the truth. A heart free from inordinate attachments to selfish desires will be docile to God's action and inspirations. That docility will give the Holy Spirit room to work, enlightening and strengthening the soul. A heart that has idolized something, however, whether it be money, pleasure, position, power, popularity, or success of any kind—or even just comfort and ease—that heart is not free to respond to God's action; it is chained to its idol. The wind of the Holy Spirit blows, but the idolatrous soul is tied to the shore and makes no progress toward the light. Often God has to send a storm to break the moorings and detach that soul from its idol. Only then can grace begin to work.

CHRIST THE FRIEND Jesus was willing to risk his own life in order to accomplish his mission, to save us and give us hope. That is love. That is friendship. St. John reminds us at the beginning of this chapter that Jesus had been forced to restrict his ministry to Galilee because the authorities in Judea had put a price on his head. But Jesus knows that he has to preach in the Temple if he is going to fulfill the Father's will. The Temple and the earthly Jerusalem were the privileged places of God's revelation and Covenant; the Messiah had to go and insistently proclaim his message there. He had to walk into the lion's den in order to save the lost sheep.

Jesus: I come to you in Holy Communion because I want to give you my own courage. I feed you with my own fortitude. I nourish you with my love. If only you knew how it saddens me when my disciples are afraid to take up their mission, to launch out to where I have sent them! And if only you knew how I rejoice—and all heaven with me—whenever one of my disciples is willing to brook opposition and rejection in order to be faithful to the truth, in order to advance the Kingdom! My Church is adorned with countless martyrs and virgins and confessors and saints who broke free from the shackles of worldly fear because they discovered my love and took the risk of letting it flood their lives. Do you think that perhaps some of them regret it? I want you to follow in their path. Trust me, be courageous, and fill each moment of your day with faith and love. I guarantee you won't regret it.

CHRIST IN MY LIFE You were entirely dedicated to your mission—the mission the Father had given you. Remind me, Lord: what is my mission? I am your disciple, your ambassador to the people around me, your messenger, just as you were the Father's messenger to Israel. O Lord, I believe that the happiness I long for can only come from living in synch with the purpose for which you created me, from fulfilling my mission in life...

I can't help wondering, Lord. Is part of me still not well disposed to your will? Do I have some secret idols stashed away in the closet of my soul? I believe in you, Lord, and I want to be wholly yours. All my hopes are in you and in your goodness. Who else can teach me and guide me to the life I long to live? Come and show me what I need to change; come and break any chains that hold me back from loving you...

Thank you for not thinking of your own personal preferences and comfort. Thank you for giving yourself entirely to fulfill the mission you had received from the Father. Teach me to do the same. Give me courage, Lord, the courage to live out all my relationships and responsibilities just as you would have me, the courage to be passionately faithful to the vocation you have given me, no matter what the cost...

Questions for
SMALL-GROUP DISCUSSION

1. What struck you most in this passage? What did you notice that you hadn't noticed before?
2. What were the different ways that people reacted to Christ's teachings? Which of those reactions do we still run across today?

3. Why are we so afraid of stirring up opposition or disdain by giving witness to Christ?

4. The people who heard Jesus teach were amazed at his eloquence and wisdom, especially since they knew he had not studied in any of the rabbinic schools that churned out scholars and preachers. Do you think there is a lesson in this for all of us?

Cf. Catechism of the Catholic Church, 1816 on the necessity of every Christian bearing witness to Christ; 769 on the necessity of suffering persecution; 675-677 on the final persecution the Church will experience; 1817-1821 on hoping in God alone; 2112-2114, 1723, 2289, and 2424 on the different types of idolatry

261. CONFLICT AND CONTRADICTION (JN 7:20-36)

"When we consider that Christ is the true light far removed from all falsehood, we realize that our lives too should be lit by the rays of the sun of justice, which shine for our enlightenment. These rays are the virtues..." – St. Gregory of Nyssa

JOHN 7:20-36

"Why do you want to kill me?" The crowd replied, "You are mad! Who wants to kill you?" Jesus answered, "One work I did, and you are all surprised by it. Moses ordered you to practise circumcision—not that it began with him, it goes back to the patriarchs—and you circumcise on the sabbath. Now if a man can be circumcised on the sabbath so that the Law of Moses is not broken, why are you angry with me for making a man whole and complete on a sabbath? Do not keep judging according to appearances; let your judgement be according to what is right." Meanwhile some of the people of Jerusalem were saying, "Isn't this the man they want to kill? And here he is, speaking freely, and they have nothing to say to him! Can it be true the authorities have made up their minds that he is the Christ? Yet we all know where he comes from, but when the Christ appears no one will know where he comes from." Then, as Jesus taught in the Temple, he cried out: "Yes, you know me and you know where I came from. Yet I have not come of myself: no, there is one who sent me and I really come from him, and you do not know him, but I know him because I have come from him and it was he who sent me."

They would have arrested him then, but because his time had not yet come no one laid a hand on him. There were many people in the crowds, however, who believed in him; they were saying, "When the Christ comes, will he give more signs than this man?" Hearing that rumours like this about him were spreading among the people, the Pharisees sent the Temple police to arrest him. Then Jesus said: "I shall remain with you for only a short time now; then I shall go back to the one who sent me. You will look for me and will not find me: where I am you cannot come." The Jews then said to one another, "Where is he going that we shan't be able to find him? Is he going abroad to the people who are dispersed among the Greeks and will he teach the Greeks? What does he mean when he says: 'You will look for me and will not find me: where I am, you cannot come?'"

CHRIST THE LORD Jesus is teaching in the Temple precincts, where long colonnades and porticos provided outdoor, spontaneous classrooms that were especially busy during the great festivals. A crowd of pilgrims surrounds him, including some of the Pharisees and Scribes and other leaders who are seeking his demise. He knows very well that ever since his earlier trip to Jerusalem and the miraculous cure of the lame man on the Sabbath, many of these leaders were contriving his death. Some pilgrims in the crowd who resided in other cities were unaware of the vehement malevolence with which the leaders viewed Jesus. But Jesus doesn't direct his remarks to them; instead, he addresses his enemies.

Once again we see Jesus practicing what he preaches. He instructed his followers to love their enemies and do good to those who hate them, and Jesus does exactly that in this and the many other conversations he has with the very men who want to do away with him. He spares no pains to open their minds to the truth. In this case, he points out the superficiality of their objection to his supposed Sabbath-breaking cure. Although the Law of Moses, which they esteemed so highly, demanded that no work be done on the Sabbath (not even medical work unless death was imminent), the Pharisees and chief priests themselves allowed for circumcision to be performed on that day because newborn male babies were circumcised on the eighth day after their birth, which often fell on the Sabbath. If this sign of their Covenant with God was permitted to trump the Sabbath restrictions, why were they so indignant at Jesus for restoring a crippled man's health and faith—thus exercising that same Covenant—on the Sabbath? His critics were so obsessed with external piety that they had lost sight of its real meaning; they were "judging according to appearances" instead of "according to what is right."

Jesus doesn't condemn those who condemn him; he instructs them. Jesus is the King who reaches out to those who reject him, meeting them on their own terms in hopes that a little bit of his light will shine through a chink in their self-righteous armor. If our Lord acts like that, we should do the same.

CHRIST THE TEACHER Jesus' teaching impresses the crowds, as does his courage—because they know that the authorities are out to get him, and yet he stands up in public and continues to preach. Reflecting on what they have seen and heard, some members of the crowd believe in him. Others raise an interesting objection, which affords Jesus an opportunity to explain once again his divine origin and mission. The objectors refer to a popular Jewish belief that the Messiah will emerge on the scene publicly, suddenly, mysteriously, and dramatically. By this standard, Jesus doesn't fit. They knew where he came from. They knew his relatives and his background. Jesus admits that, but he goes on to say that his true origin is not known to them. He has been sent by God to do God's work. He claims once again a unique knowledge of and relationship with the Father, whom they do not really know at all. If they did, they would recognize Jesus as Messiah.

Often we fall into this same mistake. We think that God's action in our lives has to be dramatic and mysterious, when most often it reaches us through the ordinary experiences of life. Jesus is both Son of God and Son of Mary; Word of God and Nazarene carpenter. God is not a tyrant, eager to show off his power and cow us into obedience. That conception was in the back of the minds of these objectors, and sometimes it lingers in the back of our minds as well. But Jesus is proof that the truth is quite different. God came into the world in the quiet of Bethlehem. He redeemed the world in the workshop at Nazareth and by suffering and dying—experiences common to all of us. He spreads his grace through normal, everyday water, oil, bread, and wine, using words and gestures that are simple and easy to understand. If we are looking for God in the extraordinary things, we may completely miss his constant love that flows continually through the ordinary things.

CHRIST THE FRIEND A touch of sadness seems to color Jesus' words when the guards show up to arrest him. The time for his Passion has not yet arrived, however, and so they do not arrest him. But their arrival makes Jesus think ahead to what he knows will happen in just a few months. He is painfully aware that his time is limited. We can hear the longing in his voice as he alludes to his Ascension—he wants people to believe in him before their hearts become so hardened that they will no longer even be able to believe. Jesus still longs for us to believe in him, to trust him, to accept him. Life is so short; time is so limited. God showers every soul with his graces and invitations, but still many souls refuse to believe.

Christ: You are a comfort to me. You have listened to my voice in your conscience and you have followed me. You have trusted me. You have let me heal you and guide you with my grace. *I am preparing a place for you in my Father's house. But I wish I could describe to you how it pains my heart to see so many souls turn their backs on me. What more could I have done for them? Each one of them is looking for me, but they keep looking in the wrong places. And the farther they distance themselves from me, the less distinct my voice becomes. Go to them and tell them that I am what they are looking for. I will be with you.*

CHRIST IN MY LIFE Keep my heart open to you, Lord. It's so easy to go to the right or the left, to fall into legalism or laxity, like the Pharisees and the Sadducees, those leaders of Jerusalem who tried to destroy you. Keep me on the right path, Lord. Teach me to do your will. Teach me to keep striving to love you with all my heart and my neighbor as myself. Push me, Lord; draw me closer to you...

I praise you for your gentle love. You come to me in the simple things of life. It delights you to show your love and your majesty in the quiet beauty of a sunset, the simple joy of a child's smile, the embrace of a loved one, the refreshing caress of a cool breeze. Teach me the wisdom I need to live in constant contact with you, so I can be a channel of your grace...

I know I only have a little time left on this earth. I want to do so much. But my job is not to save the world—that's your job, Lord. All I have to do is fulfill your will with trust and love. I ask only that you make your will clear to me each day, and then give me the strength to carry it out with love. When my last day comes, I want to be able to say: I love you Lord, and that's why I always sought to do your will...

Questions for
SMALL-GROUP DISCUSSION

1. What struck you most in this passage? What did you notice that you hadn't noticed before?

2. What has most helped your faith to grow over the years, and what has hindered it?

3. What can we do to help each other become more sensitive to God's action in the normal occurrences of everyday life?

4. If an agnostic acquaintance came up to you and asked how it is possible for Christ to be both true man and true God, how would you explain it to them?

Cf. Catechism of the Catholic Church, 464-469 on Jesus as true God and true man; 470-478 on how Jesus' divine and human faculties and knowledge coexisted; 1114-1116 on Christ at work in the sacraments

262. WATER FROM THE ROCK (JN 7:37-8:1)

"Jesus Christ is the beginning and the end, the Alpha and the Omega; he is the king of the new world; he is the secret of history; he is the key to our destiny." – Pope Paul VI

JOHN 7:37-8:1

On the last day and greatest day of the festival, Jesus stood there and cried out: "If any man is thirsty, let him come to me! Let the man come and drink who believes in me!" As scripture says: From his breast shall flow fountains of living water. He was speaking of the Spirit which those who believed in him were to receive; for there was no Spirit as yet because Jesus had not yet been glorified. Several people who had been listening said, "Surely he must be the prophet," and some said, "He is the Christ," but others said, "Would the Christ be from Galilee? Does not scripture say that the Christ must be descended from David and come from the town of Bethlehem?" So the people could not agree about him. Some would have liked to arrest him, but no one actually laid hands on him. The police went back to the chief priests and Pharisees who said to them, "Why haven't you brought him?" The police replied, "There has never been anybody who has spoken like him." "So," the Pharisees answered, "you have been led astray as well? Have any of the authorities believed in him? Any of the Pharisees? This rabble knows nothing about the Law—they are damned." One of them, Nicodemus—the same man who had come to Jesus earlier—said to them, "But surely the Law does not allow us to pass judgement on a man without giving him a hearing and discovering what he is about?" To this they answered, "Are you a Galilean too? Go into the matter, and see for yourself: prophets do not come out of Galilee." They all went home, and Jesus went to the Mount of Olives.

CHRIST THE LORD The Feast of Tabernacles was one of the most important feasts in the Jewish year. The words Christ speaks in this passage were spoken to the thousands of pilgrims who gathered in Jerusalem to celebrate that feast. On each day of the feast (and with greater drama on the last day, the day referred to in this passage), the people held a procession during which they marched around the altar of the Temple and sang hymns while the priest drew water from an ancient pool (the pool of Siloam) and poured it over the altar as an offering and a prayer to God, thanking him for the harvests that had recently been taken in and asking him to bless them with sufficient rain for the coming months. The ritual also called to mind the miracle in the desert when God had Moses draw water from a rock for his people as they made their way to the

Promised Land. This ceremony provided the backdrop for Jesus' exclamation: "If any man is thirsty, let him come to me!" He will provide them with rivers of living water flowing within their thirsty hearts.

In Christ, all the events of the Old Testament find their true meaning, for they had only been shadows of future events, as St. Paul calls them. All of God's self-revelation to mankind is summed up in Jesus Christ; he is the only rock on which it is safe to build a life, the only water that will quench the universal thirst for meaning and lasting happiness, and the new Moses who has come to turn our sin-hardened hearts into flowing fountains of life-giving love—he is the Lord.

CHRIST THE TEACHER St. John points out that the "fountains of living water" flowing within the hearts of those who come to Christ refer to the Holy Spirit, who was to make his appearance only after Jesus had ascended to the Father. The Feast of Pentecost, the tenth day after the Ascension, witnessed the descent of the Holy Spirit on the apostles, who had been gathered in expectant prayer with Mary throughout those ten days. The feast of Pentecost, in addition to being relived each year in the liturgical calendar, is also made present at the celebration of the sacrament of Confirmation. When we are confirmed, we receive a renewed outpouring of the Holy Spirit, strengthening us for our life mission of giving public testimony to Christ.

By likening the Holy Spirit's presence and action to "fountains of living water," Jesus uses imagery that would have evoked a powerful reaction from his listeners. Jewish traditions involved elaborate ceremonial cleansings, many of which occurred on a daily basis, and the Jewish Scriptures are replete with references to flowing water as a sign of God's fidelity, of life and fecundity, of happiness and promise. If the Holy Spirit is likened to water that flows within our hearts, it means that he is the source of intimate, spiritual purification, health, life, and zest. If he is "living" water, he is a constantly self-renewing source of those gifts—inexhaustible. If he is "fountains" of living water, he is a dynamic, energetic, powerful source of interior renewal, not passively pious and timidly hesitant. This is the Spirit that we who are members of Christ through Baptism and soldiers of Christ through Confirmation have received. We have a spring of pure and abundant spiritual invigoration flowing freely within us. As St. Paul puts it: "Didn't you realize that you were God's temple and that the Spirit of God was living among you?" (1 Cor 3:16).

CHRIST THE FRIEND St. John was present when Christ announced the coming of the Spirit. He mentions that on the last and greatest day of the feast,

Jesus "stood there and cried out: 'If any man is thirsty, let him come to me!'"
Every detail expresses the intensity of Christ's desire to give away the precious
gift of meaning and fulfillment that he alone can give. He waited until the
climax of the eight-day celebration. He stood up, which means that he took a
very visible posture, where the immense crowds couldn't help but see him. And
then he "exclaimed," as if to say he shouted, he cried out, he did everything
he could to make himself heard. And what did he say? "Come to me if you are
thirsty, and I will give you a drink like one you have never had before!" Clearly,
he meant more than physical thirst; he was addressing himself to the thirst of
the human soul, the thirst for meaning and true happiness that drives every
decision and action of every man and woman of every time and place. The
deepest longing of the human heart—that is what Christ came to fulfill, and
how he craves to fulfill it!

*Nicodemus: The Sanhedrin was shocked beyond description when the guards returned
empty-handed. They couldn't understand how Jesus was able to move the hearts of
everyone who listened to him. They simply refused to confront the truth—they shut it
out. I tried to make them see, but they turned on me with such violence that I was
disoriented. Wherever Jesus went, people either loved him or hated him. But he always
loved. He even loved those who despised him. I warned him and encouraged him to go
away, but he was determined to show how much he loved them. When people asked
me about him afterwards, that's what I always said, that he only wanted to convince
everyone that they were loved.*

CHRIST IN MY LIFE I am thirsty, Lord. I have already tasted the living
water that you offer. Your Holy Spirit, your wisdom, your truth, and your love
alone satisfy the yearnings of my heart. I was made for you—I was made to
know you, to feel your love, and to love you in return. But the more I taste the
living water of your grace, the more I want to drink. Send your Spirit, Lord, to
be my constant companion, my light, and my refreshment...

If your Spirit is flowing within me, refreshing me with grace at every moment, why do I get tired? Why, Lord, do I keep falling into discouragement
and frustration? O Jesus, I know that you have the answers, but sometimes
I wish I had them too. Instruct me, Lord; teach me and guide me. Show me
the way to go; purify me of everything that blocks the flow of grace in me and
through me...

Why do you care so much about me? Why does it matter to you whether I
come and drink from the springs of your grace? You hold the whole universe
in your hand, and I am just a little speck in the midst of it. And yet, you have
made this invitation resound through twenty centuries until it has reached my

ears: "Come to me!" You know my name. You want me beside you. I look at you and I know that I am loved...

Questions for
SMALL-GROUP DISCUSSION

1. What struck you most in this passage? What did you notice that you hadn't noticed before?

2. Do I eagerly strive to understand God's revelation, making an effort to know and grasp the Old Testament in the light of the New Testament, or am I a passive Catholic, taking only what comes to me and making little personal effort to delve into the riches of my faith?

3. The Holy Spirit is the third person of the Blessed Trinity, the one responsible for our growth in intimacy with God, the one who has made his dwelling in our hearts and remains there as our guest. How can we cultivate our relationship with him, learning to recognize his voice and follow his inspirations?

4. If Christ can truly quench the thirst of the human heart, why don't more people come to him? If I believe he can, why don't I bring more people to him?

Cf. Catechism of the Catholic Church, 731-741 on the meaning of Pentecost and the Holy Spirit's role in the Church; 694-701 on the Holy Spirit's individual action in each soul

"For this cause he came down upon earth, that by pursuing death he might kill the rebel that slew men. For one underwent the judgment, and myriads were set free. One was buried, and myriads rose again. He is the mediator between God and man. He is the resurrection and salvation of all. He is the guide of the erring, the shepherd of men who have been set free, the life of the dead, the charioteer of the cherubim, and the King of kings, to whom be the glory for ever and ever. Amen."

–ST. ALEXANDER OF ALEXANDRIA

263. GETTING WHAT WE DON'T DESERVE (JN 8:2-11)

"His attitude towards sinners was full of kindness and loving friendship." – St. John Bosco

JOHN 8:2-11
At daybreak he appeared in the Temple again; and as all the people came to him, he sat down and began to teach them. The scribes and Pharisees brought a woman along who had been caught committing adultery; and making her stand there in full view of everybody, they said to Jesus, "Master, this woman was caught in the very act of committing adultery, and Moses has ordered us in the Law to condemn women like this to death by stoning. What have you to say?" They asked him this as a test, looking for something to use against him. But Jesus bent down and started writing on the ground with his finger. As they persisted with their question, he looked up and said, "If there is one of you who has not sinned, let him be the first to throw a stone at her." Then he bent down and wrote on the ground again. When they heard this they went away one by one, beginning with the eldest, until Jesus was left alone with the woman, who remained standing there. He looked up and said, "Woman, where are they? Has no one condemned you?" "No one, sir," she replied. "Neither do I condemn you," said Jesus, "go away, and don't sin any more."

CHRIST THE LORD The scribes and the Pharisees—the religious leaders of Israel at the time—were constantly trying to discredit Jesus. This trap was particularly shrewd. If he forgave the woman, they could accuse him of contradicting Moses (who had taught that all women caught in adultery should be stoned to death), which was tantamount to blasphemy. If he condemned her, he would lose his popular support. Christ escapes, however, by turning the tables, showing the hypocrisy of their supposed zeal for righteousness. Christ's uncanny ability to beat these cunning adversaries at their own game is a subtle indication of his extraordinary personality. It doesn't directly prove his divinity, but it certainly shows him to be a Lord among men. The more we let ourselves be filled with his Spirit, the more we will share his deftness in building the Kingdom and defending the truth.

The scene must have been alarming. Picture the small crowd of pilgrims gathered around Jesus in the Temple courtyard, while the Lord speaks to them from a seat under the colonnade. The morning sunlight makes the marble sparkle and gives the atmosphere a clear, golden tint. The people are intent on Jesus; he is intent on them. Those sitting farther inside the courtyard, away from Jesus, hear a commotion outside the gate. They turn to see a large group of Pharisees and scribes dressed in their tassels and robes, with some Temple guards roughly escorting a frightened and disheveled woman. The crowd clears a path for the newcomers. They station themselves in front of the Master, who takes in the whole situation with his penetrating gaze. He sees the woman's scared, ashamed expression; he sees the leaders of the Pharisees with their stern look of defiance; he sees the younger ones smiling with satisfaction: finally, they have Jesus in a bind. But the Lord sees beneath their facial expressions into their hearts. His wisdom and his mercy reach out to them all, defusing their self-righteousness and pardoning their guilt with merely a word. The Lord comes to save, not to destroy.

CHRIST THE TEACHER Biblical scholars have long wondered what Christ was writing on the ground as he bent down during this encounter. Some say it was the sins of all the accusers. Others say that he was merely giving them a chance to reconsider their position so that he wouldn't have to embarrass them. In any case, the fundamental lesson is clear: we are all in need of God's mercy; we have all "sinned and forfeited God's glory" (Rom 3:23), and Christ knows it.

Significantly, the oldest accusers were the first to walk away; the younger ones were more reluctant to admit their need for God. Old and young alike, however, admitted it eventually. And so the adulteress was free to go. This brings out the corollary to the lesson that everyone is in need of God's mercy:

realizing that we need God's mercy enables us to forgive others and treat them with the charity that Christ requires. The more profoundly we have experienced God's forgiveness and the free gift of his mercy, which we don't deserve, the more readily we will communicate it to others by releasing resentment and letting grudges go—not because their sins don't matter, but because God came to save sinners.

Living on the level of God's mercy not only fills our souls with peace and supernatural strength, it also gives lost, lonely, angry, and closed hearts a whiff of God's love—and that's the only thing that can save them. If we throw stones by condemning and criticizing and judging, we drive others and ourselves away from Christ; if we give others a fresh start, whether they deserve it or not, we become the peacemakers that Jesus declared blessed: "for they will be called the sons of God" (Mt 5:9).

CHRIST THE FRIEND *Jesus: I came not to condemn the world, but to save the world. If I just wanted to condemn you, I would have had no reason to come. I know your sins and your weakness, and still I called you and continue to call you. Think for a moment about the one reason behind my incarnation, life, Passion, death, Resurrection, and Ascension. Why would I follow such an itinerary? It was only because I want your friendship. Every page and word of the Gospels, every faithful action and teaching of my Church has one, single purpose: to convince you that I want to walk with you now and spend eternity showing you the splendors of my Kingdom. I am all for you, and I ask in return only one thing, the same thing I asked of this adulterous woman: trust me, accept my love, and turn away from your sin.*

CHRIST IN MY LIFE Make me a channel of your mercy, Lord. Your mercy means that even when I offend you, you keep on loving me and wanting what's best for me. I want to be like that. I want to be like gravity: continually pulling no matter what; I want to keep on showing people your goodness and wisdom. I want to keep on leading them to you, to keep on loving even those I find hard to love...

Forgive me, Lord, for judging my neighbor. How foolish it is for me to pass judgment and criticize and pigeonhole! Can I see their hearts? The Pharisees are quick to condemn because it makes them feel important and superior. But I am even quicker to make excuses for myself and my failings. Teach me to see others as you see them and to speak about them as I would want them to speak about me...

I want to be able to defend your truth and the teachings of your Church, but so often I am at a loss for words. In the midst of conversations and encounters,

I get flustered. Afterwards, I think up great responses. You always had the right response. You always knew what to say. Fill me with your grace and your wisdom, Lord, so that I can be your faithful friend and true ambassador...

Questions for
SMALL-GROUP DISCUSSION

1. What struck you most in this passage? What did you notice that you hadn't noticed before?
2. Why do we sometimes find it hard to forgive others? What can we do to develop the capacity to forgive more fully and more freely, as Christ forgives us?
3. In what ways do our present circumstances encourage us to fall into pharisaical (hypocritical) self-righteousness?
4. How do you think the disciples reacted to this encounter?

Cf. Catechism of the Catholic Church, 456-460 on why Jesus came to earth; 1846-1851 on God's mercy and the need to admit our sinfulness

264. LIGHT FROM LIGHT (JN 8:12-20)

"That is to say, if a man follows Christ in all things, he will cross over in Christ's steps to the very throne of eternal light." – Homily of an ancient author

JOHN 8:12-20

When Jesus spoke to the people again, he said: "I am the light of the world; anyone who follows me will not be walking in the dark; he will have the light of life." At this the Pharisees said to him, "You are testifying on your own behalf; your testimony is not valid." Jesus replied: "It is true that I am testifying on my own behalf, but my testimony is still valid, because I know where I came from and where I am going; but you do not know where I come from or where I am going. You judge by human standards; I judge no one, but if I judge, my judgement will be sound, because I am not alone: the one who sent me is with me; and in your Law it is written that the testimony of two witnesses is valid. I may be testifying on my own behalf, but the Father who sent me is my witness too." They asked him, "Where is your Father?" Jesus answered: "You do not know me, nor do you know my Father; if you did know me, you would know my Father as well." He spoke these words in the Treasury, while teaching in the Temple. No one arrested him, because his time had not yet come.

CHRIST THE LORD One of the most exciting rituals associated with this festival took place at night in the second court of the Temple where the Treasury was. This courtyard was surrounded by porticoes that housed thirteen large alms-boxes, where pilgrims and worshippers could make the various offerings that Temple worship required. During the festival, a kind of grandstand was erected all around the porticoes, which could hold huge numbers of spectators. In the center of the courtyard, four gigantic candelabras were erected. When the full darkness of night had descended and the galleries were full, the candelabras were lit, creating a blaze so bright that, ancient sources record, the light spread to all the streets and courtyards throughout the city. (The Temple was located on a higher level than the rest of the city, so light there would be visible from afar.) This firelight commemorated the pillar of fire that God used to guide Israel through the desert every night during their forty-year sojourn from Egypt into the Promised Land. Throughout the night, Israel's holiest and wisest teachers would perform ceremonies of worship that included singing of psalms and dancing in praise and thanksgiving to God, whom the Scriptures repeatedly referred to as the light of his Chosen People. The faithful pilgrims would join in the celebration and enjoy the dramatic ceremony until the sun came up.

This setting gives Christ's words, "I am the light of the world," spectacular eloquence. With this experience fresh in the minds of his rapt listeners, speaking in the very courtyard where the ceremony of light had taken place, Jesus proclaims that he is the light of the world. Just as the pillar of fire had led the people of Israel into the Promised Land, and just as the great candelabras illuminated the holy city of Jerusalem, Jesus himself, his person and his teachings, is the pillar of saving fire that shines throughout the entire world, leading whoever believes in him to the fullness of life itself. That is what Jesus says about himself. Is it what we think about him?

CHRIST THE TEACHER Jesus claims to be the saving light of the world, and then he says that anyone who follows him will have the light of life. In that one phrase, he teaches us both what he came to give us, and how we can go about getting it.

He came to give us the light of life. Our lives are a journey through this wonderful but confusing and treacherous world. We live each day in search of happiness and fulfillment, but the vast majority of roads and paths and side streets lead only to frustration, futile toil, and dead ends. How true it is, as Thoreau put it, that most men lead lives of quiet desperation, knowing that there is more to life, but unable to find it. We walk in darkness, groping tentatively and anxiously—unless we have Jesus. His example, his teaching, and his presence are a "lamp to our feet and a light to our path" (Ps 119:105). With Jesus, we know where we are going and how to get there. Who are the people in history who have lived the most fulfilling, fulfilled, and fruitful lives if not the saints, who abandoned the comfort of darkness in order to launch out on the path of Christ's light? Only the saints learn the secret of rejoicing in the midst of suffering; only they conquer the conundrum of how to be happy in a fallen world. In Jesus, with him and through him, our lives grow, flourish, and blossom, like wildflowers in the sunlight of spring. Without him our potential never matures, like a seed planted in cold soil and starved of light by shadows.

CHRIST THE FRIEND How do we go about getting that light of life? By following him. The Greek word translated as "follow" has a rich deposit of overlapping meanings. It is used to describe soldiers following their commanders into battle; it is used to portray slaves who stay always at their master's side, ready to do whatever task he sets before them; it is used to describe heeding the advice or verdict pronounced by a wise counselor; it is used to describe obedience to the laws of a city or a state; and it is used to indicate someone who makes the effort to understand a teacher's line of argument.

Jesus wants to be everything for us. He wants to be our leader and teacher, our counselor and coach, our doctor and brother and friend. Most of all, he wants to walk by our side, guiding each of us along this adventure of life. He knows every road and every path, and he knows where we should go and what we should avoid. He knows where we will flourish, where we will discover our mission, and what steps we must take to fulfill it. We have to learn to listen only to his voice, which we have already learned to discern in our hearts and conscience. He has so much in store for us, so much to show us and teach us, so much for us to do. We just have to follow him, to keep following him, to trust him and not look back. He is the light of the world, the only light that will never go out.

CHRIST IN MY LIFE You are the light of the world, Lord. I believe it, and I am amazed at how easily I take you for granted. Why do the passing fancies of the world grab my attention so easily and distract me from your Kingdom and your will? You are the light that never goes out, and you have given yourself to me. Thank you, Lord. Teach me to follow you more closely. Teach me to love you and cherish your light…

The Pharisees and scribes didn't believe in you because they didn't want to. Why did you give me the desire to believe in you? How is it that you have given me the gift of faith, but so many others still don't believe? Lord Jesus, I believe in you, and I want to follow you and you alone. Only you have the light of life, and that is what I yearn for. Lead me, Lord, one step at a time; you are the light that will never fail...

You have kindled a fire in my heart, Lord. I want to spread it to other hearts. I know you want to enlighten them as well. Teach me to keep the flame of faith burning brightly. Teach me to be your witness and your herald. Make me a torch, a lamp, a star that will guide others into your embrace. How else can I show you my love, Lord, but by loving those whom you love?...

Questions for
SMALL-GROUP DISCUSSION

1. What struck you most in this passage? What did you notice that you hadn't noticed before?

2. Jesus makes it quite clear that the power exhibited by his words and deeds demonstrated that the Father was at work in and through him, and yet his enemies still refused to believe. Why?

3. Christians are those who follow Christ. What does the phrase "following Christ" mean to you? If you had to explain it to a non-believing acquaintance, how would you do so?

4. Which aspects of popular culture tend to obscure the light of Christ from our lives, and which aspects tend to magnify it?

Cf. Catechism of the Catholic Church, 2465-2470 on living in the truth of Christ's light; 781-786 on the Church's mission to continue being the light of the world; 2104-2109 on the duty of all Christians to be the light of the world

265. CHRIST'S PROGRAM OF LIFE (JN 8:21-30)

"For God, as I have said, does not work in those who refuse to place all their trust and expectation in him alone." – St. Jerome Emilian

JOHN 8:21-30

Again he said to them: "I am going away; you will look for me and you will die in your sin. Where I am going, you cannot come." The Jews said to one another, "Will he kill himself? Is that what he means by saying, 'Where I am going, you cannot come?'" Jesus went on: "You are from below; I am from above. You are of this world; I am not of this world. I have told you already: You will die in your sins. Yes, if you do not believe that I am He, you will die in your sins." So they said to him, "Who are you?" Jesus answered:

"What I have told you from the outset. About you I have much to say and much to condemn; but the one who sent me is truthful, and what I have learnt from him I declare to the world." They failed to understand that he was talking to them about the Father. So Jesus said: "When you have lifted up the Son of Man, then you will know that I am He and that I do nothing of myself: what the Father has taught me is what I preach; he who sent me is with me, and has not left me to myself, for I always do what pleases him." As he was saying this, many came to believe in him.

CHRIST THE LORD Jesus keeps telling his critics (and the crowds) that he is the Messiah. He keeps telling them that he is one with the Father, that he is the one the Father has sent, and that he is not just another rabbi. "I am from above... I am not of this world..." The force of his words must have been immense. In spite of the difficult concepts, "many came to believe in him." But some still resisted. They were so caught up in their own ideas and expectations, so centered on themselves, that this wave of heavenly light and wisdom crashed against their closed minds and hearts as uselessly as the surf crashes against cliffs on the seashore. But Jesus had a plan to penetrate even those hardened hearts: "When you have lifted up the Son of man, then you will know that I am He..." He is referring to his crucifixion, which is still six months down the road. He knows that only limitless love can win over proud, arrogant, and self-centered hearts, and by going to the cross he will show that his love has absolutely no limits. The Lord came to conquer rebellious minds and hearts and lead them into his Kingdom of light, and he is willing to go to the extreme of self-sacrifice to bring about his victory.

CHRIST THE TEACHER In this passage, Jesus reveals his program of life: "I always do what pleases him [the Father]." Sometimes we resist the virtue of obedience because we are afraid that always doing God's will is somehow going to stifle our creativity or our true self. Just the opposite is the case.

Jesus repeatedly explains that he is not doing his own thing, but what the Father has given him to do. He teaches not his own wisdom, but what he has learned from the Father, seeking only to please the one who sent him. And this is what makes his life the most fruitful and beautiful life that has ever been. Following his example has made the lives of countless saints, men and women, rich and poor, religious and laity, resound with meaning and wisdom and the kind of joy that no amount of self-seeking and self-centeredness can ever produce. The reason is simple: we were created to love and be loved, to live in relation with God and others. That ongoing relationship of love implies turning our attention away from getting things for ourselves, instead focusing on giving of ourselves for the good of the beloved. This is what it means to "always do what pleases" God. God loves us, and his love is made concrete in his will—he communicates his love by guiding us to the fulfillment we seek; we accept his love and love him in return by obeying and by following his guidance.

Far from stifling our true selves, loving God—always doing what is pleasing to him—frees us to be much more than we ever dreamed we could be, and it liberates us to be all that God has always dreamt for us to be.

CHRIST THE FRIEND *Jesus: I and my Father are one. When I called you to be my disciple, I called you to live in communion with me just as I do with my Father. And just as my Father "is with me, and has not left me to myself," I am always with you, and I will never abandon you. In your heart you know this, but even so, you often let yourself be carried away by worries and fears. When I let a cloud block out the sun, does the sun disappear? The sun is always there, and just so I am always watching over you. Every worry and fear that comes across the sky of your soul is a chance for you to exercise your faith and trust in me. That is what pleases me, and that is what sets my grace free to transform you and strengthen you and release your full potential for living as you ought to live. Seek always to do what pleases me, as I always sought to do what was pleasing to my Father, and you will discover anew my presence and grace, over and over again.*

CHRIST IN MY LIFE I, too, am sometimes hardhearted, like the Pharisees and scribes, who loved their own plans so much that they couldn't even see your plan. Cure me, Lord. Purify my heart. Show me my prejudices and self-ish tendencies. Shine the light of your love into all the shadows of my soul. I want to be completely yours. I want to become your faithful disciple, a soldier you can count on...

How simple your program of life is! You seek always and everywhere to do what is pleasing to the Father. Teach me to live like that. Free me from my obsession with pleasing myself. You didn't design me to find fulfillment by navel-gazing—you created me to flourish by self-forgetting love. With the love of your heart, Lord, inflame my heart...

Are you really always with me? Why do you let me feel alone? Why do you let so many clouds block out the sun? You want me to grow up, to mature. You want me to love you for you and not for the light and gifts that you give to me. You want me to exercise the precious virtues of faith, hope, and love, which have to be based on trust. Teach me to leave behind my cold calculations and abandon myself to your goodness...

Questions for
SMALL-GROUP DISCUSSION

1. What struck you most in this passage? What did you notice that you hadn't noticed before?

2. Why is Jesus so patient and persistent with these people who resist his teachings so systematically? Why is it so hard for us to be patient and persistent with people who resist faith in Christ?

3. In general, how can we follow Christ's example to do always what is pleasing to the Father? How can we discern what is pleasing to God in the different situations of life?

4. What has most helped you to remember that Christ never leaves you alone, that he is always with you and always in control? How can we develop this awareness?

Cf. Catechism of the Catholic Church, 2822-2827 and 2196 on what is pleasing to God; 1813 and 1817-1821 on the virtue of hope; 2656-2658 on increasing the theological virtues through prayer and the liturgy; 2779-2785 on having confidence in God the Father

266. HOME FREE (JN 8:31-41)

"This Lord of ours is the one from whom and through whom all good things come to us." – St. Teresa of Avila

JOHN 8:31-41

To the Jews who believed in him Jesus said: "If you make my word your home you will indeed be my disciples, you will learn the truth and the truth will make you free." They answered, "We are descended from Abraham and we have never been the slaves of anyone; what do you mean, 'You will be made free?'" Jesus replied: "I tell you most solemnly, everyone who commits sin is a slave. Now the slave's place in the house is not assured, but the son's place is assured. So if the Son makes you free, you will be free indeed. I know that you are descended from Abraham; but in spite of that you want to kill me because nothing I say has penetrated into you. What I, for my part, speak of is what I have seen with my Father; but you, you put into action the lessons learnt from your father." They repeated, "Our father is Abraham." Jesus said to them: "If you were Abraham's children, you would do as Abraham did. As it is, you want to kill me when I tell you the truth as I have learnt it from God; that is not what Abraham did. What you are doing is what your father does."

CHRIST THE LORD Some of the Jewish faithful listening to Jesus had the wrong idea of what it meant to live in communion with God. They thought it was sufficient to be descended from Abraham—a purely exterior condition. But Jesus demands more than biological descent; he demands spiritual descent. Abraham's greatness lay in his docility to God's will. He left his homeland and family en route to an unknown destination simply because God asked him to. He was even willing to sacrifice his own son, Isaac, when God commanded it. This faith, this docile trust in God that had enabled Abraham to recognize God's action in his life, is what made him great. The true children of Abraham and inheritors of his promise, therefore, are those who imitate his trust and docility: "If you were children of Abraham, you would do what Abraham did." But Jesus' interlocutors, by their failure to recognize Jesus as sent from God and by their desire to do away with him, exposed their self-seeking (unlike Abraham's God-seeking) hearts.

Jesus was the Word of God made flesh, a much greater revelation than Abraham had ever received, and yet these Pharisees and scribes stubbornly rejected him. They had put their trust in themselves and were seeking their own glory. Thus they were no children of Abraham and no disciples of the Lord. In Christ's Kingdom there can be only one King, and if we want to enjoy the prosperity of that Kingdom, we have to relinquish our self-made scepters and trust that King.

CHRIST THE TEACHER Every human heart yearns for freedom—the freedom to live as we suspect we ought to live, the freedom to be masters of our instincts and passions instead of their slaves, the freedom to be all that we were created to be. At the same time, every human heart feels shackled by something. Something holds us back from reaching our potential. We know we can do more, we know we can be better, and yet we find ourselves stuck in spiritual mediocrity. In this passage, Jesus reveals both the nature of our restraints, and the path to the freedom we desire.

The truth sets us free. Freedom is more than the indifferent capacity to choose between various options. Freedom is the possibility we have to achieve excellence through making choices in accordance with truth. Animals and plants and rocks don't have this possibility; only rational creatures (humans and angels) can contribute consciously and meritoriously to their own flourishing and fulfillment. But we can only do so if we direct our conscious actions in harmony with the way things are, with the way God created them to be—in other words, with the truth. This is less complicated than it seems. Think of the converse case. When does human freedom completely collapse? In the instance of insanity. When a person is no longer able to perceive reality, when they are out of touch with the way things are, they can no longer grow at all, let alone flourish.

Our inborn capacity to recognize truth—reality, the way things are, the way God designed them to be—gives us the possibility to direct our lives toward the fulfillment we long for. But that possibility is constantly being threatened and hindered by our tendency (inherited through original sin and exacerbated by personal sin—ours and others') to indulge our self-seeking appetites at the expense of what's truly fulfilling. This is sin. It is a rebellion against the way God created us to be. It is preferring our own disordered, shortsighted, and irrational preferences to God's perfectly wise and loving will. This tendency is always at work in us, and whenever we give into it, it tightens its grip, making it harder for us both to perceive our true good and also to pursue it. Thus, "everyone who commits sin is a slave." The way to overcome our tendency to selfish implosion is to "make Christ's word our home."

CHRIST THE FRIEND Christ's word is the expression of his love. He is God, and God is love, and all his actions and words are the revelation of that love. To make his word our home, then, means to dwell in God's love for us—to relish it, to accept it, to drink it in. It involves hearing and heeding his call in our life. This call takes many forms: the nudge of conscience in little and big dilemmas; the deep, insistent, resounding invitation to a particular vocation; the normal responsibilities of life; the commandments of the Bible and the Church.... When Jesus tells us to make his word our home, he is inviting us to dwell in his will and find our comfort, our solace, our rest, and our renewal in it. Jesus comes to rescue us from our vain attempts to concoct some magic formula for self-fulfillment all by ourselves. His will is his word, and his word is the expression of his love, so to dwell in his word is to be in a constant communion with the one who loves us—to live in friendship with Christ. He is the truth, and he will set us free.

CHRIST IN MY LIFE I believe in you, Lord. You are the one, true God. Only you are the Savior. I pray for those who don't believe in you. Show yourself to them. Win over their hearts. Free them from sin. And what about those around me who don't believe in you? Send me to them, Lord. I want to build and spread your Kingdom, but I need your grace to tell me what to say, what to do, and how to love them as you have loved me...

I so easily forget that I am a fallen person in a fallen world. You have redeemed me, but you didn't take away the effects of sin. You want me to exercise my faith and love by resisting my tendencies to self-seeking and by obeying the call of your truth. This is virtue, Lord. Virtue is freedom from the merciless and destructive slavery of self-centeredness. Teach me virtue; show me the way to go...

What is your will for me, Lord? Remind me. Life is so busy. Life is so unpredictable. Events and problems and activities swirl around me, and emotions and desires and temptations churn inside me. Make your word alive for me—I hear and read it so often, in Mass, in spiritual reading, and in my prayer, but I want to listen better. I don't want to dwell in my paltry self, and I don't want to dwell in the passing fads of this fallen world. I want to dwell in you, in your word, and in your will. Teach me to do your will...

Questions for
SMALL-GROUP DISCUSSION

1. What struck you most in this passage? What did you notice that you hadn't noticed before?

2. It seems that many Jews wrongly thought they were in a right relationship with God just because of their racial identity as Abraham's descendents. In what ways can today's Catholics fall into a similar mistake?

3. Where does popular culture encourage us to "make our home"? In other words, where does it encourage us to seek the meaning, fulfillment, and happiness that we long for? How does that compare with Christ's exhortation?

4. How would you explain the right and wrong views of freedom to a non-believer who claimed that freedom just means doing whatever you feel like?

Cf. Catechism of the Catholic Church, 396-406 on freedom and original sin; 407-409 on the hard battle that ensued after original sin; 144-147 on Abraham as a model of faith

267. LIES AND DEATH, TRUTH AND LIFE (JN 8:42-59)

"You who have now put on Christ and follow our guidance are like little fish on the hook: you are being pulled up out of the deep waters of this world by the word of God."
– St. Jerome

JOHN 8:42-59

"We were not born of prostitution," they went on "we have one father: God." Jesus answered: "If God were your father, you would love me, since I have come here from God; yes, I have come from him; not that I came because I chose, no, I was sent, and by him. Do you know why you cannot take in what I say? It is because you are unable to understand my language. The devil is your father, and you prefer to do what your father wants. He was a murderer from the start; he was never grounded in the truth; there is no truth in him at all: when he lies he is drawing on his own store, because he is a liar, and the father of lies. But as for me, I speak the truth and for that very reason, you do not believe me. Can one of you convict me of sin? If I speak the truth, why do you not believe me? A child of God listens to the words of God; if you refuse to listen, it is because you are not God's children."

The Jews replied, "Are we not right in saying that you are a Samaritan and possessed by a devil?" Jesus answered: "I am not possessed; no, I honour my Father, but you want to dishonour me. Not that I care for my own glory, there is someone who takes care of that and is the judge of it. I tell you most solemnly, whoever keeps my word will never see death." The Jews said, "Now we know for certain that you are possessed. Abraham is dead, and the prophets are dead, and yet you say, 'Whoever keeps my word will never know the taste of death.' Are you greater than our father Abraham, who is dead? The prophets are dead too. Who are you claiming to be?" Jesus answered: "If I were to seek my own glory that would be no glory at all; my glory is conferred by the Father, by the one of whom you say, 'He is our God' although you do not know him. But I know him, and if I were to say: I do not know him, I should be a liar, as you are liars yourselves. But I do know him, and I faithfully keep his word. Your father Abraham rejoiced to think that he would see my Day; he saw it and was glad." The Jews then said, "You are not fifty yet, and you have seen Abraham!" Jesus replied: "I tell you most solemnly, before Abraham ever was, I Am." At this they picked up stones to throw at him; but Jesus hid himself and left the Temple.

CHRIST THE LORD Jesus continues to intensify his claim to be God made man and thus the unique and everlasting Lord of life and history. In this passage, three statements would have made this claim unmistakably clear to his listeners. That some understood the claim but refused to accept it is made evident by their furious attempt to stone Jesus to death for blasphemy right there in the Temple precincts.

Besides reiterating that he is the one whom God sent (this is the role of the Messiah, the one who will fulfill God's promise to Abraham to bless all nations through his descendents, a promise Abraham rejoiced to contemplate), Jesus attests to a unique knowledge of God and a unique obedience to God's will: "I do know him, and I faithfully keep his word." Knowing and willing are the two capacities that separate spiritual beings from merely physical ones; they differentiate persons from things. By choosing to describe his union with the Father through these two activities, Jesus gives us a glimpse (and that's all we can take) of the inner life of the Blessed Trinity, in which the three divine Persons are perfectly united in knowing and willing the eternal Truth and Goodness of the divine Nature.

But lest this revelation be lost on his listeners, Jesus goes on to make yet another, unambiguous proclamation of his divine sonship: "Before Abraham ever was, I Am." To speak about the historical past in the present tense is something only God can do, because only God exists, unchanging, outside of time. To use the simple, open-ended phrase "I Am" in reference to oneself would have been to the Jewish mind a declaration of godhood; it was the same title God himself used in answering Moses' query about God's name during the encounter at the burning bush. This same Jesus, as much a human person as you and I, as close to us as it is possible to be through his self-giving in Holy Communion, is also at the same time the eternal Son and Word of God, the Second Person of the Blessed Trinity.

CHRIST THE TEACHER Jesus speaks the truth, and "whoever keeps [his] word will never know the taste of death." But the devil "is a liar, and the father of lies" and "was a murderer from the beginning." Truth and life come with Christ; lies and death come with the devil. Those who seek and heed the truth will live as they are meant to live, while those who falsify their conscience in order to satisfy their thirst for selfish glory will only experience frustration, anxiety, and spiritual infertility. This was the exact progression of original sin: Adam and Eve, tempted by the devil, chose the desire "to be like gods"—a thirst for vain glory—and ended up estranged from their Creator, from each other, and from the world around them. Jesus, on the other hand, doesn't seek his own glory; in fact, he willingly accepts the humiliation of the cross, and as a result, he rises to the fullness of eternal life. These are the two options—truth and life or lies, betrayal of conscience, and death; there is no other.

This is the dramatic structure of the human condition. Philosophers, manufacturers, entertainers, and politicians can come up with as many worldviews and programs and systems and promises as they like, but ultimately, every human heart is a battleground between two loves: love of self, which seems to promise immediate gratification but requires rebellion against or abandonment of God; and love of God, which requires self-forgetfulness and sacrifice in order to "listen to the words of God" by following Christ but leads to ever-increasing fulfillment in this life and eternal adventure in the life to come. The devil and his angels encourage the false love of self-seeking, and the Spirit of God encourages the true love of self-giving. Every choice we make, big or little, every day, strengthens one of those loves and weakens the other. One of the greatest Christian privileges consists in being privy to this knowledge of the structure that underlies the whole story of humanity and the story of every man.

CHRIST THE FRIEND *Jesus: Whoever keeps my word will never know the taste of death. Do you know what the taste of death is? It is interior darkness and the absence of hope. It is depression that gets heavier and heavier until it spawns despair. It is the sense of defeat and meaninglessness that seeps into every corner of the soul like a cold, dense fog that gets thicker and thicker and thicker. It is discovering that you are alone, that no one truly knows you, and so no one can truly love you. It is seeing the seething ugliness of sin putrefying in one's heart and being unable to do anything to wipe it away. It is watching your dreams slowly wither away, unfulfilled, or seeing them come true only to turn into nightmares as soon as you reach out to grasp them.*

No one can live at peace with themselves unless they are willing to follow me. There is no other way. Death is existence without my friendship. It is what I came to destroy. You who have embraced life, you are my prize and my delight, because you let my victory in.

Keep my word, follow me, and I will give you life.

CHRIST IN MY LIFE I have to admit, Lord, that I understand very little when it comes to the mystery of your Incarnation. I know you are true God, and I know you are true man, but how you fit those two things together boggles my mind. But I am content to know that you who created and redeemed me continue to love and accompany me. To have God as my intimate friend is more than I could ever desire...

When I think about how much my daily decisions and actions matter in your eyes, it fills me with enthusiasm. I can build your Kingdom! I know that you care most about what happens in my heart. Many people build impressive worldly empires around shriveled hearts, and when their empires wane, their lives do too. But I want to live from your love, seeking your will, giving you glory...

What would I do without your friendship, Lord? Who would I hope in? Who would I complain to? Who would I learn from? Thank you for coming into my life. Never let me be separated from you. And fill me with your own desire: to save many souls from death, from the hollow existence of life without your friendship. Make me your apostle, your disciple, your ambassador; make me a fisher of men...

Questions for
SMALL-GROUP DISCUSSION

1. What struck you most in this passage? What did you notice that you hadn't noticed before?

2. What does popular culture say about the devil and how does that compare with what Jesus says about the devil?

3. Why are lying and self-indulgence so tempting to us? What can we do to arm ourselves in advance against these temptations?

4. The Christian view of life sees the dramatic struggle between Christ-centeredness and self-centeredness that is always happening in each human heart as the fundamental structure of the human condition. Which aspects of popular culture mesh with that view, and which ones contradict it?

Cf. Catechism of the Catholic Church: 1861 on eternal death in hell; 1033-1037 on hell as eternal separation from God; 407-409 on the spiritual battle of life; 441-445 on Jesus as the only Son of God

THE GOSPEL OF JOHN
Chapter 9

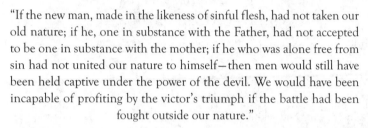

"If the new man, made in the likeness of sinful flesh, had not taken our old nature; if he, one in substance with the Father, had not accepted to be one in substance with the mother; if he who was alone free from sin had not united our nature to himself—then men would still have been held captive under the power of the devil. We would have been incapable of profiting by the victor's triumph if the battle had been fought outside our nature."

– POPE ST. LEO THE GREAT

268. A BLIND MAN SEES (JN 9:1-17)

"Let us carry bravely the shield of faith, so that with its protection we may be able to parry whatever the enemy hurls at us." – St. Cyprian

JOHN 9:1-17

As he went along, he saw a man who had been blind from birth. His disciples asked him, "Rabbi, who sinned, this man or his parents, for him to have been born blind?" "Neither he nor his parents sinned," Jesus answered, "he was born blind so that the works of God might be displayed in him. As long as the day lasts I must carry out the work of the one who sent me; the night will soon be here when no one can work. As long as I am in the world I am the light of the world." Having said this, he spat on the ground, made a paste with the spittle, put this over the eyes of the blind man, and said to him, "Go and wash in the Pool of Siloam (a name that means 'sent')." So the blind man went off and washed himself, and came away with his sight restored.

His neighbours and people who earlier had seen him begging said, "Isn't this the man who used to sit and beg?" Some said, "Yes, it is the same one." Others said, "No, he only looks like him." The man himself said, "I am the man." So they said to him, "Then how do your eyes come to be open?" "The man called Jesus," he answered, "made a paste, daubed my eyes with it and said to me, 'Go and wash at Siloam'; so I went, and when I washed I could see." They asked, "Where is he?" "I don't know," he answered. They brought the man who had been blind to the Pharisees. It had been a sabbath day when Jesus made the paste and opened the man's eyes, so when the Pharisees asked him how he had come to see, he said, "He put a paste on my eyes, and I washed, and I can see." Then some of the Pharisees said, "This man cannot be from God: he does not keep the sabbath." Others said, "How could a sinner produce signs like this?" And there was disagreement among them. So they spoke to the blind man again, "What have you to say about him yourself, now that he has opened your eyes?" "He is a prophet," replied the man.

CHRIST THE LORD As Jesus approaches his Passion (and as the Church, which reads this passage toward the end of Lent, approaches it liturgically), he shows forth his power more brilliantly, definitively claiming in word and in deed that he is "the Son of Man" (one of the Old Testament titles for the promised Messiah).

In deed, Christ does two things. First, he defies the sacred laws of the Sabbath. No work—or healing, except in case of death—was allowed on the Sabbath, according to reigning Jewish law; making clay was considered work, and anointing eyes with spittle was considered healing. This defiance shows that his authority is higher than that of the Pharisees and scribes who delineated those laws and is even equal to God's authority, since God himself had commanded the Sabbath rest in the first place. Second, he cures a man born blind. As the blind man himself says, no one had ever heard of such a thing; it was a miracle that clearly exhibited divine action. In word, Jesus attributes to himself the Messianic title, calling himself again the "light of the world," and labeling his miracle a revelation of God's glory.

That Jesus had the man wash in the pool of Siloam adds yet another dimension to the revelation of his divine nature and mission. The eight-day Feast of Tabernacles, which was just coming to an end, included a grand ceremony recalling the water that Moses made flow out of a rock during Israel's journey through the desert. During that ceremony, huge amounts of water were poured over the stone altar in the Temple's inner courtyard (the court of priests), so that they flowed through the whole Temple. This water was taken from the pool of Siloam, an artificially constructed basin fed by the only spring that supplied water to the city, a spring located outside the city walls. (The water in the pool had been "sent" from the well through a long tunnel painstakingly excavated through solid rock.) The Feast of Tabernacles also included a spectacular ceremony of light, recalling the Pillar of Fire that had guided the Israelites during the nights of their forty-year trek to the Promised Land.

Jesus' miracle reveals that the power at work in him is the same power that had formed and liberated Israel in the days of Moses: with water from the rock, he brings new light into this man's darkness. The Gospels remind us again and again that Jesus is the fullness of God's revelation, bringing light and life to this world.

CHRIST THE TEACHER Among the many lessons hidden in this passage, one deserves special mention. How odd that Jesus used spittle and mud to make clay, put the clay on the man's eyelids, and told him to go to the pool of Siloam to wash! Did he have to perform the miracle like that? Certainly not: he could have merely snapped his fingers (he was God, after all). Yet, it was appropriate to do so. Besides the obvious reason that in ancient times saliva was often used in medical procedures, through this method of curing, the blind man felt Christ touching him, heard his voice, and actively participated in the saving deed of God. In this way, Christ shows how he communicates God's grace to us in ways appropriate to our human nature—which includes both body and spirit. Jesus wants to reach into our lives, to lower himself to our level, to touch us, even physically. Christ's touch gave the blind man hope and confidence, making the miracle into a personal encounter, not a magic trick.

The Catholic Church, under the constant guidance of the Holy Spirit, has preserved this method of administering God's grace through the sacraments. The priest's words of absolution at the end of confession provide the consolation we need to bring the reality of God's forgiveness home to our hearts. The water of baptism, the bread and wine of the Eucharist, the chrism... all the material elements of the sacraments extend throughout time the reality of God's eager desire to reach out and touch us. We are not purely spiritual beings; it suits us to encounter God through the mediation of physical realities. God became man not to despoil our humanity, but to bring it to its fullness.

CHRIST THE FRIEND Everything Jesus said and did in his brief life on earth was for us. He was a constant, overflowing gift of truth and grace: "Indeed, from his fullness we have, all of us, received—yes, grace in return for grace..." (Jn 1:16). We should relish his words, his atoning sacrifice to free us from our sins, the Church that he established as his mediator through time and space, and the example he gives us of how to lead a meaningful, fulfilling, and fruitful life. In this passage, he exemplifies an especially important characteristic of that kind of life: "As long as the day lasts I must carry out the work of the one who sent me; the night will soon be here when no one can work."

Jesus lived a busy life, but his busyness was the fruit of love. The blind man had suffered so long with both the physical inconveniences of blindness and the emotional and spiritual pain of wondering why God had sent him this handicap. When Jesus saw him, he recognized all of this. His heart overflowed with love, and his love drove him to heal the man, on the inside as well as on the outside. Jesus didn't waste time, because love wouldn't let him.

Jesus: If only you could understand how brief this earthly life is! Time is so short. Eternity is always at your side. Everything that happens to you now, every opportunity I send you, every invitation I give you, is a chance for you to expand the capacity of your soul for love by exercising self-forgetfulness and self-giving. And the more you expand that capacity, the more I will be able to fill you with the light of my glory when you come home to my Father's house. Think more about this. Work for my Kingdom as if you had little time left to do so, because the truth is that you do have little time left, so little time!

CHRIST IN MY LIFE Never let me forget your majesty and glory. This world seems to delight in watering down your magnificence. But I believe in your greatness and your goodness. I want to live in the reality of your presence, like the saints. I want to learn to hear your voice calling out to me in all things, as I know you are doing, because you have promised that your love for me is constant, personal, and determined...

Too frequently, I take your sacraments for granted. You are so humble and gentle; you want to pour the balm of your grace into my life through signs that I can recognize and understand. I want to be grateful and attentive to your gifts. I want to appreciate them as I should and teach others to do the same. Open my eyes, Lord...

You know that I tend to be lazy, Lord. I gravitate toward idleness and self-indulgence. Please take this tendency away so I can be more energetic and constant in doing good and fulfilling your will. O Lord, please pour your Spirit into my heart, purge my soul from the self-seeking habits that hold me back. Make me an apostle, a soldier, a worker—teach me to live with the fervor of someone whose love never grows cold...

Questions for
SMALL-GROUP DISCUSSION

1. What struck you most in this passage? What did you notice that you didn't notice before?

2. Sometimes we tend to resist Christ's Lordship, like the Pharisees. What causes such resistance, and what can we do to diminish it?

3. What can we do to live the different sacraments better, to make them the kind of personal encounter with Christ that God wants them to be?

4. Think of the liturgical gestures that the congregation performs during Mass (kneeling, standing, making the sign of the cross in different ways at different times...). How would you explain their meaning to a non-Catholic?

Cf. Catechism of the Catholic Church: 2466 on Jesus as the Light of the World; 547-550 on the meaning of Christ's miracles; 1076 on the nature of the sacramental economy; 1084-1090 on Christ's continued work through the sacramental economy

269. THE SEEING GO BLIND (JN 9:18-41)

"God is watching us as we battle and fight in the combat of the faith. His angels are watching us, and so is Christ." – St. Cyprian

JOHN 9:18-41
However, the Jews would not believe that the man had been blind and had gained his sight, without first sending for his parents and asking them, "Is this man really your son who you say was born blind? If so, how is it that he is now able to see?" His parents answered, "We know he is our son and we know he was born blind, but we don't know how it is that he can see now, or who opened his eyes. He is old enough: let him speak for himself." His parents spoke like this out of fear of the Jews, who had already agreed to expel from the synagogue anyone who should acknowledge Jesus as the Christ. This was why his parents said, "He is old enough; ask him." So the Jews again sent for the man and said to him, "Give glory to God! For our part, we know that this man is a sinner." The man answered, "I don't know if he is a sinner; I only know that I was blind and now I can see." They said to him, "What did he do to you? How did he open your eyes?" He replied, "I have told you once and you wouldn't listen. Why do you want to hear it all again? Do you want to become his disciples too?" At this they hurled abuse at him: "You can be his disciple," they said "we are disciples of Moses: we know that God spoke to Moses, but as for this man, we don't know where he comes from."

The man replied, "Now here is an astonishing thing! He has opened my eyes, and you don't know where he comes from! We know that God doesn't listen to sinners, but God does listen to men who are devout and do his will. Ever since the world began it is unheard of for anyone to open the eyes of a man who was born blind; if this man were not from God, he couldn't do a thing." "Are you trying to teach us," they replied "and you a sinner through and through, since you were born!" And they drove him away. Jesus heard they had driven him away, and when he found him he said to him, "Do you believe in the Son of Man?" "Sir," the man replied, "tell me who he is so that I may believe in him." Jesus said, "You are looking at him; he is speaking to you." The man said, "Lord, I believe," and worshipped him. Jesus said: "It is for judgement that I have come into this world, so that those without sight may see and those with sight turn blind." Hearing this, some Pharisees who were present said to him, "We are not blind, surely?" Jesus replied: "Blind? If you were, you would not be guilty, but since you say, 'We see,' your guilt remains."

CHRIST THE LORD Jesus continues insisting on his identity as the Son of God and the Messiah. He claims for himself the title of "Son of Man," commonly held to refer to the Messiah and used that way by the prophets. Then he accepts the blind man's calling him "Lord" (the title used by Jews to address God in prayer) and worshipping him—in Israel worship was reserved for God alone. Then Jesus declares that he came for judgment, to set free those who accept his Lordship and to condemn those who refuse to admit their need for him. These unheard of claims stir up the entire city of Jerusalem, throwing its leaders into a frenzy of agitation and its people into a state of excitement.

Jesus Christ came to earth to establish an eternal Kingdom, nothing less; when he comes into our lives, we can also expect him to shake things up—one way or another. That's the way the Lord works.

CHRIST THE TEACHER What did Jesus teach the blind man? He opened the eyes of his soul as well as the eyes of his body. He gave him the joy of physical sight. For the first time in his life, he could see. All of the things that he had known just by words and sound and touch suddenly came alive to him. Color entered his mind like a flood and filled him with wonder. The visual symphony of the sky and the landscape, the subtle beauty of expressions on people's faces emphasizing the meanings of their words, the look of love and tenderness from his mother, which he had never seen—Jesus opened up to this man a new, glorious, awe-inspiring world of human experience. Joy, amazement, and gratitude filled the man's mind and heart so that he experienced an intensity of life that he had never even dreamed of.

But Jesus also gave him spiritual sight – the gift of faith. He enabled the blind man to see God through himself. He enabled him to encounter his Creator knowingly, face to face. And the man worshipped as he had never worshipped before, pouring out all the love and faith he could muster at the feet of Christ, fulfilling the first and greatest commandment more passionately than we can imagine. This, too, must have overwhelmed him with ineffable spiritual delight.

Which gift did the man value more? Perhaps at first he valued his physical sight, but by the end of the day he was willing to stand up to the powerful Pharisees in order to defend the Lordship of Jesus Christ, knowing that such resistance could incur severe punishment. He did not let the gifts of God blind him to the goodness of God. In this, there is a lesson for us all: God, Jesus Christ, deserves our loyalty, friendship, and worship; if we ever find ourselves forgetting this by following him only for what he can do for us (cure us, give us gifts, work miracles), we will have become spiritually blind.

CHRIST THE FRIEND The blind man was interrogated twice, maligned, and insulted by the Pharisees for his allegiance to Jesus Christ. As soon as Christ found out, he went looking for him, and rewarded him with the gift of a deeper, more complete faith. Jesus must have been pleased and consoled by the man's courage, just as he is pleased and consoled whenever any of his followers stay faithful to him in the face of difficulties or persecution. In hard times, friends show what they're really made of.

Jesus: I am always the Good Shepherd, always seeking out and protecting my sheep and leading them to rich pastures and flowing streams. I never abandon you – I never have and I never will. I will never leave you alone. How could I? I died in order to give you life. You can always count on me to feel your needs deeply and hear your prayers, even before you feel them or voice them. Only those, like the Pharisees, who refuse to put aside their illusory, but comfortable, self-sufficiency and accept me as their Lord and companion, need ever fear being separated from me.

CHRIST IN MY LIFE I know you love me, Lord. And I know you are always on the lookout to teach me, guide me, protect me, and heal me. Your goodness is as broad as the sky and as deep as the ocean. Your faithfulness is as steadfast as the snow-capped mountains. I beg you, Lord, to increase my faith. Let these truths that I know in my mind seep into the depths of my heart. I want to experience your joy...

I fear spiritual blindness. The Pharisees were the most learned of men, and yet they didn't recognize you. They were experts, consultants, and guides, yet they themselves fell into the dark pit of arrogance. If they fell so low, how can

I pretend to be immune from the temptations to self-sufficiency, pride, vanity? Keep me humble, Lord; how much I need your constant help... Your will has never let me down. Make me a faithful friend, a trustworthy worker, loving and dependable in all my relationships, especially in the most ordinary and day-to-day ones. If you were faithful, it was in order to give me an example, a clue to true happiness. With your grace, I can be faithful too. I want to be faithful to you, to the Church, to those around me—faithful unto death...

Questions for
SMALL-GROUP DISCUSSION

1. What struck you most in this passage? What did you notice that you hadn't noticed before?

2. Christ's miraculous intervention in the blind man's life changed his heart and his behavior as well as his eyesight. Christ still intervenes in our lives. How does he do so, and how should we react?

3. The blind man was willing to defend Jesus even in the face of persecution, knowing that Christ was not going to let him down. What opportunities do our life situations give us to defend Jesus and bear witness to him?

4. What are some circumstances or occurrences that could start moving us in the direction of pharisaical spiritual blindness, and how can we guard against that?

Cf. Catechism of the Catholic Church: 2088-2089 and 2091 on sins against faith and hope; 1420-1421 on Christ's continued work of healing through his sacraments of penance and anointing; 1866, 2094, 2733, and 2755 on sloth and not taking advantage of the opportunities God presents during this life

"So the sheep find the Lord's pastures; for anyone who follows him with an undivided heart is nourished in a pasture which is forever green. What are the pastures of these sheep if they are not the deepest joys of the everlasting fresh pastures of paradise? For the pasture of the saints is to see God face to face; when the vision of God never fails, the soul receives its fill of the food of life forever. And so, dear brethren, let us seek these pastures and there join in the joy and the celebrations of so many citizens of heaven. Let their happiness and rejoicing be an invitation to us. Let our hearts grow warm, brethren, let our faith be rekindled, let our desires for heavenly things grow warm; for to love like this is to be on the way."

– POPE ST. GREGORY THE GREAT

270. LIFE TO THE FULL (JN 10:1-10)

"Christ my God, you humbled yourself in order to lift me, a straying sheep, on to your shoulders." – St. John Damascene

JOHN 10:1-10
"I tell you most solemnly, anyone who does not enter the sheepfold through the gate, but gets in some other way is a thief and a brigand. The one who enters through the gate is the shepherd of the flock; the gatekeeper lets him in, the sheep hear his voice, one by one he calls his own sheep and leads them out. When he has brought out his flock, he goes ahead of them, and the sheep follow because they know his voice. They never follow a stranger but run away from him: they do not recognise the voice of strangers." Jesus told them this parable but they failed to understand what he meant by telling it to them. So Jesus spoke to them again: "I tell you most solemnly, I am the gate of the sheepfold. All others who have come are thieves and brigands; but the sheep took no notice of them. I am the gate. Anyone who enters through me will be safe: he will go freely in and out and be sure of finding pasture. The thief comes only to steal and kill and destroy. I have come so that they may have life and have it to the full."

CHRIST THE LORD Israel had long been a shepherding people, and none of these details would have been lost on Jesus' listeners. Israel's greatest king was a shepherd (David), and it is one of the favorite images of God in the psalms and the prophets: "Yahweh is my shepherd, I lack nothing..." (Ps 23). By assuming this identity, Christ asserts both our need for his guidance and care and his great willingness to provide it.

When a lamb is particularly rambunctious or adventurous, repeatedly putting itself in danger, a shepherd will sometimes purposely break one of its legs. He then puts the lamb around his neck until its leg is healed. By that time, the little lamb has become attached to the shepherd, and it never again strays far from its master's protection and guidance.

Jesus wants us to know who he is: the Good Shepherd who protects and cares for the people of God just as a shepherd does his sheep. He does not claim to be one among many, but the only one: "All others who have come are thieves and brigands." Some religious leaders and philosophers throughout history have claimed to be saviors, claimed to have all the answers, but they were really consumed by pride, greed, or lust. Others sincerely sought to better this world, but simply did not have enough wisdom or power to provide the human family with the kind of hope we long for and need. Jesus Christ, on the other hand, not only wants to give us abundant life, but he can. Omniscient, omnipotent, and eternal, he combines utter goodness with unlimited wisdom and power. With his flock, the problem is not the shepherd's powerlessness or ignorance, but the sheep's lack of docility: we stray from the flock and trap ourselves in thistles and swamps. As Christians, we don't only have a good Shepherd, but the perfect Shepherd; now all we need is to be sensible sheep and listen to the voice of the One we know.

CHRIST THE TEACHER A flock of sheep needs both protection and nourishment. The corral (sheepfold) provides the protection, and the fields provide the food and water. Without the corral, they are vulnerable to attack (sheep are notoriously bad at self-defense), and without the pasture, they starve. When Christ calls himself the "gate" for the sheep, he is claiming to provide us with everything we need, both the sheepfold and the pasture.

In Palestine, shepherds often sleep in the opening of the sheepfold, which is made out of a large circle of thick, high shrubbery. In this way, the shepherds both scare away the wolves and keep the sheep together: wolves smell their presence and are afraid to make midnight raids, while the sheep have no desire to walk over the shepherd to escape through the opening, since they recognize him as a sign of security. When day finally dawns, the shepherd will rise and lead his sheep out to pasture. Thus the gate, the door to the sheep pen, symbolizes the complete attention and care given by a good shepherd. Christ chooses this image to teach us what he wants to be for each of us: everything.

CHRIST THE FRIEND Sheep grow accustomed to their shepherd, and vice versa. When a shepherd leads his sheep out to graze, he walks in front of them, speaking or singing to them. They recognize his voice and follow along. Very different is the cattle driver, who pushes the herd from behind by force. A shepherd knows which sheep tend to wander off from the flock, which tend to lead others astray, and which he can count on to stay close beside him—he knows each by name.

Sheep are also infamously dependent. They are defenseless against their carnivorous predators. They will gnaw a little patch of grass down to dirt and then starve instead of looking over the next hill for fresh pasture. They will follow one another to their deaths over the edge of a cliff before breaking ranks. If any animal needs husbanding, it's the sheep; sheep depend on their shepherd. And shepherds always want their sheep to be healthy and happy. They want them to have the best grass, fresh water, and safety, so that they can grow and multiply as much as possible. A sheep has no greater friend than a good shepherd, and we have no greater friend than Christ. He invented life, he gave us life, and he came so that, in him, we might learn to live it "to the full."

CHRIST IN MY LIFE If I believed in you the way I really ought to, I would pray more, study the Scriptures more, and make a more concerted effort to discover and embrace your will in the daily hustle and bustle of life. I'm not a very good sheep, Lord. I get distracted by the seductions of other shepherds—the ones who are thieves and robbers. Forgive me, Lord. Teach me to do your will…

So many people are wandering through life like lost sheep, Lord. They are looking for good pastures, for guidance. They are fearful of wolves, and they don't know how to distinguish friends from enemies or wise counselors from charlatans. Call out to them. They need you. Teach me to be a loudspeaker for your voice, so those around me can find you and come into the fold where they belong…

It is hard for me to admit that I need you as much as I do. Why is that, Lord? Why do I think I can be so self-sufficient, when in fact I know very well that I am constantly stumbling along and messing things up? You are a God who comes to watch over me and guide me. My greatest glory, Lord, is to be loved by you. Free me to trust wholly in your goodness and obey fully your will…

Questions for
SMALL-GROUP DISCUSSION

1. What struck you most in this passage? What did you notice that you hadn't noticed before?

2. This speech takes place right after Jesus cured the man born blind, when the man defends Jesus as the Messiah in front of the threatening Pharisees. What special relevance does that context give to this speech?

3. In this passage, Christ gives a summary of his life's mission: "I have come so that they may have life and have it to the full." What do you think he means by "life" and "to the full"?

4. Who embodies the role of the good shepherd in our world today? Who do people look to for guidance and protection when they don't look to Christ?

Cf. Catechism of the Catholic Church: 754, 874 on the flock of sheep as an image for the Church; 896 on the image of the Good Shepherd as a model for the ministry of priests and bishops

271. ONE FLOCK, ONE SHEPHERD (JN 10:11-18)

"Death is certain, and life is short and vanishes like smoke. Therefore you must fix your minds on the Passion of our Lord Jesus Christ who so burned with love for us that he came down from heaven to redeem us." – St. Francis of Paola

JOHN 10:11-18

"I am the good shepherd: the good shepherd is one who lays down his life for his sheep. The hired man, since he is not the shepherd and the sheep do not belong to him, abandons the sheep and runs away as soon as he sees a wolf coming, and then the wolf attacks and scatters the sheep; this is because he is only a hired man and has no concern for the sheep. I am the good shepherd; I know my own and my own know me, just as the Father knows me and I know the Father; and I lay down my life for my sheep. And there are other sheep I have that are not of this fold, and these I have to lead as well. They too will listen to my voice, and there will be only one flock, and one shepherd. The Father loves me, because I lay down my life in order to take it up again. No one takes it from me; I lay it down of my own free will, and as it is in my power to lay it down, so it is in my power to take it up again; and this is the command I have been given by my Father."

CHRIST THE LORD Jesus Christ was sent to the Jews to be their Messiah in accordance with God's ancient promises to his Chosen People. Yet God was not satisfied to save only one group of people— he wants his blessing to reach all nations, every corner of the earth. Christ the Savior, then, receives Lordship not only over the little flock of Israel and Judah but over all the flocks of the earth. In him, we all come under one Lordship, that of the Good Shepherd, who is the one pastor of the one flock. The effect of the wolf (the devil) is to catch and scatter the sheep; Christ frees and unites us. And even if the wolf attacks the shepherd himself, as he will during Christ's Passion, the shepherd has the power both to lay down and raise up his life, so the one flock will never perish, never be scattered, never be captured. Because Christ the Good Shepherd is our Lord, the Church (the one flock) will never fail. Our membership in this flock is perhaps the greatest gift we have received from the Lord after the gift of life itself. Unfortunately, we often take them both for granted.

This is one of the most compelling reasons behind the Church's missionary mandate. We are all called to spread the Good News of Christ, to "make disciples of all nations," bringing everyone into this one flock. Only the Catholic Church has the divine guarantee that it will never fail (never be scattered by wolves). Other churches and other religions may have sincere believers and parts of the truth, but only Christ's one flock gathered around his vicar's staff is guaranteed never to fail. Building the Kingdom of the Lord, then, means building up his Church.

CHRIST THE TEACHER The fall of Adam and Eve came about as a result of their lack of trust in God. Jesus Christ came to win back that trust. By giving up his own life to atone for our sins, he showed that the Father is worthy of our trust, that he will forgive us, protect us, and lead us to rich pastures. God will never abandon us in our need—never. The Passion, death and Resurrection of Jesus Christ are his proof. Though the wolf (the devil) attacked and scattered Christ's disciples on that first Good Friday, Christ did not flee; he gave up his own life, freely suffering what in truth we, because of our sins, deserved to suffer and freely obeying with the total obedience that Adam and Eve had lacked. Because of his docility in embracing the Father's will, the Father rewarded him by raising him from the dead. Christ was faithful to his mission, even knowing what it was going to cost him. That mission consists in saving us from sin and estrangement from God. He is the Good Shepherd, the one we can trust, the one who cares more about our lives than we do ourselves, the Lord who came not to be served, but to serve, and to give his life as a ransom for ours.

Note how this mission of carrying out the Father's plan, of obeying the Father's will, consumes Jesus and constitutes in his mind the entire meaning of his life: "The Father loves me, because I lay down my life in order to take it up again... and this is the command I have been given by my Father." This is how Christ, the perfect man, lived out his human existence, focusing wholly on the Father's will, being passionately faithful to his sonship. To discover and fulfill our own identity as children of God, and thus experience life as he created us to live it—both now and in eternity—Jesus invites us to do the same: "The sheep follow, because they know his voice" (Jn 10:4).

CHRIST THE FRIEND *Jesus: I know my own and my own know me. When I created you, I built two needs into your soul: the need to love and the need to be loved. If you don't learn to love, you will never flourish, and if you don't discover that you are loved, you will never learn to love. Love is always a two-way street—an exchange, an embrace. It's much harder for you to let yourself be loved than it is to love, because to be loved, you have to let yourself be known. You cannot be loved fully by someone who doesn't know you fully. This is why every earthly love is precarious; you never know if the person who loves you will continue to do so when they know you better.*

I know you through and through, completely, even better than you know yourself. I know all the things you keep hidden from others, all the things about you that you barely understand yourself. I know you so thoroughly because I gave you life, I brought you into existence, and I have been holding you and sustaining you every instant of your life. I know you uniquely and totally, so I can love you as no one else can. You never have to worry about my love waning because I have already shown you, while you were still a sinner, still a rebel, that my love endures to the end, even to death on a cross. You have nothing left to fear. Nothing is hidden from me, and yet I still love you without an ounce of ambiguity or reluctance. I know you, and now you know me. I love you, so come now and love me...

CHRIST IN MY LIFE How can I thank you for bringing me into your flock and saving me from so many dangers? You have called out to me, and you have given me ears to hear your voice. Never let me be separated from you, Lord. Only you love me enough to lay down your life for my sake. Teach me to be worthy of your love. Teach me to be docile, to stay at your side no matter what...

I am so used to thinking about your sacrificial love. I look at crucifixes all the time. But I know that I haven't plumbed the depths of this lesson. You gave your life because you loved me. How can I discover the full import of that truth? I think it's only by following in your footsteps. Only by giving my own life for your Kingdom, by sacrificing myself for the good of my neighbor and those around me...

How can I love you, Lord? Love wants to give, but what can I give you that you don't already have? I know the answer, Lord. I can love you by loving those you put into my life. Every one of them. You love them, and so you are within them, and when I love them, I am loving you. May our wills become one...

Questions for
SMALL-GROUP DISCUSSION

1. What struck you most in this passage? What did you notice that you hadn't noticed before?

2. If we were more aware of our need for God, which Christ likens to the sheep's need for the shepherd, how would that affect our everyday attitudes and choices?

3. What can we do to foster a healthier awareness of our membership in the universal Church, by which we should rejoice with our fellow Christians when they rejoice, and mourn with them when they mourn?

4. What more can we do to help those in our community draw closer to the Good Shepherd—or enter into the flock?

Cf. Catechism of the Catholic Church: 754, 874, and 2686 on the flock of sheep as an image for the Church; 830-856 on the universality of the Catholic Church; 396, 397, and 227 on the role of trusting God in the life of a Christian; 846-856 on the Church's missionary responsibility and salvation

272. A Shepherd's Lament (Jn 10:19-42)

"Let us have recourse to that fatherly love revealed to us by Christ in his messianic mission, a love which reached its culmination in his cross, in his death and resurrection."
– St. John Paul II

JOHN 10:19-42
These words caused disagreement among the Jews. Many said, "He is possessed, he is raving; why bother to listen to him?" Others said, "These are not the words of a man possessed by a devil: could a devil open the eyes of the blind?" It was the time when the feast of Dedication was being celebrated in Jerusalem. It was winter, and Jesus was in the Temple walking up and down in the Portico of Solomon. The Jews gathered round him and said, "How much longer are you going to keep us in suspense? If you are the Christ, tell us plainly." Jesus replied: "I have told you, but you do not believe. The works I do in my Father's name are my witness; but you do not believe, because you are no sheep of mine. The sheep that belong to me listen to my voice; I know them and they follow me. I give them eternal

life; they will never be lost and no one will ever steal them from me. The Father who gave them to me is greater than anyone, and no one can steal from the Father. The Father and I are one."

The Jews fetched stones to stone him, so Jesus said to them, "I have done many good works for you to see, works from my Father; for which of these are you stoning me?" The Jews answered him, "We are not stoning you for doing a good work but for blasphemy: you are only a man and you claim to be God." Jesus answered: "Is it not written in your Law: I said, you are gods? So the Law uses the word gods of those to whom the word of God was addressed, and scripture cannot be rejected. Yet you say to someone the Father has consecrated and sent into the world, 'You are blaspheming,' because he says, 'I am the son of God.' If I am not doing my Father's work, there is no need to believe me; but if I am doing it, then even if you refuse to believe in me, at least believe in the work I do; then you will know for sure that the Father is in me and I am in the Father." They wanted to arrest him then, but he eluded them. He went back again to the far side of the Jordan to stay in the district where John had once been baptising. Many people who came to him there said, "John gave no signs, but all he said about this man was true"; and many of them believed in him.

CHRIST THE LORD "I and the Father are one." When the Jewish leaders heard him say that, they picked up rocks in order to stone him to death—for a man to claim equality with God was, for them, the purest blasphemy, the grossest idolatry. Indeed, what other man in history has claimed to be God—not just "a" god or a "manifestation" of a higher power, but the God? It is an outrageous claim, and it makes it impossible to write Jesus off as merely a great teacher, philosopher, or religious leader. Even believing Christians, however, can fall into those errors, at least in practical terms—treating their Christianity like a cold body of doctrine or a mere personal opinion. Therefore, although Christ has made this claim frequently throughout the Gospels, we should never tire of considering it, of letting it sink deeper and deeper into our understanding of the Lord we follow.

Someone who makes such a claim can only be one of two things: a lunatic or exactly what he says he is. The Gospels give no evidence for lunacy in Christ; in fact, his teaching and his behavior are more lucid and brilliant than anyone else's, and his miracles (the "works" he constantly refers to) are incontrovertible. And in the centuries after his Ascension, his followers and doctrine have not waned—as would a lunatic's—but have only grown, contributing immeasurable good to a human race beset with evil. Therefore, we have to conclude that Christ wasn't a lunatic. Only one option remains. But if he is indeed who he says he is, then we must follow him. That takes humility; it takes listening to him and trusting him, as sheep do with their shepherd. Indeed, he is the Lord—that is clear; what's problematic is our reluctance to surrender our personal kingdoms into his hands.

Another level of meaning can be ascribed to this phrase. On the one hand, as the Jews understood it, Jesus was claiming equality with God. On the other hand, Jesus alludes to the Old Testament texts that refer to judges who have been set aside to do God's work as "gods"—i.e., men set aside to represent God to other men through the administration of justice (e.g., Ps 82:6 and Ex 21:6). In this sense, then, Jesus' phrase "I and the Father are one" emphasizes the interpersonal union between the Son and the Father, a union of love that Jesus manifests more perfectly than anyone else who has ever been sent by God through his flawless and loving obedience. From this perspective, the Lord's claim to be one with the Father is actually an invitation for his listeners to enter into the same union; if they "listen to [his] voice and follow [him]," they will enter into the "eternal life" that he shares with his Father.

CHRIST THE TEACHER The scene St. John describes is picturesque. It is winter, cool and blustery, during the celebration of Hanukkah, a commemoration of the cleansing and rededication of the Temple in 164 B.C. after its three years of being polluted by pagan squatters (this had occurred with the successful completion of the Maccabees' wars against the Greek Hellenistic ruler of Palestine, Antiochus Epiphanes). Jesus is spending his days in the outer courtyard of the Temple precincts. This courtyard was flanked by two huge covered colonnades that were over forty feet high. He and his apostles and other residents and pilgrims are walking up and down the colonnades discussing the meaning of the Scriptures, the nature of the Messiah, and the way of salvation. Jesus is strolling along the porticoes arguing and explaining and teaching and exhorting. It is no dry, difficult to comprehend, boring philosophical lecture, but a passionate, enthusiastic, fiery exchange in which the eager words of Jesus stir his listeners to question him and themselves. Their comments, questions, and reactions pour out, not waiting for the others to finish, talking over each other, full of intent and enthusiasm. God is walking among men, speaking their language, engaging with them on their own turf, joyfully pleading with them to open their minds and hearts to his revelation.

This is still his methodology. Jesus is still walking among men through his ordained ministers and his missionaries, through his catechists and his disciples in every walk of life. He dwells and speaks and accompanies all men through those who by his grace have become his ambassadors. And he still backs up his words with incontrovertible deeds, with signs that prove his credibility and dependability—the greatest of which is the continued existence and expansion of his Church. In spite of twenty centuries of nonstop crises and attacks, the Church marches on, giving light to the world and reminding men and women of all times and places that they are loved by a merciful God who invites them to join him in the everlasting adventure of eternal life.

CHRIST THE FRIEND "I give them eternal life." Shepherds want their sheep to thrive. They want their sheep to stay safe, to eat well, to be healthy and happy—the shepherds' livelihood depends on it. Christ is our shepherd.

Jesus: All I want is for you to flourish, to experience the fullness and wonder of life as I designed it to be. Every invitation I make, every indication I give through my words, my example, the commandments, the teachings of my Church, the nudges in your conscience, all has but one purpose: to lead you into the incomparably rich pastures of a life in communion with me, a communion that can begin here on earth but will only reach its fulfillment when you come home to heaven. I want to be your Good Shepherd, and my greatest joy is when you decide to be my good sheep.

CHRIST IN MY LIFE You and the Father are one, and you invite me to be one with you. I can't get over how strange it is that you, Creator of all things, deign to come into my life and address me, guide me, and patiently invite me to follow you and assume responsibility in your Kingdom. You and I both know that I don't deserve this kind of attention. It flows from your abundant goodness, which will never run dry...

Only you know how hot the desire for meaning and fruitfulness burns in my heart. How strange this life is! It is so full of joys and sorrows and yet so incomplete. You are the bread of life. Keep guiding me, Lord; keep leading me. You know what I need and hope for—you are my hope. Never let me slow down or be satisfied when you still have more in store for me...

You were eager to dwell among men because you had something to give them—your love, your wisdom, your grace. And now you have made me your messenger. Am I as eager as you were to engage my neighbors, to bring them your light? I am reluctant sometimes. I don't love enough. But you know that I want to love more. And that's all you need—you will work wonders through those who trust in you...

Questions for
SMALL-GROUP DISCUSSION

1. What struck you most in this passage? What did you notice that you hadn't noticed before?

2. How can we increase our confidence in Christ's unique Lordship enough so that we are able to defend and explain it calmly and charitably (inoffensively) in conversations with those who don't believe in it?

3. In what ways can we be true to our need for God throughout the day? In other words, in what situations do we tend to forget about God or act like we don't really need him?

4. When God asks something difficult of us, why is it often so hard to react with faith and trust, obeying promptly and joyfully?

Cf. Catechism of the Catholic Church: 754, 874, and 2686 on the flock of sheep as an image for the Church; 830-856 on the universality of the Catholic Church; 396, 397, and 227 on the role of trusting in God in the life of a Christian

"The Lord, our Savior, raised his voice and spoke with incomparable majesty. 'Let all know,' he said, 'that after sorrow grace follows; let them understand that without the burden of affliction one cannot arrive at the height of glory; that the measure of heavenly gifts is increased in proportion to the labors undertaken. Let them be on their guard against error or deception; this is the only ladder by which paradise is reached; without the cross there is no road to heaven."

– ST. ROSE OF LIMA

273. God's Timing (Jn 11:1-16)

"Rather, my dear brothers, let us be ready for all that God's will may bring, with an undivided heart, firm faith, and rugged strength." – St. Cyprian

JOHN 11:1-16

There was a man named Lazarus who lived in the village of Bethany with the two sisters, Mary and Martha, and he was ill. It was the same Mary, the sister of the sick man Lazarus, who anointed the Lord with ointment and wiped his feet with her hair. The sisters sent this message to Jesus, "Lord, the man you love is ill." On receiving the message, Jesus said, "This sickness will end not in death but in God's glory, and through it the Son of God will be glorified." Jesus loved Martha and her sister and Lazarus, yet when he heard that Lazarus was ill he stayed where he was for two more days before saying to the disciples, "Let us go to Judaea." The disciples said, "Rabbi, it is not long since the Jews wanted to stone you; are you going back again?" Jesus replied: "Are there not twelve hours in the day? A man can walk in the daytime without stumbling because he has the light of this world to see by; but if he walks at night he stumbles, because there is no light to guide him." He said that and then added, "Our friend Lazarus is resting, I am going to wake him." The disciples said to him, "Lord, if he is able to rest he is sure to get better." The phrase Jesus used referred to the death of Lazarus, but they thought that by "rest" he meant "sleep," so Jesus put it plainly, "Lazarus is dead; and for your sake I am glad I was not there because now you will believe. But let us go to him." Then Thomas—known as the Twin—said to the other disciples, "Let us go too, and die with him."

CHRIST THE LORD Jesus is drawing close to the end of his earthly mission. His disciples have been accompanying him, learning from him, and witnessing his miracles for almost three years. Here once again St. John shows that Jesus had knowledge that was not merely human—he knew how Lazarus's sickness would end, and he knew, without any need for a messenger, when Lazarus had died.

And yet, even at this late point in his ministry, even when Jesus shows his divine knowledge, we see that his disciples still don't understand him. They still misconstrue his words and even doubt his good sense and power. Any lesser Lord would have long ago given up on his slow and artless followers, but not Jesus. He is a Lord who serves his subjects, teaching them and guiding them to the fullness of life. The needier they are, the more he condescends to stay with them, put up with them, and give them whatever they need in order to make them believe in, trust, and follow him. And besides all this, he entrusted his greatest gift to their care—his Church. The Lord rules, but he rules with love.

CHRIST THE TEACHER St. John points out that "Jesus loved Martha and her sister and Lazarus." And yet he let Lazarus die. He told the messengers, "This sickness will end not in death but in God's glory, and through it the Son of God will be glorified." Jesus loves them, and yet he lets them suffer. He lets them experience their helplessness, their weakness, the separation of death, and the loss of a loved one. Did he do it to punish them? Did he do it because he had no power to remedy the evil? No, he let them suffer precisely because he loved them. He wanted to give them the great gift of knowing him more deeply and more intimately, and he wanted them to experience his power and his love more profoundly. The suffering afforded him an opportunity to act in their lives in a new way, revealing himself to them more completely. This is God's glory—that we know him and love him and experience his love more completely.

We urgently need to contemplate this moment in our Lord's life. Suffering, death, pain, and sorrow touch us all. If we exercise our faith in Christ's wisdom as shown in his relationship with this family from Bethany, we will be more ready to find and embrace him when suffering strikes closer to home.

CHRIST THE FRIEND The messengers arrive tired and breathless; they have traveled in haste. The circle of apostles opens up so they can come close to the Master and deliver their message. Their faces are anxious, fearful, but with a glint of hope that Jesus will come to save the dying Lazarus. And they deliver their message, the simplest and subtlest of messages, composed by Mary and Martha, close friends of Jesus (and probably relatives on Jesus' mother's side according to the scholars): "Lord, the man you love is ill." The messengers look earnestly and eagerly at Christ's face, and the apostles alternate their gazes between Jesus and the messengers. Silence. Then Jesus, looking warmly at the messengers, smiles and answers: "This sickness will not end in death..."

Jesus: Look into my heart at the moment when I heard that message, "The man you love is ill." How it filled my soul with joy! It was the perfect prayer. Martha and Mary knew me so well. They knew that I loved, and they knew that I can't hold back from acting on my love. They could have said, "Lord, the one who loves you is ill," as though because Lazarus loved me, he deserved to be healed. But who loved more, Lazarus or I? I loved him infinitely more than he could ever love me! They could have said, "Lord, come and heal Lazarus, who is ill." But they knew that my love would do much more than they could ever think of. This was the perfect prayer. It throws all their needs and hopes and sorrows into the bottomless ocean of my love. You, too, can pray this prayer. Do you have a need, a worry, a sin that has to be forgiven? Say to me, "Lord, the one you love is ill," and how will I be able to hold myself back from coming to your aid? Do you have someone else who is in need? Tell me, "Lord, the one you love is ill." Can my heart resist that prayer? Is it possible? It may seem that I delay my response, but trust me. My love only seeks fullness of life for you and greater glory for my Father.

CHRIST IN MY LIFE I am slow and artless, clumsy and inelegant by nature, Lord. You have to teach me the same lesson a hundred times before I start getting the gist of it. But you are willing to do that. I think that one of the best ways I can praise you is simply by rejoicing in your love, your patience, and your goodness. You are all-powerful, all-loving, and all-good—you are all mine, so I can always rejoice...

You have something for me to do in your Kingdom, just as you had something for each of your apostles. You have given me a mission in life, and because I am united to you through grace, that mission will resound through all eternity. Without you, what worthwhile thing would I have to do? What could I do that would last? You have given me what I yearn for most: meaning, purpose, a mission...

Lord, I am here, the one you love, and I am ill. I am sick with the infection of selfishness, vanity, arrogance, and self-indulgence. I am weighed down by troubles and worries. Lord, the one you love is ill. I trust in you. You are mercy. You are love...

Questions for
SMALL-GROUP DISCUSSION

1. What struck you most in this passage? What did you notice that you hadn't noticed before?

2. Why is it often so hard to trust in Christ during times of crisis and suffering?

3. How does our popular culture's view of suffering and sickness compare with the Christian view?

4. St. John tells us that Jesus said to his apostles, "For your sake I am glad I was not there because now you will believe." That implies that they still did not believe. What did you think they didn't believe, and why didn't they? Does this detail have some kind of a lesson for us?

Cf. Catechism of the Catholic Church: 547-550 on the meaning of Christ's miracles; 551-553 on the special role of the Twelve Apostles in the Kingdom of Christ; 478 on the heart of Christ; 1500-1513 on the place of sickness in the lives of Christians

274. THE FORCE OF FAITH—THE POWER OF LOVE (JN 11: 17-44)

"Since Christ is our peace, we shall be living up to the name of Christian if we let Christ be seen in our lives by letting peace reign in our hearts." – St. Gregory of Nyssa

JOHN 11:17-44

On arriving, Jesus found that Lazarus had been in the tomb for four days already. Bethany is only about two miles from Jerusalem, and many Jews had come to Martha and Mary to sympathise with them over their brother. When Martha heard that Jesus had come she went to meet him. Mary remained sitting in the house. Martha said to Jesus, "If you had been here, my brother would not have died, but I know that, even now, whatever you ask of God, he will grant you." "Your brother," said Jesus to her, "will rise again." Martha said, "I know he will rise again at the resurrection on the last day." Jesus said: "I am the resurrection. If anyone believes in me, even though he dies he will live, and whoever lives and believes in me will never die. Do you believe this?" "Yes, Lord," she said, "I believe that you are the Christ, the Son of God, the one who was to come into this world." When she had said this, she went and called her sister Mary, saying in a low voice, "The Master is here and wants to see you." Hearing this, Mary got up quickly and went to him. Jesus had not yet come into the village; he was still at the place where Martha had met him. When the Jews who were in the house sympathising with Mary saw her get up so quickly and go out, they followed her, thinking that she was going to the tomb to weep there.

Mary went to Jesus, and as soon as she saw him she threw herself at his feet, saying, "Lord, if you had been here, my brother would not have died." At the sight of her tears, and those of the Jews who followed her, Jesus said in great distress, with a sigh that came straight from the heart, "Where have you put him?" They said, "Lord, come and see." Jesus wept; and the Jews said, "See how much he loved him!" But there were some who remarked, "He opened the eyes of the blind man, could he not have prevented this man's death?" Still sighing, Jesus reached the tomb: it was a cave with a stone to close the opening. Jesus said, "Take the stone away." Martha said to him, "Lord, by now he will smell; this is the fourth day." Jesus replied, "Have I not told you that if you believe you will see the glory of God?" So they took away the stone. Then Jesus lifted up his eyes and said: "Father, I thank you for hearing my prayer. I knew indeed that you always hear me, but I speak for the sake of all these who stand round me, so that they may believe it was you who sent me." When he had said this, he cried in a loud voice, "Lazarus, here! Come out!" The dead man came out, his feet and hands bound with bands of stuff and a cloth round his face. Jesus said to them, "Unbind him, let him go free."

CHRIST THE LORD Jesus raises Lazarus from the dead. He had been in the tomb for four days, and Jesus Christ calls his name, orders him to come out, and he does. Death itself submits to Christ the Lord. The crowd must have been stupefied, wide-eyed with disbelief, awe, and wonder that gathered in deadly silence as Lazarus stepped out from the tomb and then burst forth in a storm of joy and celebration. Martha and Mary were so full of natural jubilation and supernatural elation that they wouldn't have known who to embrace first, their brother or their Lord. Lazarus, as soon as the cloths were removed, surely gazed into his Lord's shining eyes with the deepest love and most determined, courageous loyalty that he had ever experienced. The whole scene was a prelude to heaven and the final resurrection.

The Church presents this reading to us toward the end of the Lenten liturgical crescendo: Christ told the woman at the well that he was the Messiah; he cured the man born blind, something never done before; and now he tops everything by raising Lazarus from the dead, once again "for God's glory; through it the Son of God will be glorified." Jesus knows that in order to fulfill the Father's plan, he will soon suffer humiliation, torture, and death. As that moment draws near, he performs miracle after miracle to bolster his disciples' faith, so that the coming events of his Passion will not snuff out their hope in him.

How many great figures throughout history have made (and continue to make) wild claims and fabulous promises! And yet none have made such a claim as Christ: "I am the resurrection...." Unlike so many others, however, Jesus Christ backs up his claims with incontrovertible deeds. He is a Leader we can count on—forever.

CHRIST THE TEACHER Martha and Mary had different personalities. Martha was the organizer, the practical one, the quick-thinking one, attentive to details. She doesn't interrupt Mary's prayer when she gets word that Jesus has arrived—she quietly tiptoes away. She comes to Jesus and discusses the situation with him, eliciting explanations and words and instruction from the Master. She is the one who arranges that her sister, too, can come to be with the Lord. She whispers to Jesus that if they take away the stone the stench of the tomb will be terrific. Mary, on the other hand, was the contemplative one, the intense and more emotional one, the natural, effortless leader. Everyone followed her out of the house when she rushed to see Jesus. She throws herself at his feet when she sees him. She moves his heart and elicits his tears.

Did either one love Jesus more? Did Jesus love either one more? Not at all. The lesson St. John teaches us by presenting these distinct portraits is that each one of us has a unique relationship with Christ. Mary and Martha shared a friend in Jesus, but each one's friendship was personal, intimate, and customized. Learning this lesson is essential to achieving peace of heart and maturity in our spiritual lives. What would have happened if Mary had wanted to relate to Jesus the way Martha did? She would have been frustrated and anxious and off balance. And what if Martha wanted to relate to Jesus the way Mary did? She, too, would have been dissatisfied and experienced insincerity and incompleteness in her relationship with Christ. Too often we fall into that trap, trying to gear our friendship with Christ in accordance with someone else's standard or style. We envy what others have instead of being true to what God has given us.

CHRIST THE FRIEND This passage contains the shortest verse in the New Testament: "Jesus wept." Jesus Christ is not a distant God. Look how intimately and familiarly Martha and Mary treat him! He never relinquishes his Lordship, and they never forget that he is the Lord. But he is unlike any other Lord; he not only gives us protection, security, life, and peace, he gives us his very heart. The heart of Christ yearns for us to give him as much love and confidence as Mary and Martha; he yearns to be let into the presence of our hearts so as to share our sorrows and troubles. "Jesus wept." No other god ever shared our tears; only Christ is Emmanuel, "God with us."

Lazarus: How differently I lived from that day on! It was like a fog had lifted and I could see everything clearly. I wasn't anxious for praise and acceptance and recognition anymore because I finally realized how fleeting such things were. I thought less about myself and my problems because I knew so clearly that God was holding me in the palm of his hand. I was so free! I was free to bring joy and comfort to those around me, to be a delight for my sisters and our friends. I was free from the fears that made me hesitate to speak to everyone about Jesus. When he called my name and drew me out of the tomb, it really was a brand new start, a brand new life. And he's willing to do the same for everyone, if only they will trust in him and take the first step toward the opening of the tomb.

CHRIST IN MY LIFE Death is the great equalizer. It comes for everyone, and it brings an end to all illusions. And yet you are Lord over death. You have conquered death. With you, death is just a door to an even truer life. Death—so many fear it; so many avoid thinking about it. With you at my side, Lord, I have nothing to fear, nothing to avoid thinking about. Death is my sister; she will lead me deeper into your presence...

Teach me to be as close to you as Mary and Martha were. Teach me to speak to you right from my heart, to share all my thoughts with you. Teach me to be sincere and spontaneous, yet still full of reverence and respect. I, too, believe in you, I know you are the Resurrection; you are the life. Teach me to trust in you and do your will...

Do you still weep with me, Lord? Do you still feel the losses I feel, the struggles that weigh me down? Can you understand them? Can you come and rescue me from my sorrow as you did with Mary and Martha? I know you do and I know you can. O Lord, increase my faith! Increase my faith! Increase my faith! You don't want me to suffer alone. Let me know your presence, Lord...

Questions for
SMALL-GROUP DISCUSSION

1. What struck you most in this passage? What did you notice that you hadn't noticed before?

2. Why do you think Jesus spends so much time questioning Martha?

3. If Jesus already knew that Lazarus was dead even before he reached Bethany, why do you think he suddenly started weeping and sighing once he saw the sorrow of all the mourners?

4. Why do you think Jesus had some of the bystanders remove the stone from the entrance to the tomb and then take off Lazarus's burial cloths? If he had the power to raise the dead man to life, he certainly had the power to take care of those details as well, didn't he? Do you think these details harbor any lessons for us and for the Church?

Cf. Catechism of the Catholic Church: 992-1004 on the meaning of the Resurrection for Christ and for us; 456-460 on why Jesus became man in the first place; 547-550 on Jesus' miracles as signs of the Kingdom

275. PAR FOR THE CHRISTIAN COURSE (JN 11:45-57)

"He was crucified on behalf of us all and for the sake of us all, so that, when one had died instead of all, we all might live in him." – St. Cyril of Alexandria

JOHN 11:45-57

Many of the Jews who had come to visit Mary and had seen what he did believed in him, but some of them went to tell the Pharisees what Jesus had done. Then the chief priests and Pharisees called a meeting. "Here is this man working all these signs," they said, "and what action are we taking? If we let him go on in this way everybody will believe in him, and the Romans will come and destroy the Holy Place and our nation." One of them, Caiaphas, the high priest that year, said, "You don't seem to have grasped the situation at all; you fail to see that it is better for one man to die for the people, than for the whole nation to be destroyed." He did not speak in his own person, it was as high priest that he made this prophecy that Jesus was to die for the nation—and not for the nation only, but to gather together in unity the scattered children of God. From that day they were determined to kill him. So Jesus no longer went about openly among the Jews, but left the district for a town called Ephraim, in the country bordering on the desert, and stayed there with his disciples. The Jewish Passover drew near, and many of the country people who had gone up to Jerusalem to purify themselves looked out for Jesus, saying to one another as they stood about in the Temple, "What do you think? Will he come to the festival or not?" The chief priests and Pharisees had by now given their orders: anyone who knew where he was must inform them so that they could arrest him.

CHRIST THE LORD Caiaphas rightly declared that Christ was to die for the sake of the whole nation, but he declared it without fully understanding what he was saying. In his own mind, he meant the preservation of the status quo in Palestine, the continued occupation by the people of Israel of the Promised Land, even though they were under Roman rule. By doing away with Jesus, he thought he would save that relative stability; by letting Jesus continue his ministry, he feared its annihilation by the Romans. In the mind of God, however, the death of Jesus, by giving him a chance to exhibit utter fidelity and perfect, loving obedience, was the antidote to the death of the human race that had occurred because of Adam's infidelity and disobedience. The salvation that God was working out through the actions of Caiaphas was far beyond Caiaphas's wildest imaginings. Instead of maintaining a precarious, merely political status quo, God was laying the foundation for a new and everlasting covenant between God and man.

This incident is a striking example of the great mystery of Providence. God is able to guide the history of the world and of each person's life toward his own wise and glorious ends without violating the freedom of his spiritual creatures. He is a Lord both just and merciful, all-powerful but all-loving. Though we cannot completely understand how this happens, the coming Passion, death, and Resurrection of Jesus is the most astonishing and incontrovertible evidence that it does indeed happen. Nothing on earth walks aimlessly; all things are working together for the good of those whom God loves.

CHRIST THE TEACHER Think for a minute about the recent sequence of events. Jesus shows up in Bethany to visit some of his closest friends, only to find them and their acquaintances mourning Lazarus's death. He is moved with compassion and asks to be taken to the grave. In the midst of the general gloom and sadness, he performs one of the most dramatic miracles of his whole ministry—one of the most dramatic miracles of all human history. He brings Lazarus back from the dead with a mere word of command. Joy, gratitude, celebration, and amazement abound. The news spreads, people come to see for themselves, and the undeniable evidence leads them to believe in Jesus' claims to be the Messiah. They are filled with hope, joy, and humble faith. But not all are rejoicing. For some of the Jewish leaders, the miracle is the straw that breaks the camel's back. They decide finally and definitively to apprehend and destroy the miracle worker.

Is this a logical reaction? Shouldn't even his enemies realize by this point that Jesus was from God? They should have, but they don't. And they flex their political and social muscles so threateningly that Jesus is forced to go into hiding as he waits for the Passover. Anyone who associates with him or even fails to tell the police where he's hiding is menaced with punishment. All because Jesus raised Lazarus from the dead!

The stark contrast between the pure goodness of Christ and the violent opposition his goodness stirs up is a composite of the history of the Church and of every Christian. Where Jesus Christ is truly being preached and taught, where he is changing lives and raising dead souls to hope and enthusiasm, the forces of evil will not tarry in throwing up clouds of adversity. If this happened to Jesus himself, whose goodness and trustworthiness were incontrovertibly confirmed by his extraordinary miracles, only the most foolish or naïve Christian will ever be surprised, scandalized, or discouraged by the opposition that necessarily shows up wherever serious Kingdom-building operations are under way.

CHRIST THE FRIEND The Pharisees appear monstrous to us. Yet we can be just like them. When we are stuck in our sins or wallowing in self-centeredness, the good deeds of others agitate us; they prick our conscience. We try to stamp them out. We try to minimize them. Instead of rejoicing in goodness wherever we find it, we resent it, and we rejoice instead in our neighbor's fall, since it brings them down to our level. Christ is never like that with us. The more we experience his unquenchable generosity toward us, the more it will purify our stinginess and free us to love our neighbors as he does.

Jesus: Do you think I despised these corrupt men who countenanced my death and scattered my sheep? How could I? They were as much my sheep as the others. They were more lost than the others, and I longed for their hearts to turn around and come to me. It was for them that I went to the cross. They needed to see the extent of my love for them; they needed to see that nothing they could do to me was able to stop me from loving them. Rest in my heart for a moment now, and see how I love those who hate and persecute me. Since you know that I am always with you, always loving and guiding and protecting you, you have the strength to do the same.

CHRIST IN MY LIFE Thinking about your Providence fills my soul with peace. I know that you are always watching over me and guiding me and those around me. In some hidden way, the many Good Fridays of human history, and of my story, will all erupt into Easter Sundays. You are my Father, and in addition to loving me intensely and tenderly, you hold the reins of the universe and put everything at the service of that love...

How do I react to difficulties and opposition in life? How did you react? You accepted them, and you continued steadfastly on the path of the Father's will. Why do they upset me so much? Jesus, increase my faith! Convince me that you can handle these injustices and persecutions and this endless gauntlet of obstacles. Lord Jesus, I believe that you are the Lord of life and history, and I trust in you...

Lord Jesus, I can barely keep myself from lashing out at colleagues who show up late... how can I learn to love actual enemies, people who willfully destroy reputations and good works? And how can I refrain from criticizing those who exert their energy and influence in resisting your action and your Spirit? Teach me the science of the cross, Lord, and teach me the lesson of Christ-like love...

Questions for
SMALL-GROUP DISCUSSION

1. What struck you most in this passage? What did you notice that you hadn't noticed before?

2. What do you think was really at the root of Caiaphas's and the other leaders' resistance to Christ?

3. In what ways do faithful Christians find themselves opposed and persecuted today?

4. Many people believed in Jesus after this miracle, but many still didn't believe in him. What should that teach us about our own evangelizing efforts?

Cf. Catechism of the Catholic Church: 302-314 on the mystery of God's providence and how it combines with the realities of evil and human freedom; 305, 322, 2215, 2547, and 2830 on childlike abandonment to the providence of God; 2608 and 1825, 2443 and 2844 on loving the poor and one's enemies as Christ did; 595-598 on the leaders of Jerusalem and Jesus' death

THE GOSPEL OF JOHN
Chapter 12

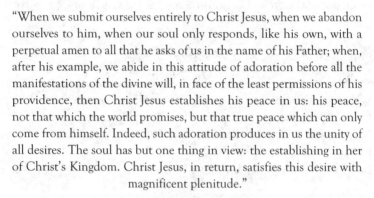

"When we submit ourselves entirely to Christ Jesus, when we abandon ourselves to him, when our soul only responds, like his own, with a perpetual amen to all that he asks of us in the name of his Father; when, after his example, we abide in this attitude of adoration before all the manifestations of the divine will, in face of the least permissions of his providence, then Christ Jesus establishes his peace in us: his peace, not that which the world promises, but that true peace which can only come from himself. Indeed, such adoration produces in us the unity of all desires. The soul has but one thing in view: the establishing in her of Christ's Kingdom. Christ Jesus, in return, satisfies this desire with magnificent plenitude."

–BLESSED COLUMBA MARMION

276. THE SWEET SCENT OF LOVE (JN 12:1-11)

"An egg given during life for love of God is more profitable for eternity than a cathedral full of gold given after death." – St. Albert the Great

JOHN 12:1-11
Six days before the Passover, Jesus went to Bethany, where Lazarus was, whom he had raised from the dead. They gave a dinner for him there; Martha waited on them and Lazarus was among those at table. Mary brought in a pound of very costly ointment, pure nard, and with it anointed the feet of Jesus, wiping them with her hair; the house was full of the scent of the ointment. Then Judas Iscariot—one of his disciples, the man who was to betray him—said, "Why wasn't this ointment sold for three hundred denarii, and the money given to the poor?" He said this, not because he cared about the poor, but because he was a thief; he was in charge of the common fund and used to help himself to the contributions. So Jesus said, "Leave her alone; she had to keep this scent for the day of my burial. You have the poor with you always, you will not always have me." Meanwhile a large number of Jews heard that he was there and came not only on account of Jesus but also to see Lazarus whom he had raised from the dead. Then

the chief priests decided to kill Lazarus as well, since it was on his account that many of the Jews were leaving them and believing in Jesus.

CHRIST THE LORD Mary's exquisite gesture of love illustrates in three ways the utter uniqueness of Christ and the corresponding uniqueness of our friendship with him.

First, she gives Jesus her best. The ointment was rare, expensive, and precious. Jesus deserves our complete loyalty, not our leftovers. We have received everything from him; we will live forever in his company because of his mercy and love. The only appropriate response to God's generosity is complete abandonment to his goodness and unflinching obedience to his will. Mary shows that she understands this by pouring out upon him her "very costly ointment."

Second, she anoints his feet. The common way to show honor to a guest was through anointing his head. But Mary understood that she could confer no honor upon Christ; he was the Lord, he already possessed infinite dignity. Instead of bestowing honor from a position of superiority, as hosts could normally presume to do for guests who entered their own homes, she humbles herself. In an absolute sense, we cannot do favors for Christ—what does he lack that we can supply? But we can give thanks to him for the favor he has given to us—his coming among us and taking up residence in the needs of our neighbors provides us an opportunity to return love for love. Serving the Lord requires humility of heart.

Third, she wipes his feet with her hair. In Palestine at the time, women covered their hair in public. Mary defies this protocol. Her love for the Master frees her from the shackles of convention and the fears of ridicule. Christian faith is creative. The Lord always has more to give, so when we follow him sincerely, he shatters our human limitations and leads us to new horizons of generosity, new levels of fruitfulness, and new experiences of his goodness.

CHRIST THE TEACHER Jesus defends Mary's gesture on the grounds that the time for such deeds is short. This applies to every human life. Opportunities for love—for the creative, beautiful, saving deeds of self-forgetful generosity—present themselves each day. But if they are not seized, they disappear. How many times have we regretted not issuing a word of encouragement when the idea occurred to us? How many spouses, children, and friends have gazed sadly on the corpse of a loved one, desperately yearning to turn back the clock, to have just five more minutes to express the love that they had failed to show? How many chances to brighten up our neighbor's day or give glory to God in a detail of fidelity or with a brief prayer hover around us as we rush through life thinking only about ourselves? The time to love, the time to give, the time to be the noble child of God that in our hearts we know we are called to be—that time is now.

CHRIST THE FRIEND "Martha waited on them..."

Martha: How can I describe to you that scene? Something new was in the Lord's eyes in those last days before his Passion. It was a new intensity, a new determination. Maybe "new" isn't the right word—it was just more of what had always been there, more intensity, more determination, more attention, more love. And it spread to everyone around him. I will never forget watching him at dinner, surrounded by his apostles, with Mary, so content, sitting at his feet and the other guests unable to look away from him. He was like a glowing hearth that drew in and warmed everyone around him. His presence filled everyone with light and vigor and a freshness of life. What the aroma of Mary's perfume was for our senses, Jesus had already been for our minds and hearts. Whenever I smelled perfume after that day, it reminded me of the gentle power of his presence, which since then has never left me. And I knew that just as the perfume filled the house with its sweet and delicious scent, just so the Lord's life-giving presence was going to spread and fill every corner of history and the world.

CHRIST IN MY LIFE Teach me to love you as I should, Lord. Turn me around—I don't want to keep gazing in the mirror and worrying about what others think of me and how I can achieve more than them. I want to gaze at you, at your truth, at the beauty of your Kingdom. I want to care only about pouring out my life in your service, like Mary's perfume, so that I can spread the fullness of life to those around me...

I wonder if I have it too easy, Lord. Maybe if my life were a bit less comfortable and pleasant I would more easily remember that I am here to fulfill a mission, not just to have a good time. You lived your life so intensely, focusing on your Father's will and the mission he had given you. And that intensity, that focus, was the source of your joy and fruitfulness. Help me, Lord, to follow your example...

Lord Jesus, you have already given me so much, but I want to ask you to come anew into my life, to make me experience again the sweet aroma of your presence. I forget so easily, Lord. The troubles of life dull my faith and hope. I need you to come and dine with me, to let me sit at your feet and drink in your wisdom. I want to keep fighting for your Kingdom. Lord Jesus, give me strength...

Questions for
SMALL-GROUP DISCUSSION

1. What struck you most in this passage? What did you notice that you hadn't noticed before?

2. Judas' criticism sounded good on the outside, but in reality it stemmed from his selfishness. Can you think of any criticisms currently being launched against the Church that might fall in the same category?

3. If St. John knew that Judas was pilfering from the community bank account, surely Jesus knew as well. Why do you think he hadn't taken that responsibility away from Judas? Do you think there is a lesson in this for us?

4. Some people claim that the Church should sell its works of art and give the money to the poor. Do you think that's a good idea? Why or why not?

Cf. Catechism of the Catholic Church: 2096-2097 and 2626-2628 on adoration of God; 2559-2565 on authentic prayer; 2639-2643 on the prayer of praise

277. THE CONQUEROR COMES (JN 12:12-19)

"Just as what brings heat makes things expand, so it is the gift of love to stretch hearts wide open; it is a warm and glowing virtue... For there is nothing which so draws a man to return love, as when he understands that he who loves him is urgently longing for his affection." – St. John Chrysostom

JOHN 12:12-19

The next day the crowds who had come up for the festival heard that Jesus was on his way to Jerusalem. They took branches of palm and went out to meet him, shouting, "Hosanna! Blessings on the King of Israel, who comes in the name of the Lord." Jesus found a young donkey and mounted it—as scripture says: Do not be afraid, daughter of Zion; see, your king is coming, mounted on the colt of a donkey. At the time his disciples did not understand this, but later, after Jesus had been glorified, they remembered that this had been written about him and that this was in fact how they had received him. All who had been with him when he called Lazarus out of the tomb and raised him from the dead were telling how they had witnessed it; it was because of this, too, that the crowd came out to meet him: they had heard that he had given this sign. Then the Pharisees said to one another, "You see, there is nothing you can do; look, the whole world is running after him!"

CHRIST THE LORD Two crowds converged on the Lord as he joined the hundreds of thousands of pilgrims who flooded Jerusalem for the celebration of Passover. With him was the crowd that accompanied him from Bethany. Many of the pilgrims stayed in Bethany during the Passover; Jerusalem was too small to hold the masses of people who came for the festival, and Bethany was designated by law as one of the overflow cities. But another, even larger crowd surged out of the city gates as Jesus approached, riding down the small mountain situated to the east of the ancient city. Word had spread that the wonder-working rabbi from Nazareth, whom the authorities had condemned and put a bounty on, was arriving in full daylight. The common people were stirred by curiosity, but also by an intuitive sense of significance. How could it be that this man, whom the rich and powerful were hunting like an outlaw, was brash enough to make such a public appearance? It was a deliberate challenge, as if Jesus was looking the authorities in the eye and daring them to just try and stop him. Such was the viewpoint of the crowds. A man who could show such courage might indeed be the one who would set Israel free from Roman domination, clear out the corrupt collaborationists who ran the Temple and the Sanhedrin, and reestablish the greatness of the Chosen People. If Jesus could raise the dead to life, maybe he was the new conqueror and deliverer.

Jesus accepted their homage, though it was only partially correct. He was the new conqueror, but he came to conquer evil and sin so as to free men's minds and hearts, not to build a political empire. He was the new deliverer, but he came to deliver God's truth, grace, and love through his self-sacrifice on the cross, not to impose the rule of sword and spear. The shouting and frenzy of the crowd precluded him from speaking, but he told them this all the same: he didn't enter on a mighty horse, as kings who were going to war; he came on a meek donkey colt, as kings who come in times of peace.

To this day the world and even many of his believing disciples continue to mistake the nature of Christ's Kingdom. We keep hoping he will bring us heaven on earth, instead of accepting his message of how to live this passing, earthly life in a way that will prepare us for heaven.

CHRIST THE TEACHER St. John, who saw this dramatic event with his own eyes—in fact, he was probably walking right beside the Master the whole time, basking in the Lord's glory—makes a point of telling us that "At the time the disciples did not understand this, but later, after Jesus had been glorified, they remembered."

This is often the case in our journey of faith. God is always at work in our lives, but we don't always recognize or understand his action until later. Like parents who have to teach children to do certain things even before the children can fully understand the reasons behind them, God is constantly preparing us for the future, filling our spiritual supply depots. The example of the disciples who didn't understand the meaning of what Jesus was doing while he was doing it should encourage us. The important thing is simply to stay with Christ, to continue to live in his presence and fulfill the commitments of our friendship with him. If we do, little by little the Holy Spirit will coach us until we reach the fullness of holiness and happiness that he has in store for us. Jesus can see the whole picture even when we can't, so we should continue following his lead with enthusiasm and trust, no matter where it takes us.

CHRIST THE FRIEND "The whole world is running after him!"
A Pharisee: That was the day I started to believe in Jesus. Up until then I was convinced that he deserved to be silenced. But I was standing on the city walls when he came to Jerusalem, and I watched the crowds behind and before him surge together like two great tides colliding. As he approached, I could see his face. The look he gave them wasn't the look of a power-hungry and self-absorbed demagogue. It was calm, glad, and, well, it sounds rather anticlimactic, but I think the best word to describe it is – good. His countenance irradiated goodness. The irrepressible ebullience of that immense mass of humanity would have made any normal man drunk with their adoration. But not Jesus. And for some reason, I recognized immediately why he was riding on the donkey. I had just been meditating on the prophesy of Zechariah that described how the Messiah would enter into his reign just this way. I had a kind of intuitive flash as I watched him make his way slowly and gently through the forest of palm branches and the din of cheers. I seemed to see that this was the first swell of something entirely new, of a Kingdom that would surpass all of our small and antiquated expectations. And then – you may not believe me, but I promise you, it's true – then, just before he passed through the gate, he looked up, and his eyes met mine. His gaze gripped me and shone right through me as sunlight shines through glass; I couldn't resist it, but I didn't want to. It was just for a split second. And with that look he said to me, "Yes, it is so" – just as if he had known everything I had been thinking while I watched his triumphal entry! And he had known it. He knew it all, because in his mercy and love he had been inspiring those thoughts. From that day forward, I believed.

CHRIST IN MY LIFE I want your Kingdom to come, Lord. I want your wisdom to drench my mind and your love to infuse my heart. I want to be a riverbed through which your saving grace can flood the world around me. I am not looking for comfort and bliss and ease, but for ways of spreading the good news of your salvation. Teach me to be your faithful disciple, right here where I live. I want to live as you would have me live...

I think I am too intent on understanding everything. I get frustrated if I can't figure everything out. But how could I ever comprehend the immensity of your glory and knowledge? Why am I so greedy as to demand an explanation for everything? Lord Jesus, teach me the sweet wisdom of humility and keep me faithful. Show me the way to go and never let me stray from your path...

I believe in you, Lord. I believe that you are the One the Father sent, that you are the Savior of all people, that you are the way, the truth, and the life. Do you know, Lord, how many people don't believe in you? Give them the gift of faith. Increase my faith, so that I can go and tell them the truth. Every soul is searching for you, Lord. Let them find you. Let them discover your love...

Questions for
SMALL-GROUP DISCUSSION

1. What struck you most in this passage? What did you notice that you hadn't noticed before?

2. The Church puts this prayer—"Hosanna in the highest, blessed is he who comes..."—on our lips during Mass, right before the prayer of consecration. Why do you think this is so?

3. Why do you think Jesus chose to make his final entry into Jerusalem so dramatic? Why didn't he come quietly, as he had in the past?

4. Do you think Jesus was pleased or displeased by the crowd's welcome? Why?

Cf. Catechism of the Catholic Church: 559-560 on the meaning of Jesus' Messianic entry into Jerusalem; 2302-2317 on the Christian understanding of peace and war; 736, 1424, 1468, and 1832 on peace as the fruit of the Spirit and a gift from God

278. THE HOUR HAS COME (JN 12:20-33)

"In Christ and through Christ God has revealed himself fully to mankind and has definitively drawn close to it..." – St. John Paul II

JOHN 12:20-33
Among those who went up to worship at the festival were some Greeks. These approached Philip, who came from Bethsaida in Galilee, and put

this request to him, "Sir, we should like to see Jesus." Philip went to tell Andrew, and Andrew and Philip together went to tell Jesus. Jesus replied to them: "Now the hour has come for the Son of Man to be glorified. I tell you, most solemnly, unless a wheat grain falls on the ground and dies, it remains only a single grain; but if it dies, it yields a rich harvest. Anyone who loves his life loses it; anyone who hates his life in this world will keep it for the eternal life. If a man serves me, he must follow me, wherever I am, my servant will be there too. If anyone serves me, my Father will honour him. Now my soul is troubled. What shall I say: Father, save me from this hour? But it was for this very reason that I have come to this hour. Father, glorify your name!" A voice came from heaven, "I have glorified it, and I will glorify it again." People standing by, who heard this, said it was a clap of thunder; others said, "It was an angel speaking to him." Jesus answered, "It was not for my sake that this voice came, but for yours. Now sentence is being passed on this world; now the prince of this world is to be overthrown. And when I am lifted up from the earth, I shall draw all men to myself." By these words he indicated the kind of death he would die.

CHRIST THE LORD We are on the verge of Christ's Passion. Jesus knows exactly what is going to happen to him. "His hour" has arrived. He will suffer ignominy, public humiliation, abandonment by his closest companions, betrayal at the hand of an intimate friend, rejection by the very people he came to save, supreme and drawn-out physical torture, even a kind of separation from his Father—and then he will die. By announcing this to his disciples beforehand, he demonstrates to them that he suffers it willingly for the sake of the Father's glory and the eternal Kingdom. Thus, Christ's Passion signifies the unbreakable strength of his divine love, the ultimate freedom shown forth by obeying God's will under the most trying circumstances. It is the reversal of Adam's tragic weakness that led him to give in to temptation and disobey God's wise commands. Now the "passing sentence on this world," through the unshakable love and trust that he will demonstrate by his obedience unto death on a cross, "the prince of this world [the devil] is to be overthrown." We are on the verge of the climax of human history.

So that the crowds will grasp meaning of this pivotal moment in human history, the Father himself audibly affirms what the Son is going to do. Jesus was speaking to the people, but he must have looked up as he addressed his Father. His listeners had been focused on Jesus throughout his impassioned speech, and suddenly, as he lifts his gaze and utters his prayer to the Father, they hear a voice from heaven respond! It must have been a shock—exhilarating to those who had already come to believe in Jesus and disconcerting to those who doubted him. Jesus Christ is the champion of the human race, the savior of mankind, the everlasting Lord; he knows it; the Father knows it; how deeply do we know it?

CHRIST THE TEACHER During his public ministry, Jesus laid down the condition for being his disciple: "If anyone wants to be a follower of mine, let him renounce himself and take up his cross every day and follow me" (Lk 9:23). Now, as his Passion draws near, he forcibly reiterates this same condition: "Unless a wheat grain falls on the ground and dies, it remains only a single grain; but if it dies, it yields a rich harvest."

To be a Christian is to be where Christ is ("If a man serves me, he must follow me, wherever I am, my servant will be there too"), and Christ is always pouring out his life for others on the cross, giving himself for the good of others through self-forgetful love. St. Paul learned this lesson well: "... the only knowledge I claimed to have was about Jesus, and only about him as the crucified Christ" (1 Cor 2:2). Love is self-giving: "A man can have no greater love than to lay down his life for his friends" (Jn 15:13). And Jesus calls us to love: "This is my commandment: love one another as I have loved you" (Jn 15:12). Therefore, our lives must bear the sign of the cross — of self-giving, of self-sacrifice. When we decide to follow Christ, we should expect crosses, we should expect difficulties, and we should expect persecution: "If they persecuted me, they will persecute you too" (Jn 15:20). Christ's is the "narrow gate and the hard road" that leads to life (Mt 7:14), and Christian joy is deep and strong because it sinks its roots into the rich soil of sacrifice, suffering, and sorrow. There is no greater lesson than that of Christ's cross, and there is no better time to learn it than now.

CHRIST THE FRIEND The Greek visitors (non-Jews who were sympathizers with Judaism) wanted to see Jesus. When Jesus hears this, he responds with a long explanation of "his hour." It seems that he denies their request. But his last statement shows that he will grant it: "And when I am lifted up from the earth, I will draw everyone to myself."

By his crucifixion, he reveals himself to everyone (the Greek visitors included). Christ wants everyone to find him, to see him, to learn to know and love him; and so he allows himself to be crucified, he exposes his heart for all to see — a heart blazing with so much love that it is willing to die for our sake, to suffer unspeakable pain in order to reopen for us the gates of heaven. The crucifix is the great revelation of the heart of God; if we want to "see Christ," to see and know God, we have only to raise our eyes to behold him dying on the cross in order to give us true life. There Christ is most attractive to us—and we should always remember that we are no less attractive to him when we bend under the weight of our own cross and weakness.

CHRIST IN MY LIFE Christianity seems so strange, Lord. You saved us from sin by taking sin upon yourself. You conquered evil by absorbing in yourself all the venom that evil could spit out. You ended the tragic meaninglessness of human suffering not by eliminating it, but by turning it into a way to exercise the virtues that reunite our souls to God: faith, hope, and love. Help me to understand this mystery, Lord...

All your saints loved and embraced their crosses. Why do I still resist mine? What is it that makes me carry my crosses reluctantly and halfheartedly? I know that if you gave me a choice, I would probably choose a path without crosses. But you who did have a choice chose the way of the cross. Lord Jesus, purge my heart of the selfishness that clings so desperately to me. I want to live; I want to love as you love...

I take my crucifix in my hands again, Lord, right now. There you are. Agonizing. Your life slowly, excruciatingly ebbing away—only because you love me. You have told your saints, and your Church teaches, that if I had been the only sinner in the universe, you would have suffered all of that just for me, just so I wouldn't have to suffer it, just so I could hope with assurance to enjoy the Father's embrace...

Questions for
SMALL-GROUP DISCUSSION

1. What struck you most in this passage? What did you notice that you hadn't noticed before?

2. What can we do to participate more fruitfully in the liturgical celebration of Christ's Passion, death, and Resurrection that happens at every Mass?

3. What has helped you most to bear your crosses as Christ bore his?

4. What should we think when we gaze on a crucifix or make the Sign of the Cross?

Cf. Catechism of the Catholic Church: 595-623 on the meaning of Christ's Passion and death; 2015, 407-409, and 2725 on the role of the cross and self-denial in the life of Christians

279. BELIEF AND UNBELIEF (JN 12:34-50)

"When I begin to pray I do not see Jesus with my eyes, but I know he is there before me, and my soul finds rest in his presence." – St. Gemma Galgani

JOHN 12:34-50

The crowd answered, "The Law has taught us that the Christ will remain for ever. How can you say, 'The Son of Man must be lifted up?' Who is this Son of Man?" Jesus then said: "The light will be with you only a little longer now. Walk while you have the light, or the dark will overtake you; he who walks in the dark does not know where he is going. While you still have the light, believe in the light and you will become sons of light." Having said this, Jesus left them and kept himself hidden. Though they had been present when he gave so many signs, they did not believe in him; this was to fulfil the words of the prophet Isaiah: Lord, who could believe what we have heard said, and to whom has the power of the Lord been revealed? Indeed, they were unable to believe because, as Isaiah says again: He has blinded their eyes, he has hardened their heart, for fear they should see with their eyes and understand with their heart, and turn to me for healing. Isaiah said this when he saw his glory, and his words referred to Jesus. And yet there were many who did believe in him, even among the leading men, but they did not admit it, through fear of the Pharisees and fear of being expelled from the synagogue: they put honour from men before the honour that comes from God.

Jesus declared publicly: "Whoever believes in me believes not in me but in the one who sent me, and whoever sees me, sees the one who sent me. I, the light, have come into the world, so that whoever believes in me need not stay in the dark any more. If anyone hears my words and does not keep them faithfully, it is not I who shall condemn him, since I have come not to condemn the world, but to save the world: he who rejects me and refuses my words has his judge already: the word itself that I have spoken will be his judge on the last day. For what I have spoken does not come from myself; no, what I was to say, what I had to speak, was commanded by the Father who sent me, and I know that his commands mean eternal life. And therefore what the Father has told me is what I speak."

CHRIST THE LORD We who believe in the Lord continue to battle the shadows. Doubts assail us, fears constrain us, and hesitancy and infidelity are always knocking at the door of our hearts. Why? Why has Christ still not conquered our hearts completely?

It is because we are too much like those many Pharisees who believed in Jesus, but who "put honor from men before the honor that comes from God." The human heart has an imperishable need to be accepted, to be loved, and to be valued. We want to be part of the popular crowd, the inner circle, the winning team. In a fallen world, this fundamental need for solidarity, as all of our fundamental needs and desires, has gone awry. It tends to override other values that matter more: truth, justice, and fidelity, to name a few. We want to follow Christ because his call resonates in the depths of our hearts, but we don't want to risk following him to the cross because a little voice in the back of our minds still thinks that happiness and meaning can be had by our own efforts, by arranging our lives according to our own natural preferences. It's the old temptation behind every temptation: eat the forbidden fruit and you can be like gods—completely fulfilled—without having to submit to God.

It didn't work for Adam and Eve, and it doesn't work for us. Disobeying the voice of conscience in order to win praise from the voices of peers hardens the heart. Gossiping or welcoming gossip to get into someone's good graces nullifies the grace of God. If we really believe that the Lord is Lord, we will lay aside once and for all anything and everything that interferes with our faithful following of his will.

CHRIST THE TEACHER The unbelief of so many who experienced Jesus face-to-face is one of the most vexing mysteries of the Gospel. Still today, unbelief in the face of twenty centuries of saints and miracles and the ineffable wonder of the Catholic Church's unceasing expansion and fruitfulness boggles the mind. And yet, at first glance, St. John's explanation of this phenomenon is entirely unsatisfying. He quotes the prophet Isaiah, who seems to attribute this unbelief to God's own action, as if God had forced these people to reject his Son. Certainly that cannot be the case, since some did believe. God cannot contradict himself, sending Jesus to save his people while at the same time inspiring those people to turn away from Jesus. We can only understand St. John's explanation if we understand the context in which Isaiah uttered those words. They came after his own mission of preaching had failed. He was sent to the northern tribes of Israel to convince them to repent from their idolatry, but they refused to repent. And afterwards he writes those words, "He [God] has blinded their eyes." His prophecy is a bewildered complaint. He can't explain why they won't believe God's message, so he throws up an impassioned complaint, "It's as if God himself didn't even want them to believe!"

Jesus' contemporaries were free to accept or reject Jesus' message, just as every man and woman continues to be. Ultimately, St. John is saying, only God knows why and how so many human hearts that were created to live in communion with God freely turn aside from that communion. Only God knows why, and God can still take those refusals and somehow weave them into his plan of salvation. We cannot expect to understand and control all things; it is enough for us to know that God does.

CHRIST THE FRIEND *Jesus: I have not come to condemn the world, but to save the world. My child, have you understood this? So many of my followers have not. They condemn and judge and criticize. I know that most of the time they mean well; they truly think they know what's best. But condemning each other does no good. It hardens hearts. Did I condemn my enemies? Did I condemn sinners? Did I condemn you? I forgave, I taught, I exhorted, I encouraged, I insisted, I invited, I invited again, and that's what I still do. Those who condemn forget that they too ought to be condemned. Those who criticize forget that they too deserve to be criticized. I long for disciples who leave all that behind. I long for followers who bring my light into darkened hearts. I am the light. Let me shine through you. That will scatter the shadows. Leave aside all rancor and useless criticism and condemnation. Build up, plant, work. Say little, do much. You have only a short while—spend it loving, not berating, and teach others to do the same.*

CHRIST IN MY LIFE Father, how can I root out these fears and vain ambitions that infest my heart? You want me to follow in the footsteps of your Son. Pour your Spirit into my mind and my soul, cleanse every vestige of self-seeking, and infuse me with courage and purity of heart and poverty of spirit. Hallowed be thy name...

Jesus, if you don't teach me how to use my words to build up my brothers and sisters, how can I do it? You have never condemned me, although I have so often deserved it. Your patience and your goodness are inexhaustible. You hang from the cross and forgive me, and still I dare to pass judgment on my neighbor. Have mercy on me, Lord, and teach me to love as you love...

Mary, how hard it must have been for you to see so many of your brothers and sisters refuse to believe in Jesus! You were there in Jerusalem during these last days. Did you encourage him? Did he encourage you? You continued to believe and trust. I am your child too; Jesus is my brother. I try to build his Kingdom, but I run into so many dead ends, just like Jesus. Stay by my side, as you stayed by his...

Questions for
SMALL-GROUP DISCUSSION

1. What struck you most in this passage? What did you notice that you hadn't noticed before?

2. Why do you think Jesus continues to insist so much on his identity with the Father and on his unique link to the Father?

3. According to St. John, this was Jesus' last public preaching. Considering that, how does it change your interpretation of his speech?

4. How can we apply Jesus' example of dealing with people who reject his message to our own efforts to spread the gospel?

Cf. Catechism of the Catholic Church: 1084-1090 on the centrality of Christ in the Liturgy; 2598-2616 on the centrality of Christ in prayer; 587-591 on Jesus and Israel's faith; 238-248 on the relationship between the Father, the Son, and the Spirit

THE GOSPEL OF JOHN
Chapter 13

"Man cannot live without love. He remains a being that is incomprehensible for himself, his life is senseless, if love is not revealed to him, if he does not encounter love, if he does not experience it and make it his own, if he does not participate intimately in it."

– POPE JOHN PAUL II, *Redemptor Hominis, 10*

280. THE FINAL LESSON (JN 13:1-20)

"'Consider well,' he says to us, 'that in loving I was first. You had not yet come forth into the light, not even the world itself had come into existence, when already I was loving you. Throughout my eternal existence I have loved you.'" – *St. Alphonsus Liguori*

JOHN 13:1-20

It was before the festival of the Passover, and Jesus knew that the hour had come for him to pass from this world to the Father. He had always loved those who were his in the world, but now he showed how perfect his love was. They were at supper, and the devil had already put it into the mind of Judas Iscariot son of Simon, to betray him. Jesus knew that the Father had put everything into his hands, and that he had come from God and was returning to God, and he got up from table, removed his outer garment and, taking a towel, wrapped it round his waist; he then poured water into a basin and began to wash the disciples' feet and to wipe them with the towel he was wearing. He came to Simon Peter, who said to him, "Lord, are you going to wash my feet?" Jesus answered, "At the moment you do not know what I am doing, but later you will understand." "Never!" said Peter. "You shall never wash my feet." Jesus replied, "If I do not wash you, you can have nothing in common with me." "Then, Lord," said Simon Peter, "not only my feet, but my hands and my head as well!" Jesus said, "No one who has taken a bath needs washing, he is clean all over. You too are clean, though not all of you are." He knew who was going to betray him, that was why he said, "Though not all of you are."

When he had washed their feet and put on his clothes again he went back to the table. "Do you understand," he said, "what I have done to you? You call me Master and Lord, and rightly; so I am. If I, then, the Lord and Master, have washed your feet, you should wash each other's feet. I have given you an example so that you may copy what I have done to you. I tell you most solemnly, no servant is greater than his master, no messenger is greater than the man who sent him. Now that you know this, happiness will be yours if you behave accordingly. I am not speaking about all of you: I know the ones I have chosen; but what scripture says must be fulfilled: Someone who shares my table rebels against me. I tell you this now, before it happens, so that when it does happen you may believe that I am He. I tell you most solemnly, whoever welcomes the one I send welcomes me, and whoever welcomes me welcomes the one who sent me."

CHRIST THE LORD Most of the world's great teachers and philosophers shy away from adulation. They draw people's attention to their doctrine while they themselves shun the spotlight. Jesus Christ, whose doctrine is more complete, powerful, and veracious than anyone's, breaks this mold. He constantly invites people to hear and heed his doctrine, but at the same time, and even more vehemently, he draws his listeners and disciples to himself; he wants them to cling with all their hearts and minds to him. Nowhere is this personal, heart-to-heart appeal of Christ more clearly expressed than in this passage. But to appreciate it properly, we have to put ourselves into the scene.

The Twelve are gathered with their Master for the most sacred meal of the year. The stone walls of the upper room are lit with the warm light of flickering torches and lamps. The apostles and Jesus are reclining at the low table, glad to be together once again, eager to share the lamb, the bread, the wine, and the bitter herbs. They know each other so well by now. They can feel something different in the atmosphere tonight. Something has changed in the Lord's attitude. It has some new sense of urgency. He is looking at them with even greater emotion than usual.

St. John's introduction to the Last Supper recreates the atmosphere of solemnity that surrounded that climactic meal. He reminds us that Jesus' mission was coming to its dramatic conclusion, that Jesus knew it, and that he was consciously intensifying the revelation of his love because of it, "... now he showed how perfect his love was." The words of Jesus on this occasion ring with an even greater intimacy, majesty, and solemnity than we have heard throughout this Gospel. The apostles sense the added intensity, and their own expectations rise to a higher pitch than ever before. When Jesus interrupts the

Passover ritual by standing up, all their eyes are fixed on him. Conversation ceases. Eating stops. Jesus walks over to the large water jug (water was habitually kept nearby for the many ritual washings), and the silence deepens. They watch Jesus as he puts on the garment used by slaves and, slowly, deliberately, but still without a word, begins washing their feet. Only Peter breaks the silence, but he quickly quiets down. It takes a good amount of time to make the circle of his Twelve Apostles. Then Jesus gets up, replaces his normal outer garment and once again takes his place among them. The apostles are turned to him, their looks are begging for an explanation. They are humbled, all their attention is on the Lord. He doesn't speak right away, but looks at each of them. Then he finally breaks the long silence, which makes his quiet but momentous words reverberate all the more: "... You call me Master and Lord, and rightly; so I am."

CHRIST THE TEACHER In ancient Palestine, washing feet was a job reserved for slaves. It was one of the most unpleasant and humiliating tasks. People wore sandals or went barefoot, and the roads and paths that they walked were the same ones used by herdsmen to drive their animals to market, as well as travelers and traders who moved their goods by ox and camel. The dirt of these unpaved byways, therefore, was blended with dung. Even a short jaunt would cake one's sandal-exposed feet with the pungent mix. This earthy combination of elements, this unattractive mire was what Jesus washed from the feet of his disciples. Jesus, God made man, the King of kings and Lord of the universe, lowered himself to the status of a slave and freely, willingly, and gladly "showed how perfect his love was" by this utterly self-forgetful act of service. He didn't have to do it. He certainly felt no natural pleasure in doing it. But still he did it, at the most solemn moment of his ministry, when common sense would dictate that he be more focused on his coming Passion. Why? "... You should wash each other's feet. I have given you an example so that you may copy what I have done to you."

The mark of the Christian is self-forgetful love. Sin divided once and still divides the human family. Christ, the conqueror of sin, reunites all people. He does this through his love, which reaches out to all the ends of the earth through his disciples. And love is not feelings; it is not noble desires; love is self-giving. Love is costly. In Jesus, God came down from heaven to dwell among men, to serve the needs of men, the very men who had rebelled against him and usurped the world he had entrusted to them. In so doing, they ruined themselves. God wanted to save them, even though they deserved to die. So he takes the first step; he reaches out to them by serving them. The washing of his disciples' feet was an icon of Jesus' entire mission and a revelation, a miniature portrait of the heart of God. And so he tells us that if we wish to regain our place in the family of God, we are to enter into the same dimension of self-forgetful love. There is no other way: "You should wash each other's feet."

For our fallen nature, this is a hard lesson. For that very reason, Jesus taught it so insistently and so graphically. The cross of self-sacrifice repels us, so Jesus climbed onto it before us to make sure that we make no mistake about what he means. But although the lesson is hard, it is not sad. It is the truth that will set us free, and Jesus finishes with a glow in his eyes and a smile on his lips: "Now that you know this, happiness will be yours if you behave accordingly."

CHRIST THE FRIEND Judas was still at the Last Supper at this point. He had already decided to follow through with his plan of betrayal, but he had not yet left to set it in motion. What was in Jesus' mind when he came to Judas, poured water over his feet, and began to wash them? As Jesus finished drying Judas' feet with the towel, and as he laced up the sandals again, he looked into Judas's face and caught his eye. Jesus hadn't given up on him. Jesus never gives up on us; he is the ever-faithful friend. The tragedy is that we are the ones who sometimes give up on him.

Judas: I was more disgusted than ever at this repellent display of weakness. It confirmed yet again all my suspicions: this man had not come to restore Israel to its glory, but to enervate it and despoil it. I wanted nothing to do with such an imposter, such a weak dreamer. I have to admit, though, that when he looked up at me—well, it made me think of the first time we had met, when I heard him speaking in the Temple and my heart surged with hope. He had looked at me then too, and I seemed to see in his eyes all the strength and wisdom and life that I knew existed somewhere but hadn't been able to find. He invited me to come with him then, and I couldn't resist. I had never been moved like that before. And then there were the miracles, and the huge crowds, and his mastery over the Pharisees. It was all so promising, and I could even taste victory just around the corner. But he never took the final step. And then he started talking about the cross. The others ignored it, but I knew he was serious. And how could a crucified rabbi be the Messiah? How could weakness reclaim our glory? That last night, for a split second after he replaced my sandals, it occurred to me that maybe there was more to it than I understood. But then I looked at him again, wrapped in that towel like a slave, washing my feet. It was repugnant. Peter was right—who would ever let a real Messiah sink so low as to wash our feet? But Peter was weak too; he caved in. I could never serve a Lord like that.

CHRIST IN MY LIFE I glory in being able to call you Lord. I know that there is order in the universe. I know that my life has purpose. I know that the world is safe in your hands and history is marching forward according to a law of hidden progress, surely guided by your invincible Providence. Jesus, my Lord, my Master! Here is my life. I put it at your feet and at your service. I offer myself to you...

So many items are on my to-do list. I have so many plans and hopes. I want to do so much for you, Lord. But in the midst of my programs and activities, I too often forget about the only law of your Kingdom: I am to wash my neighbors' feet. Only there will I ever find the happiness you intend for me. I must learn self-forgetful love. And each day you provide so many chances for me to give myself in this way! Give me courage...

You have washed my feet so often, Lord. Every time I go to confession, you humble yourself and wash my feet. Thank you for washing Judas's feet. I am like Judas. Have I not betrayed you at times? You knew I would; you knew my heart as you washed my feet. A Judas is within me; don't let me forget. As soon as I forget it, I will follow his example. Make me faithful, Lord; never let me be separated from you, never...

Questions for
SMALL-GROUP DISCUSSION

1. What struck you most in this passage? What did you notice that you hadn't noticed before?

2. In our current life situations, what are some ways that we can follow Christ's example of service on a daily basis?

3. Why is it often so hard for us to serve those around us? In your experience, what circumstances have made self-forgetful service easier, and what can we learn from that?

4. If an agnostic acquaintance asked you why you think Christianity is so unique, what would you say?

Cf. Catechism of the Catholic Church: 459, 852, 1022, 1823-1825, 1844, 1337, 2055, 2104, 2196, 2443, and 2822 on the commandment to love one's neighbor as Christ has loved us; 221 on God's nature as an exchange of love

281. THE NEW COMMANDMENT (JN 13:21-38)

"But he was not satisfied with giving us all these beautiful things. He went to such lengths to win our love that he gave himself wholly to us. The Eternal Father gave us even his only Son." – St. Alphonsus Liguori

JOHN 13:21-38

Having said this, Jesus was troubled in spirit and declared, "I tell you most solemnly, one of you will betray me." The disciples looked at one another, wondering which he meant. The disciple Jesus loved was reclining next to Jesus; Simon Peter signed to him and said, "Ask who it is he means," so leaning back on Jesus' breast he said, "Who is it, Lord?" "It is the one," replied Jesus, "to whom I give the piece of bread that I shall dip in the dish." He dipped the piece of bread and gave it to Judas son of Simon Iscariot. At that instant, after Judas had taken the bread, Satan entered him. Jesus then said, "What you are going to do, do quickly." None of the others at table understood the reason he said this. Since Judas had charge of the common fund, some of them thought Jesus was telling him, "Buy what we need for the festival," or telling him to give something to the poor. As soon as Judas had taken the piece of bread he went out. Night had fallen.

When he had gone Jesus said: "Now has the Son of Man been glorified, and in him God has been glorified. If God has been glorified in him, God will in turn glorify him in himself, and will glorify him very soon. My little children, I shall not be with you much longer. You will look for me, and, as I told the Jews, where I am going, you cannot come. I give you a new commandment: love one another; just as I have loved you, you also must love one another. By this love you have for one another, everyone will know that you are my disciples." Simon Peter said, "Lord, where are you going?" Jesus replied, "Where I am going you cannot follow me now; you will follow me later." Peter said to him, "Why can't I follow you now? I will lay down my life for you." "Lay down your life for me?" answered Jesus. "I tell you most solemnly, before the cock crows you will have disowned me three times."

CHRIST THE LORD By issuing a new commandment, Christ manifests unambiguously his unique claim to be sent by God and to be God's own Son. In the Old Testament, only God issued commandments; no one else had the authority to make precepts binding on the whole nation. Repeatedly, the texts in the Pentateuch point out that Moses delivered to Israel the commandments he had received from God. Here, however, Christ says, "I give you a new commandment," not "Here is a commandment that I pass on to you from God." He speaks calmly and confidently with the authority of God himself. Notice that Christ says he is giving them a "new" commandment. That means that the old commandments were somehow insufficient. (In truth they were a preparation for the new covenant, a first stage toward definitive communion with God in Christ.) If the old ones, however, came from God, only God could enhance them. Thus, in that one sentence, Christ makes clear yet again that he is no mere philosopher or above-average rabbi—he is the Messiah, the Son of God, the only Savior: the Lord. These details would not have been lost on the Twelve Apostles. We should make sure it is never lost on us—Christ is close; he is our intimate friend, but he is also God, all-powerful, all-knowing, and all-loving. He is worthy of our praise and adoration, worthy to be our Lord.

And what is the defining characteristic of Christ's Lordship? Wherein lies his glory? As he has repeated again and again throughout this whole Gospel, it is in his perfect, loving obedience to the Father's will. It is the Father's will that Jesus suffer and die, and Judas is the instrument through which that will be accomplished. Jesus knows this, but his "soul is troubled" at the thought of it. Deeply troubled—anguished, as we see later in the Garden of Gethsemane. And yet, in spite of the repugnance and resistance of his human nature, he accepts his mission. He expresses this acceptance by telling Judas, "What you are going to do, do quickly." And this is what glorifies God. The glory of God and the glory of the human person converge, as the Lord displays, in our loving obedience to God's will, no matter the cost.

CHRIST THE TEACHER This glory of God is, as the *Catechism* tells us, the entire reason behind the existence of all things: "The world was created for the glory of God." It is an inexhaustible concept, but that doesn't mean we shouldn't reflect on it a bit more.

God's glory is different than we might think. We tend to think of it in Hollywood terms—bursts of brilliant light, thunder claps, swirling vortexes of power and color and smoke. Such extraordinary phenomena may be used now and again to call attention to the extraordinariness of God, but his glory is something deeper. When Judas begins to carry out his betrayal, Christ says, "Now the Son of Man is glorified, and God is glorified in him." What's the connection? Love. Love means self-giving; by accepting the suffering and death that Judas's betrayal brings on, Jesus is revealing, making visible, God's immeasurable love for each one of us. He loves us so much that he is willing to suffer in our place, even while we were still sinners (as St. Paul later points out). It's like sitting in the electric chair in place of the man who murdered your children so that he doesn't have to suffer and die—crazy love, incalculable love, unfathomable love. And that is God's glory: making known God's love, the love that gives existence to the universe, the love that calls us into being and reaches out to bring us into the eternal Kingdom.

CHRIST THE FRIEND If we value our friendship with Christ, we will try to please him, make him happy, and stay close to him. And he (unlike many human friends) is able to tell us exactly how to do that. If we love him, we will keep his command, and his command is for us to love one another, to put our lives at the service of those around us, just as he did for us. It is the touchstone of the Christian: "By this... everyone will know that you are my disciples...." Without it, no matter how much theology we may know, no matter how good we may be at winning arguments, no matter how many awards we may win—without learning to love as Christ has loved, we simply cannot consider ourselves his friends.

When Judas left Christ to betray him, St. John tells us that "night had fallen." It is the counterpoint to Christ's insistent self-appellation throughout the Gospel that he is the light of the world and that whoever heeds his word will not walk in darkness. Only friendship with Christ illuminates the meaning of the human condition and the path to human happiness. To reject this friendship is to willingly plunge into the darkness.

Jesus: I was looking ahead to my sufferings. They loomed over me. Yet I wanted them because I wanted to glorify the Father; I wanted to show forth his goodness. I wanted them, too, because of you. They would rebuild the bridge between God and man, a bridge that you could then walk across into my Kingdom. If only you knew how ardent my love for you is! That is what I wanted to show you. Let me show you. Open your mind to see the intensity of my love reflected in the intensity of my suffering.

CHRIST IN MY LIFE Teach me to do your will, Lord. What more could I desire than for your goodness to shine through my life? Your will is love and wisdom. Your will is my salvation, fulfillment, and happiness. I have only to follow your example, the teachings of your Church, and your voice in my conscience. Make your will the whole quest of my heart...

Mary, you knew all the apostles, including Judas. Why was Satan able to enter into him? I want to know. I don't trust myself. I don't want to betray Christ. Maybe I should ask instead why the others, who also abandoned him, were able to come back to him. They fell because of weakness, but Judas initiated his own rebellion. Mother, save me both from weakness and from pride...

Father, you sent us your Son so that we would not have to stumble in the darkness anymore. Yet so many people continue to reject him, and so many others have never known him. Move their hearts, Lord. Send out messengers—convinced, courageous, determined messengers. Send me. Reach into the hearts of those around me through my words, actions, and prayers...

Questions for
SMALL-GROUP DISCUSSION

1. What struck you most in this passage? What did you notice that you hadn't noticed before?

2. How can we live out Christ's new commandment more fully in our present circumstances?

3. In our relationship with Christ, how should we manifest the reverence and respect that we ought to have for the Son of God?

4. How does Christ's commandment to love and serve everyone (not just those people we naturally get along with) compare with the behavior patterns encouraged by popular culture?

Cf. Catechism of the Catholic Church: 2093-2094 on love toward God; 2084-2109 on reverencing God; 2196 on the importance of love for one another; 1822-1829 on the "new commandment"

THE GOSPEL OF JOHN
Chapter 14

"It is surely unnecessary to prove, what experience constantly shows and what each individual feels in himself, even in the very midst of all temporal prosperity—that in God alone can the human will find absolute and perfect peace. God is the only end of man. All our life on earth is the truthful and exact image of a pilgrimage. Now Christ is the 'Way,' for we can never reach God, the supreme and ultimate good, by this toilsome and doubtful road of mortal life, except with Christ as our leader and guide."

–POPE LEO XIII

282. Untroubled Hearts (Jn 14:1-12)

"Contradictions, sickness, scruples, spiritual aridity, and all the inner and outward torments are the chisel with which God carves his statues for paradise." – St. Alphonsus Ligouri

JOHN 14:1-12
"Do not let your hearts be troubled. Trust in God still, and trust in me. There are many rooms in my Father's house; if there were not, I should have told you. I am going now to prepare a place for you, and after I have gone and prepared you a place, I shall return to take you with me; so that where I am you may be too. You know the way to the place where I am going." Thomas said, "Lord, we do not know where you are going, so how can we know the way?" Jesus said: "I am the Way, the Truth and the Life. No one can come to the Father except through me. If you know me, you know my Father too. From this moment you know him and have seen him." Philip said, "Lord, let us see the Father and then we shall be satisfied." "Have I been with you all this time, Philip," said Jesus to him, "and you still do not know me? To have seen me is to have seen the Father, so how can you say, 'Let us see the Father?' Do you not believe that I am in the Father and the Father is in me? The words I say to you I do not speak as from myself: it is the Father, living in me, who is doing this work. You must believe me

when I say that I am in the Father and the Father is in me; believe it on the evidence of this work, if for no other reason. I tell you most solemnly, whoever believes in me will perform the same works as I do myself, he will perform even greater works, because I am going to the Father."

CHRIST THE LORD Christ is not Lord just because he is more intelligent than anyone else, or more charismatic, or more ruthless, or filled with magic powers. Christ is Lord because he is God become man. To see him is to see God; he is in the Father and the Father is in him. But seeing him requires more than bodily eyes; it requires faith. Philip had followed Christ for almost three years, and he still did not recognize him. How many Catholics have been going to Mass for years but still do not know the Lord? If we look at Christ and find it hard to see the Father, it is our eyes — our lives — that need adjusting, not him.

If we do adjust them, trusting more in Jesus and less in our own limited understanding and talent, our lives will gradually take on proportions far beyond what we can imagine: "Whoever believes in me will perform the same works as I do myself, he will perform even greater works." To live in a communion of friendship and obedience with Christ is to live united to God himself, the Creator and Sustainer of the universe, the Lord of life and history. His knowledge and power and love become ours; we become sharers in the divine nature (2 Pet 1:4). The lives of the saints, past and present, continue to cry out their confirmation of this promise. They are our brothers and sisters who, under the impulse of God's grace, have relinquished their vain attempts at controlling their destiny and the world and truly believed in Christ, trusting that he, the only Lord, knows better and that his plans, his will, are better than theirs.

Too often we relegate our relationship with the Lord to one section of our agenda. Christ's presence and will should be much, much more for us. He should be everything. As Christians, our life is a mission. We are called to be other Christs in the world — in the specific circumstances, relationships, and possibilities of our own personal worlds. If our first concern is truly to live as Christ would live in our place, we will release the full power of grace in our lives, and we will become saints. If following the Lord is just one action item among many, grace will have no room to work.

CHRIST THE TEACHER From ancient times philosophers have summed up the human condition as a quest to answer three fundamental queries: What should I do? What can I know? What can I hope for? Jesus Christ answers them all, not merely with doctrine, but with his very person. "I am the way" can translate into: What should you do? Follow me! Do what I have done. "I am the truth" means: What can you know? You can know everything, if only you know me. Knowing me, you know the truth; you know the secret behind the workings of the whole universe and the yearnings of the human heart. "I am the life" means: What can you hope for? In me, through me, you can hope for and expect the fullness of life that you long for, even though you may not be able to put that longing into words. Christ is truly the living water that quenches every thirst. He is truly the light that scatters every kind of darkness. The quest of every man and woman to satisfy the heart's deepest needs is the quest to seek his face, and it leads either to Christ and the place he has prepared for us in heaven or to a dead end.

CHRIST THE FRIEND The atmosphere of the Last Supper was tense. The apostles knew that something was up, and they were afraid, or at least disquieted. Jesus reassures them by inviting them to believe in him, to trust in him. He goes to prepare a place for us in the Father's house, in heaven. And he promises to come back for us, so that he can take us where we will always be with him. Christianity is about entering into the family of God, becoming a member of that family. Jesus wants to dwell with us; he wants to dwell in us, and he longs to share his eternal and ever-new joy with us. This is why he came. He is the friend who "gave his life up for his friends." With a friend like that, how could our hearts be troubled?

Mary: My child, Jesus tells you: "Do not let your hearts be troubled... Trust in me...." *If he tells you that, it means that it is possible for you to live in his peace. He does not say that troubling things won't happen—they will. But in him, if you exercise your trust in him, you can keep your heart in peace, like a little child in its mother's arms. He always holds you in his sure embrace. When troubles come, bring your heart back to the sure knowledge of his love and his wise providence. It is a mark of all true followers of Christ that they have learned to be steady in the storm; they have learned to rejoice in the depths of their souls even in the midst of tears. He is worthy of your trust.*

CHRIST IN MY LIFE Lord, you wanted to be known, and so you came to reveal yourself to us. I already know you; you have given me the gift of faith. I want to be for you what you were for the Father. When people see me, especially those closest to me, I want them to see you. Make me like you, Lord...

I believe in you, Lord, and I am so grateful to you. What thousands of people for thousands of years have been searching for, you have given me. You have given me the pearl of great price, the hidden treasure. I know the answers to the deepest questions because I know you. You are not just the endpoint of my search; you are the beginning of my adventure, my way, my truth, my life...

Mary, my mother, how can I trust in Jesus when everything is collapsing around me? How can I be at peace when my mind and heart are in turmoil? You can teach me. On this night of the Last Supper, you were close by. You knew that Jesus' hour had come. Your mother's heart quaked and shook and wept, and yet you never ceased trusting, accepting, or offering. Teach me to not be afraid...

Questions for
SMALL-GROUP DISCUSSION

1. What struck you most in this passage? What did you notice that you hadn't noticed before?

2. What do you think was most on Jesus' mind and heart during this intense emotional moment of the Last Supper?

3. Why would the Church give us this Gospel passage to read during the liturgical season of Easter?

4. Why do you think Christ invites us to trust in him when our hearts are troubled, instead of just making sure that our hearts never get troubled in the first place?

Cf. Catechism of the Catholic Church, 464-478 on Jesus Christ as true God and true man; 459, 1698, 2037, 2614 on Jesus Christ as "the way, the truth, and the life"

283. THE SUPREME GIFT (JN 14:13-21)

"The spiritual building-up of the body of Christ is brought about by love..."
– *St. Fulgentius of Ruspe*

JOHN 14:13-21
"Whatever you ask for in my name I will do, so that the Father may be glorified in the Son. If you ask for anything in my name, I will do it. If you love me you will keep my commandments. I shall ask the Father, and he will give you another Advocate to be with you for ever, that Spirit of truth whom the world can never receive since it neither sees nor knows him; but you know him, because he is with you, he is in you. I will not leave you orphans; I will come back to you. In a short time the world will no longer see me; but you will see me, because I live and you will live. On that day you will understand that I am in my Father and you in me and I in you. Anybody who receives my commandments and keeps them will be

one who loves me; and anybody who loves me will be loved by my Father, and I shall love him and show myself to him."

CHRIST THE LORD Jesus is gathered with his disciples on the evening before his Passion. The intense intimacy of the moment is marked by his apostles' rapt attention. He begins to speak to them of what is about to happen. He knows that he is going to suffer, die, rise, and ascend into heaven. His earthly mission is coming to a close, and he is preparing them for the next stage, the epoch of the Church, which he will guide through the work of the Holy Spirit, the "Advocate."

To us, this is normal. We know the full story, so we know what Christ is referring to. But put yourself in the position of the apostles. How odd it must have been for them to hear these words—even mystifying! Jesus is predicting the future with an uncanny specificity and confidence. His mastery over other men, over nature, over sickness and demons, all this was familiar to the Twelve. But mastery over future events? Seemingly contradictory references to being unseen and then seen again? Allusions to the Father sending an "Advocate" to be with them always? Surely they must have sounded almost like the words of a madman...or of the Son of God. If with our imagination we try to enter into this scene, placing ourselves at the apostles' side and listening to these words as if for the first time, perhaps we will hear once again the untamed grandeur, tender love, and mysterious truth that radiated from Christ the Lord on the first Holy Thursday.

CHRIST THE TEACHER During the Last Supper discourse, Christ's constant refrain is: if you love me, you will keep my commandment. That commandment is to "love one another as I have loved you" (Jn 13:34), the commandment of charity. In a sense, the Last Supper is Jesus' last earthly encounter with his beloved companions (the later Resurrection appearances already have an otherworldly feel). These are his parting words, then, the last flow of love from his Sacred Heart before it is broken and pierced. They are special words. We need to hear them; we need to let them sink in.

He knows that these twelve men, so normal and yet so privileged, love him. He earnestly desires to teach them how to live out that love. It is not in pretty words, it is not merely in rituals and prayers, it is not in lengthy theological treatises—it is in obedience to the wishes of his heart; it is in imitating his love for them. Love made into action, into serving our brothers and sisters, giving our lives for them—just like Christ's love from Calvary's cross—is the only mark of a follower of Christ. Jesus never tires of repeating this. He wants to convince us that everything else is in a distant second place. If, having discovered his love for us, we courageously and trustingly leave behind our self-absorption and launch out on the enlivening and everlasting adventure of loving in the same way, we will finally discover and experience what we were created for and what we long for. In the end, we will be judged on our love – our love for God lived out in love for our neighbor.

CHRIST THE FRIEND "I will not leave you orphans." How painful for the Twelve to hear their Lord, their Leader, speaking about his imminent departure! They had left all to follow him, and he was going to leave them. But not really... He would send them the "Advocate to be with them always" – the "Paraclete," the Holy Spirit. In the Holy Spirit, Jesus knows that he will be present to his disciples in a more intimate way than ever before. The Holy Spirit, the third person of the Blessed Trinity, is the love between the Father and Son lived so intensely that it is a person itself. When we are baptized, that same Spirit takes up residence within our souls, and his field of action is increased when we are confirmed. This gift surpasses all other gifts. In the Holy Spirit the prophecy of "Emmanuel" (God-with-us) takes on unimaginable proportions: not merely God among us, as in the Incarnation, but God within us, a guest in our souls, a guide for our life's journey, a personal trainer for our spiritual fitness. What greater gift could Christ have left us? What other friend could match such a gift?

Jesus: I was longing to complete my mission and go back to the Father because I was longing to come and live in your heart forever, in an intimacy that only the Spirit can give. And I was longing to go and sit at the Father's right hand so that I could be there interceding for you all the time, so that you could finally ask the Father for all that you need and desire in my name. Now that I have repaired the breach through my sacrifice on the cross, the floodgates of grace are open, and all that I have and all that the Father has is all yours.

CHRIST IN MY LIFE You speak with such assurance, Lord. You are Master of all time and space. You are Master of my life. What confidence this should give me! Increase my faith, Lord. Give me the faith and trust of a child who is incapable of doubting, of being anxious, of wondering what will become of him. You love me more than any human mother or father ever could. And you are all-powerful. Jesus, I trust in you...

Mary, the Church calls you the Mother of Fairest Love. But you didn't do big and impressive things. You did all things with the purest and most humble self-forgetfulness and dedication to God the world had ever seen. You had two mottos: "Let it be done to me..." and "My soul magnifies the Lord." Why do

I keep seeking satisfaction in other mottos? Mother, pray for me, teach me to love...

Holy Spirit, pour out your gifts into my soul. My mind is weak and benighted; renew and restore its vigor and clarity. My will is shrunken and misdirected; breathe into it your force and goodness. My heart—I don't even want to talk about it. You know that way down at its very core is a tiny spark of love. Blow on it, feed it, build it into a blazing fire of zeal for God's glory and the salvation of souls...

Questions for SMALL-GROUP DISCUSSION

1. What struck you most in this passage? What did you notice that you hadn't noticed before?

2. Why do you think Christ insists so vehemently on loving him through obeying his command? Does that mean that prayer and the sacraments don't really matter? How pleased do you think he is with how his disciples (throughout the ages) have responded to this insistence?

3. Why do you think Christ says that he will reveal himself to those who love him? Why wouldn't he reveal himself so that we would love him?

4. How can we take better advantage of the priceless gift of the Holy Spirit?

Cf. Catechism of the Catholic Church, 539, 1850, 1991, 2087 on the relationship between love and obedience; 683-747 on the nature and role of the Holy Spirit; 232-248 on the nature of the Holy Trinity: "Father, Son, and Holy Spirit"

284. THE GIFT OF PEACE (JN 14:22-31)

"In all this he offered his own self, so that when you suffered you would not lose heart, but rather would recognize that you are a man, and would yourself expect to receive what he received from God." – St. Hippolytus

JOHN 14:22-31

Judas—this was not Judas Iscariot—said to him, "Lord, what is all this about? Do you intend to show yourself to us and not to the world?" Jesus replied: "If anyone loves me he will keep my word, and my Father will love him, and we shall come to him and make our home with him. Those who do not love me do not keep my words. And my word is not my own: it is the word of the one who sent me. I have said these things to you while still with you; but the Advocate, the Holy Spirit, whom the Father will send in my name, will teach you everything and remind you of all I have said to you. Peace I bequeath to you, my own peace I give you, a peace the world cannot give, this is my gift to you. Do not let your hearts be troubled or afraid. You heard me say: I am going away, and shall return. If you loved me you would have been glad to know that I am going to the Father, for the Father is greater than I. I have told you this now before it happens, so that when it does happen you may believe. I shall not talk with you any longer, because the prince of this world is on his way. He has no power over me, but the world must be brought to know that I love the Father and that I am doing exactly what the Father told me. Come now, let us go."

CHRIST THE LORD Jesus knows what is going to happen. He knows what will happen to him, what will happen to his disciples, and what will happen to the Church. But he not only knows what will happen, he is in charge of it. Therefore, when he says, "Do not let your hearts be troubled or afraid," we can trust him. He is the Lord; he is in control; he is watching out for us. In Christ, we have someone we can count on—absolutely.

Jesus bequeathed peace to his apostles. The battle of his Passion issued in the definitive victory over the "prince of this world," the devil, who rules by fear and intimidation and by providing a false sense of security. When Jesus commands a life, he brings peace. Peace to the ancient Jews was God's greatest gift. It was much more than a temporary feeling of contentment, like the feeling we get after a good meal. Peace implied the fullness of prosperity and fruitfulness, the hum of a life being lived to the max, like the hum of a healthy beehive. What greater gift could he have given? What does the human heart seek if not the deep joy of knowing that we are loved unconditionally, the strength and opportunity to love fully in return, the certainty that our lives have a meaning that no earthly power can take away, the invigoration of having a mission with eternal consequences? By coming to "dwell" in us, by sending us the Holy Spirit to be our guide, God wishes to imbue us with this peace. But we have to claim it and make it our own. We have to activate the faith and hope we have received, counteracting every disturbance with prayer and trust and overcoming all trouble and fear by turning to our Lord.

CHRIST THE TEACHER If Christ had not returned to the Father ("I am going to the Father"), he would have remained limited by time and space, as he was during his earthly life. But since he now dwells body and soul in heaven, he can be present to each one of us at all times, through the Holy Spirit. The Church has long called the Holy Spirit the "sweet guest of the soul," as the ancient hymn puts it. He is the same Spirit that animated and animates Christ. When we were baptized, he came to dwell within us as well, to be our intimate friend, as if Christ climbed into our hearts to accompany us throughout the rest of our life's journey. The Holy Spirit is like our own personal trainer, but instead of honing our physique, he polishes our love, our holiness, our very hearts. Unfortunately, we often forget about him. He is polite; he knows he is only a guest, because even though he created us, he completely respects our freedom. And so he waits for us to listen to him, to ask him for guidance and strength. And if we listen, he will teach us, just as Christ taught his disciples during those three years when they walked together through the hills of Galilee and Judah.

Even though the Holy Spirit will be with us to remind us of Christ's lessons and to teach us more and more about the Kingdom, Christ wants to be sure to give us the most important lesson before he leaves. He tells us explicitly how to love him, how to live in communion with God, which is the meaning of human existence. If we love him, we will "keep his word,"—i.e., we will follow his new commandment to love one another as he has loved us, and then the Father and the Son will come and take up their dwelling in our hearts. Do we want to live close to God? Here's the recipe...written by God himself.

CHRIST THE FRIEND *Jesus: What I said to my apostles that night, I say to all of my followers: "I have told you this now before it happens, so that when it does happen you may believe." I explained everything to them – the betrayal, the arrest, the trial and condemnation, the scourging and mockery and crucifixion, and most importantly, my rising and ascension and the delivery of the Holy Spirit. When I told them these things, they didn't understand. Only as the events unfolded did they recognize them, and as they did, they were able to grasp their meaning. I am doing the same with you. You have the Gospels and the lives of my saints, and so you know that as you follow me you will face your own Gethsemanes and Calvaries, your own Resurrections and Pentecosts. You must pass through all that I passed through in order to grow to maturity in me. But I have told you this beforehand, so that whatever happens, you will find in me the comfort and light that will protect you from being troubled and afraid. You will never be caught off guard. I am always with you. You have believed in me and obeyed me, and I have made my home in your heart.*

CHRIST IN MY LIFE Blessed Trinity, you have taken up residence in my heart. How do you do that? How can my Creator dwell within me? But this is what love does. Wherever I go, you are with me. Whatever I do or say, you are with me. Whatever I look at or think about, you are there within me. I believe in you. Yet I have to ask: Why am I not more aware of you? Grant me that grace, Lord—teach me never to walk alone...

I believe in you, Lord, but help me to believe more fully. Help me to believe so completely that my life and yours become one. In all my activities, conversations, and relationships, I want to live and communicate the joy and peace that only you can give. Lord Jesus, I trust in you...

Mary, it was the Holy Spirit who overshadowed you and conceived Jesus in your womb. And how did he form Jesus in you? Through all the normal channels and processes, so subtly and quietly, from inside the depths of your being. Teach me to let the Holy Spirit teach and guide and form my Christian life. I want to know how, so that I can cooperate better. May Jesus be formed within me...

Questions for
SMALL-GROUP DISCUSSION

1. What struck you most in this passage? What did you notice that you hadn't noticed before?

2. How can we cultivate a deeper friendship with the Holy Spirit?

3. When have you experienced most palpably the peace that Jesus promises?

4. Jesus' promise of peace is repeated during every Mass right before we receive Holy Communion. Why do you think the Church puts his words in that particular place in the Liturgy?

Cf. Catechism of the Catholic Church, 687-741 on the Holy Spirit; 227 on trust in God in all circumstances

THE GOSPEL OF JOHN
Chapter 15

"O Lord Jesus, I surrender to you all my will. Let me be your lute. Touch any string you please. Always and forever let me make music in perfect harmony with your own. Yes, Lord, with no ifs, ands or buts, let your will be done in this family, for the father, for the children, for everything that concerns us, and especially let your will be done in me."

– ST. JANE DE CHANTAL

285. Bearing Fruit for Christ's Kingdom (Jn 15:1-8)

"Others may have their wealth, may drink out of jeweled cups, be clad in silks, enjoy popular applause, find it impossible to exhaust their wealth by dissipating it in pleasures of all kinds, but our delight is to meditate on the Law of the Lord day and night..."
– St. Jerome

JOHN 15:1-8

"I am the true vine, and my Father is the vinedresser. Every branch in me that bears no fruit he cuts away, and every branch that does bear fruit he prunes to make it bear even more. You are pruned already, by means of the word that I have spoken to you. Make your home in me, as I make mine in you. As a branch cannot bear fruit all by itself, but must remain part of the vine, neither can you unless you remain in me. I am the vine, you are the branches. Whoever remains in me, with me in him, bears fruit in plenty; for cut off from me you can do nothing. Anyone who does not remain in me is like a branch that has been thrown away—he withers; these branches are collected and thrown on the fire, and they are burnt. If you remain in me and my words remain in you, you may ask what you will and you shall get it. It is to the glory of my Father that you should bear much fruit, and then you will be my disciples."

CHRIST THE LORD The world's greatest leaders influence people from the outside in; their speech, their ideas, their example, their presence—they move us and motivate us, they draw us and stir us. Christ, however, goes much deeper. He not only calls us from the outside, but he also unites himself to us so intimately that his very life flows through our veins. "I am the vine, you are the branches." Where does the vine stop and its branches begin? Their union is too complete to tell. The same sap gives life to the vine and to its branches. He is Lord from within, renewing hearts from the inside, as only God can do. Once again, Jesus Christ stands alone among great historical figures; not only does he excel over all others in their own game, but he plays in an entirely different league; he is a leader, but he is also the Lord.

CHRIST THE TEACHER Jesus tells us point blank what the Father wants. God wants us to "bear much fruit" and to "be [his] disciples." God wants our lives to show forth his goodness, to bring lost souls back into the fold, and to fill human society and culture with the justice and beauty they need to flourish. Our desire to do something with our lives is a gift from God; we are created in his image, and he is the Creator—we too yearn to build, to contribute, to make a difference that will last not only in this life, but into all eternity.

Bearing this fruit requires in the first place our own efforts to stay united to the vine, through prayer, the sacraments, and loving obedience to God's will. And it also requires our being pruned—the purification of our selfishness that comes through suffering and sacrifice. Love and sacrifice, as all the lives of the saints attest to, and as Christ himself exemplifies, keep the sap flowing. They yield the fruit we yearn for most: living a life that resounds with meaning and energy, a life that positively impacts others and exudes joy and enthusiasm, a life that changes this world for the better in as profound a way as Christ's own life did, and a life whose meaning and impact overflow into eternity. This is what God wants for us; this is why Jesus came to earth. Bearing such fruit makes life worth living; without it we are dry, dead branches good for nothing except the fire—pretty simple lesson, pretty dire consequences if we don't learn it well.

CHRIST THE FRIEND Christ goes on to tell us how to achieve this fruitfulness: "Remain in me...cut off from me you can do nothing." As long as we stay united to the vine, whatever apostolic activities we engage in will yield a harvest—even a small branch dangling near the ground will produce its fruits as long as it's united to the vine. Separated from Jesus Christ, no one can live in communion with God, the only source of lasting fruit. How much we need to learn how to pray and make this the center of our lives! This is Christ's constant refrain from the moment of his Incarnation: Come to me, learn from me, follow me... My heart yearns for you to make my friendship the highest value of your life, so that I can fill you with true peace, meaning, and joy—the kind that you long for but can never achieve on your own. The sacraments, the Church, prayer, the Bible—these are all extensions of my effort to stay intimately united with you, to guide you along the path of everlasting life, and to reveal to you the glories of my love. These were my final words before I went to death on the cross, my last lesson, and I really mean them: remain in me; stay close to me; do not forsake me; trust in me.

CHRIST IN MY LIFE Lord, your very life flows through my veins. Why don't I think of this more? Why do I let myself act as if this world were all there is? I know that my life now is a training ground of love, a chance to exercise the virtues of faith, hope, and love that you have grafted into my soul, an opportunity to spread your Kingdom to those around me. In my fidelity to that mission is your pleasure; in it is my joy...

No one loves me more than you. No one has given me more than you—no one can. If I succeed on my own, the satisfaction is real, but it passes; I need another success to feel satisfied again. If I possess something nice, I enjoy it for a while, but then it gets old. You want me to enjoy fruit that will last, the undying fruits of the Spirit: "love, joy, peace, patience, kindness, goodness, gentleness, self-control" (Gal 5:22)...

Of all the people I know, how many are united to the vine of your friendship, Lord? Half? A little less, a little more? You are yearning for all of them to live close to you, so you can make their lives bear fruit, the kind they yearn for. So I ask you, why don't I feel a bigger burden to pray for them and to show them your love? Why am I satisfied in my comfort zone? Let the light of your heart illumine my heart...

Questions for
SMALL-GROUP DISCUSSION

1. What struck you most in this passage? What did you notice that you hadn't noticed before?

2. Christ wants nothing more than to remain united to each of us in intimate friendship. This is his greatest desire. How can we measure if our greatest desire is the same?

3. What are some signs that we can look for in order to determine whether our lives are "bearing fruit" in the way that God desires?

4. What can we do to make sure that we always stay united to the vine? What do you think is the surest and most visible sign that we have cut ourselves off from the vine?

Cf. Catechism of the Catholic Church, 2558-2565 on the importance of a vital union between Christ and the Christian; 1382-1401 on the Eucharist as the efficacious sign of this communion of life with God in Christ; 1718-1724 on our desire for happiness from God's perspective; 1812-1829 on union with God through the theological virtues

286. You Are My Friends (Jn 15:9-17)

"He had no need of us in order to save us, but we can do nothing without him… So let us love one another as Christ loved us and gave himself for us." – St. Augustine

JOHN 15:9-17
"As the Father has loved me, so I have loved you. Remain in my love. If you keep my commandments you will remain in my love, just as I have kept my Father's commandments and remain in his love. I have told you this so that my own joy may be in you and your joy be complete. This is my commandment: love one another, as I have loved you. A man can have no greater love than to lay down his life for his friends. You are my friends, if you do what I command you. I shall not call you servants any more, because a servant does not know his master's business; I call you friends, because I have made known to you everything I have learnt from my Father. You did not choose me, no, I chose you; and I commissioned you to go out and to bear fruit, fruit that will last; and then the Father will give you anything you ask him in my name. What I command you is to love one another."

CHRIST THE LORD The moment is solemn. Jesus is at table with his intimate collaborators, his handpicked Twelve Apostles, and he knows that this is the last time they will be gathered in this way until they meet again in eternity. Nothing is carelessly said. Everyone on their deathbed has their final words, what they want to leave as their legacy. Jesus explains that he has loved us, and that he longs for us to remain in his love, to stay in his friendship, so that we may experience the indescribable joy that flows from true love. And then he lays down his one commandment, the new commandment, the summary of all his teaching and of his entire life: "Love one another as I love you." The law of Christ, the law of Christ's Kingdom, the only eternal law, is the law of love. Christ is Lord, because he commands with authority. But he is Lord of love, in love, and because of love, and his "command" is a heartfelt invitation to follow his example.

We can think of this part of his discourse as his battle plan—indeed, he is on the verge of heading into battle, his final battle against evil and all the forces of darkness. And with the consummating sacrifice of his life he will give birth to his Church militant, the body of believers who will take that same battle to the ends of the earth and the far corners of human history and culture. The plan is simple and straightforward. It is all summed up in his single, final, definitive command: love one another as I have loved you. To fight for the Lord and his Kingdom is to fight to fulfill that command.

CHRIST THE TEACHER Jesus, God himself, teaches us the nature of love. Love is self-giving: the greater the self-giving, the greater the love. "A man can have no greater love than to lay down his life for his friends." When we put our lives at the service of others, when we live in order to give and not to take, when we are willing to suffer so that someone else can rejoice, then we may call ourselves his disciples.

Just to make sure we don't misunderstand this lesson, he illustrated it by his own suffering and death. He accepted mockery, humiliation, torture, rejection, injustice, misunderstanding, betrayal, and finally death, not because he was too weak to resist, but to show us what love really is: self-giving, self-forgetting generosity. Jesus Christ hanging on the cross, bearing the weight of our sins and the punishment these sins have earned, thinking not of himself but of the souls he came to save, even pleading for their forgiveness up until the very end—this is love. Far from warm fuzzies and dreamy emotions, the love of Christ—and therefore the love of the Christian—is a love that gives without ever counting the cost, a love that gives without ever asking for something in return, a love that gives and gives and gives, just like God. And the more it gives, the more it has; the more it loves, the better it loves. We learn to love by loving. When we learn this lesson of true love and self-giving, we tap into the inexhaustible source of energy and enthusiasm that is God himself.

CHRIST THE FRIEND *Mary: My child, Jesus has now told you the most important thing that is in his heart. He has looked into your eyes, he has chosen you, and he has revealed his soul to you. He has held nothing back. You know him. He has come to offer you his friendship. If you reciprocate, if you also bare your heart to him in prayer, heed his call to follow him, and fulfill his commands, then your life will bear "fruit that will last" and your "joy will be complete." It is his promise, and he keeps his promises. Following Jesus Christ is a matter of the heart, a personal response to a personal invitation. And* *since the heart is the core of your being, anything that touches your heart touches every aspect of your life. Jesus wants to abide in your heart so that his friendship can color every nook and cranny of your life. Let him in again, today, right now.*

CHRIST IN MY LIFE Lord Jesus, you have wished to be my friend. I have so many friends. Friendship seems so simple, so natural. Do you really want to live like that with me? Don't you want something more dramatic, more impressive, more historic? After all, you are the King of the universe. But no, you just want my friendship. And I want yours. It is all I want. Increase my faith, Lord, and teach me to walk always by your side...

You keep repeating the same lesson, Lord, that you want me to love as you have loved. Why do you keep insisting? Because I still haven't learned it. It's like when I was a kid and my coaches and teachers kept drilling the fundamentals. How many times I had to write out the alphabet! How many times I had to shoot a layup! The fundamentals of eternal life—help me get them right, so I can help others...

I am so grateful that you have made me your soldier. You didn't need me; you could have conquered without me. But you chose to include me, to make me your ambassador, to give me a mission, a responsibility, a field of action. Now I can show you that I love you, that I am thankful for the innumerable gifts you have given me. I can show it by giving myself wholly to the mission you have entrusted to me...

Questions for
SMALL-GROUP DISCUSSION

1. What struck you most in this passage? What did you notice that you hadn't noticed before?

2. What does "love one another as I have loved you" mean for us right here and now?

3. Why do you think Christ insisted so much on his followers obeying that commandment?

4. What has most helped your relationship with Christ grow toward the heartfelt friendship that he wants it to be?

Cf. Catechism of the Catholic Church, 1822-1829 on the law of charity; 1965-1974 on the "new commandment" of charity and the new law of the gospel; 2558 on the importance of a vital and personal relationship with God

287. HARD TIMES WILL COME (JN 15:18-27)

"Though our ancestors' institutions failed, public affairs are in tumult, and everything human is confused, the Catholic Church alone never vacillates, but instead looks confidently to the future." – Pope Benedict XV

JOHN 15:18-27

"If the world hates you, remember that it hated me before you. If you belonged to the world, the world would love you as its own; but because you do not belong to the world, because my choice withdrew you from the world, therefore the world hates you. Remember the words I said to you: A servant is not greater than his master. If they persecuted me, they will persecute you too; if they kept my word, they will keep yours as well. But it will be on my account that they will do all this, because they do not know the one who sent me. If I had not come, if I had not spoken to them, they would have been blameless; but as it is they have no excuse for their sin. Anyone who hates me hates my Father. If I had not performed such works among them as no one else has ever done, they would be blameless; but as it is, they have seen all this, and still they hate both me and my Father. But all this was only to fulfil the words written in their Law: They hated me for no reason. When the Advocate comes, whom I shall send to you from the Father, the Spirit of truth who issues from the Father, he will be my witness. And you too will be witnesses, because you have been with me from the outset."

CHRIST THE LORD As Jesus draws his final discourse toward its conclusion, he returns to the themes that have been present throughout John's Gospel: he is the one who has been sent from the Father, he is one with the Father, and in spite of all the works he has done and signs he has given, many have still rejected him, and so they have also rejected the Father. But Jesus knows that God's power, wisdom, and love can take even such tragic rebellion and weave it into his providential plan of salvation, and so he invokes yet another Old Testament prophecy to explain the mystery, as if to say, simply, that God's plan includes and absorbs even the abuse of human freedom; he is the Lord.

Nevertheless, if we read between the lines, we can detect an air of sadness, a dose of regret. He quotes the Scripture almost to comfort himself, because his heart has been broken by their refusal to accept him. He tries to make an excuse for them, "If I had not come... If I had not performed such works..." But their rejection stands, and it pains him. It is the same sadness that colored the very beginning of John's Gospel, "He came to his own domain, and his own people did not accept him.... He was in the world...and the world did not know him" (Jn 1:11, 10). If we are to be true followers of the Lord, we need to remember that he is not a cold tyrant or a distant judge; his human heart beats for all his subjects—for those who obey as well as for those who rebel. If we truly love the Lord, ours will too.

CHRIST THE TEACHER Jesus is on the brink of his passion. The hatred and persecution that have long been simmering are about to boil over. He knows it's coming. But even in its very jaws, his mind stays focused on his apostles and on his mission. He comforts them now for the trials they will have later. He prepares them to accept his suffering as part of God's plan of salvation and also to accept the similar suffering that will come their way as part of that same plan. They too, if they faithfully follow the Master's call in their life, will both win converts, as he did, and suffer persecution and the violence of hatred, just like him. Persecution will help show that they are authentic disciples of Christ, and it will give them a chance to show that their love and fidelity are authentic too. In this context, it is no wonder that throughout the centuries, saints have desired and prayed for persecutions; they wanted to follow Christ more closely.

The same applies to us and to Christians of all times and places. A fundamental division gives dramatic tension to human existence. This world is fallen and yet redeemed. We are sinners and yet still destined for glory. As long as the age of the Church lasts, this division will continue to erupt here and there in waves of hatred, persecution, and conflict. We cannot prevent it, and so we must be ready for it. We must decide ahead of time how we will react, following in the footsteps of Christ. Then we will be his witnesses, as he has chosen us to be—not only with our words, but with our lives and our deaths as well.

CHRIST THE FRIEND *Jesus: My choice withdrew you from the world. There was never a time when I wasn't thinking of you. I have watched over you since the moment of your conception, and I have loved you since before time began. I searched you out as you grew up, whispering in your heart and preparing you to hear my invitation in your life. I kept inviting you many times until you accepted. I am the one who chose you to be my companion, disciple, and ambassador. And I am the one who will give you the strength and light you need to persevere in this labor of faith and love. You must never think that everything depends on you. That is too much for you. You are my adjutant, my helper, my messenger. I will protect you. I will teach you and show you the way to go. You have committed your life to me, and now you belong to me, and so all your challenges and troubles are mine. You are my problem now; let me carry you.*

CHRIST IN MY LIFE Part of me is still mystified at why so many people who witnessed your presence and your miracles didn't accept you and believe in you. But another part of me isn't, because I can see in my own heart that same hard-heartedness. I know you and believe in you, and yet I still lash out at my neighbor, I still wound others with my tongue, and I still indulge my self-centeredness. With the mercy of your heart, soften my heart...

If I think of soldiers in wartime, it is impossible to picture them being surprised at having to engage in battle. That's what soldiers do; that's what war is. Then why am I surprised when I am tempted, when I am misunderstood or ridiculed for trying to advance your Kingdom? Part of me still resists thinking of history in terms of a battle. But it is: you are my general; my weapons are love, forgiveness, and truth...

Mary, why did Jesus choose me? Why did he choose you? Why does he even care about us at all? I know; it is because he is sheer goodness and doesn't want to live without me. He would rather be scourged, crowned with thorns, and crucified than live without me. Mother, teach me to know him, to love him, and to follow him...

Questions for
SMALL-GROUP DISCUSSION

1. What struck you most in this passage? What did you notice that you hadn't noticed before?

2. What more do you think Jesus could have done to convince his antagonists that he really was the Messiah?

3. In this passage Jesus speaks of the world as hating him and his disciples. It seems that the world is the enemy. But earlier in the Gospel, St. John told us that "God so loved the world that he sent his only begotten Son..." (Jn 3:16). If the world is so evil, how can God love it so much?

4. What are the most common kinds of battles in the Christian life? What's the difference between accepting persecution when it comes and imprudently stirring it up?

Cf. Catechism of the Catholic Church, 402-409 on the Christian life as a hard battle; 1-3, 50, 279-281, 295-301 and 2559-2565 on God's taking the initiative in our lives

"The providence of our God and Savior in regard to man consists of his recall from the fall and his return to close communion with God from the estrangement caused by his disobedience. This was the purpose of Christ's dwelling in the flesh, the pattern of his life described in the gospels, his sufferings, the cross, the burial, the resurrection; so that man could be saved, and could recover, through imitating Christ, the adoption of former times. So, for perfection of life it is necessary not only to imitate Christ, in the examples of gentleness, and humility, and patience which he gave us in his life, but also to imitate him in his death…"

–ST. BASIL

288. AFTER THE COMING STORM (JN 16:1-15)

"It is better to be alone with God. His friendship will not fail me, nor his counsel, nor his love. In his strength, I will dare and dare and dare until I die." – St. Joan of Arc

JOHN 16:1-15

"I have told you all this that your faith may not be shaken. They will expel you from the synagogues, and indeed the hour is coming when anyone who kills you will think he is doing a holy duty for God. They will do these things because they have never known either the Father or myself. But I have told you all this, so that when the time for it comes you may remember that I told you, but now I am going to the one who sent me. Not one of you has asked, 'Where are you going?' Yet you are sad at heart because I have told you this. Still, I must tell you the truth: it is for your own good that I am going because unless I go, the Advocate will not come to you; but if I do go, I will send him to you. And when he comes, he will show the world how wrong it was, about sin, and about who was in the right, and about judgement: about sin: proved by their refusal to believe in me; about who was in the right: proved by my going to the Father and your seeing me no more; about judgement: proved by the prince of this world being already condemned.

"I still have many things to say to you but they would be too much for you now. But when the Spirit of truth comes he will lead you to the complete truth, since he will not be speaking as from himself but will say only what he has learnt; and he will tell you of the things to come. He will glorify me, since all he tells you will be taken from what is mine. Everything the Father has is mine; that is why I said: All he tells you will be taken from what is mine."

CHRIST THE LORD Jesus knows that his mission will not come to an end after he returns to the Father—rather, it will just be the beginning. He established his Kingdom through his life, Passion, death and Resurrection, and he will spend the rest of history expanding it. The instrument of that expansion will be his Church, guided "to all truth" by the Holy Spirit. Jesus did not leave us a book; he left us the living Church, animated by the Holy Spirit, indestructible, guaranteed to last until he comes again at the end of time. (The Church, through the inspiration of the Holy Spirit, subsequently put together the world's best-selling book, the Bible.)

Christ is the only King whose Kingdom will have no end. Even now, through his Spirit he is here among us, guiding our hearts "to the complete truth." If ever we get bored with the faith, we can be sure that the faith is not to blame—rather, we will have stopped listening to the words of our Lord.

CHRIST THE TEACHER In words that can hardly sustain the meaning he hoists upon them, Jesus teaches us about the very structure of God. The Spirit can only speak what he hears from the Son, and everything the Son has he has received from the Father—each communicates the other. God is a total unity of persons, a community of love, of self-giving. Whatever one has, the others receive. There is no holding back, no hidden agendas, no manipulation—it's absolute generosity and unlimited self-donation. And, just think, we are created in his image. We are meant to interact with one another with that same generosity. This was the new commandment that Christ gave us during the Last Supper, that we "love one another" as he has loved us, which means to love as the Father has loved him. We can't grasp completely the mystery of the Trinity, but we can enter into it by loving, and loving is better than grasping anyway.

One of the Spirit's first jobs will be to vindicate Jesus, who was about to be wrongly condemned to death. In so doing, the Spirit will reveal to the world, all throughout history, the truth about sin, justice ("who was in the right"), and judgment. Through the enlightenment that comes at Pentecost, all will recognize that Jesus was not the sinner his accusers claimed him to be;

rather, their rejection of him will be shown up as the sin of disbelief. At the same time, it will become clear that all Jesus had said about himself and his mission was right, and the criticisms of his antagonists were wrong. Finally, in the epoch of the Church, what seemed like Christ's defeat in the face of a false judgment will turn out to have been the definitive and lasting judgment that dethrones Satan—idolatry and demonic possession will roll back as the Church rolls forward.

In the light of the Holy Spirit, the truth about Jesus will shine without interruption, exposing evil and pushing back injustice in every generation and every nation. When we renew our faith in the truth of Jesus, we make that light shine brighter, and make reparation for those who still prefer the darkness.

CHRIST THE FRIEND Jesus knows what we need, and he offers it to us—he is always thinking about what we need. He told his apostles just enough on that first Holy Thursday so that their faith would endure the coming storm—both the storm of his passion and that of the persecutions they would face afterwards. And although he still had "many things to say," he knew that it "would be too much for them" then. And so he waited. How humble our God is to adjust himself to the paltry limitations of our fallen human nature! How glad we should be to have someone we can trust so completely! He is perfect wisdom, unlimited power, and undying love, and he puts himself at our service, paying attention to our needs just as a loving mother would. And what does he get out of it? Nothing but the joy of bringing us into his Kingdom—for some reason, he wants to enjoy our friendship from now through eternity, and he's willing to be very patient in order to do so.

How different the world would be if every Christian followed our Lord's example! Patience, kindness, determined love, and attention to the needs of those around us in all circumstances... a simple formula for a worldwide revolution, a moral coup d'état.

CHRIST IN MY LIFE I feel as if every sentence, every phrase you utter is overflowing with meaning that goes way beyond me. Your words are a waterfall of light, and they dazzle me. Dear Lord, take me by the hand and guide me. Every day, help me to understand just a little bit more about you and your Kingdom and how to follow you. This is all I desire, this is all I hope for. Teach me the way to go...

I want to lead those around me into the truth of your friendship, Lord, but how? You revealed yourself gradually to your disciples, before and after your Passion. You befriended them and lived with them. You spoke the truth, but above all you lived the truth. And you drew them closer and closer to you. Help me to do the same. Help me to love others with your love, so I will know exactly what to do…

Mary, you watched over the apostles, the fledgling Church, between Christ's Ascension and the coming of the Holy Spirit. You took care of the infant Church just as lovingly and energetically as you took care of the infant Jesus. I am still just a child, just a beginner in my journey of discipleship. Take care of me, too. My mind is so dark and weak and confused; my heart so scrawny. Mother, make me like Jesus…

Questions for
SMALL-GROUP DISCUSSION

1. What struck you most in this passage? What did you notice that you hadn't noticed before?

2. How can we make our faith more and more Christian—in other words, how can we cultivate a relationship with God the Father, God the Son, and God the Holy Spirit, not just with God "in general"?

3. One of the consequences of the doctrine of the Trinity is that love itself is the force behind the existence of the universe and the life of the Church. What impact should that truth have on our daily lives?

4. How can we live with a greater awareness that we are temples of the Blessed Trinity? How should the fact that others are, at very least potentially, also temples of the Trinity affect our interpersonal relationships?

Cf. Catechism of the Catholic Church, 238-260 on the Trinity; 50-67 on God's plan of "loving goodness"; 849-856 on the "missionary mandate" of the Church

289. In Christ's Name (Jn 16:16-33)

"There is nothing more beautiful than to be surprised by the gospel, by the encounter with Christ. There is nothing more beautiful than to know Him and to speak to others of our friendship with him." – Pope Benedict XVI

JOHN 16:16-33
"In a short time you will no longer see me, and then a short time later you will see me again." Then some of his disciples said to one another, "What does he mean, 'In a short time you will no longer see me, and then a short time later you will see me again' and, 'I am going to the Father?' What is this short time? We don't know what he means." Jesus knew that

they wanted to question him, so he said, "You are asking one another what I meant by saying: In a short time you will no longer see me, and then a short time later you will see me again. I tell you most solemnly, you will be weeping and wailing while the world will rejoice; you will be sorrowful, but your sorrow will turn to joy. A woman in childbirth suffers, because her time has come; but when she has given birth to the child she forgets the suffering in her joy that a man has been born into the world. So it is with you: you are sad now, but I shall see you again, and your hearts will be full of joy, and that joy no one shall take from you. When that day comes, you will not ask me any questions. I tell you most solemnly, anything you ask for from the Father he will grant in my name. Until now you have not asked for anything in my name. Ask and you will receive, and so your joy will be complete.

"I have been telling you all this in metaphors, the hour is coming when I shall no longer speak to you in metaphors, but tell you about the Father in plain words. When that day comes you will ask in my name; and I do not say that I shall pray to the Father for you, because the Father himself loves you for loving me and believing that I came from God. I came from the Father and have come into the world and now I leave the world to go to the Father." His disciples said, "Now you are speaking plainly and not using metaphors! Now we see that you know everything, and do not have to wait for questions to be put into words; because of this we believe that you came from God." Jesus answered them: "Do you believe at last? Listen; the time will come — in fact it has come already — when you will be scattered, each going his own way and leaving me alone. And yet I am not alone, because the Father is with me. I have told you all this so that you may find peace in me. In the world you will have trouble, but be brave: I have conquered the world."

CHRIST THE LORD Christ's words during the Last Supper were spoken in intimacy. He was not aloof from his disciples, delivering a discourse from a lectern or distant podium. He was sitting beside them, eating with them. They could see every expression of his face, hear every inflection in his voice; they could feel the table move with the gestures of his hands. This is how he wishes to speak these words to us — intimately.

Part of the Christian mystery consists in Christ's decision to ascend into heaven after his Resurrection. In doing so, he inaugurated the era of the Church, to which the action of the Holy Spirit belongs in a special way. But Jesus is still involved. He sits at the right hand of the Father, meaning that he shares fully—both as the eternal Son and as true man, in his human nature and with his human body—in the divine splendor. He is the bridge that reestablishes communion between God and mankind. So whenever we address God in his name, our prayer shares the efficacy of his prayer—a perfect efficacy.

During the Last Supper, Jesus is overjoyed at this prospect. As the risen and ascended Lord, the fully accepted sacrifice of atonement, he will be able to unfurl his love in ways that he couldn't while he was still here on earth. He is looking forward to our being able to ask the Father for our needs and desires in his name: "Until now you have not asked for anything in my name. Ask and you will receive, and so your joy will be complete." Imagine how he spoke those words, "Ask and you will receive." Picture him spreading his arms wide in a sign of generosity, holding nothing back, his face eager and animated, his eyes glowing and shining and burning with anticipation. He is Lord not for himself, but for us. His Kingdom is our Kingdom, if only we have the childlike simplicity and faith to claim it.

CHRIST THE TEACHER Jesus teaches his apostles the true relationship between sorrow and joy. The fallen world has a distorted vision of this relationship. It considers them opposites; either you experience sorrow or you experience joy—all sorrow is to be avoided, and all joy is to be embraced. But precisely because the world is fallen, this vision is false. In a fallen world, the bad must be purged before the true good can be experienced. An abandoned and trampled garden has to be weeded, tilled, and cultivated before it can produce beautiful flowers and healthy fruit. An injured limb has to be operated on and rehabilitated before it returns to the vigor it is meant to have. Just so, to experience the life we were meant to experience, the life of grace and communion with God, requires the weeding and cultivating and healing of our minds and hearts. Every advance in the spiritual life is a new birth necessarily preceded by birth pangs. The apostles could only experience Christ's victory after going through the darkness of his apparent defeat.

The pattern of spiritual growth is always death to sin and self (the sorrow, the pain, and the purification of our fallen nature), making more and more room for life in Christ. Here on earth this purification can occur more efficiently and less painfully than in purgatory because we are free to cooperate with it, as an athlete cooperates with his trainer. Any purification that remains to be done after death is completely passive, as a patient under the scalpel of a surgeon. In both cases, however, the goal remains the same. The more that self-love gives way to Christ-love, the more fully we will taste the peace and joy that no one can take away, because it flows from the One who has risen and who reigns forever: "In the world you will have trouble, but be brave: I have conquered the world."

CHRIST THE FRIEND *Mary: "I am not alone..." Jesus could say that, because he was always united to his Father through prayer and obedience. But he also wants you to be able to say that. He never wants you to have to feel the angst of loneliness, of not being known and loved by someone close at hand. Hell is eternal, unrelieved loneliness, because in hell there is no love. But you are never alone. He dwells in your heart, and he is always speaking with you, guiding you, and loving you. He has given you his presence in the Eucharist and his grace in all the other sacraments. He has extended his Incarnation through the living Church. He sends you the messengers of creation and art and beauty of every sort as gifts and reminders that he is always thinking of you and looking forward to welcoming you home to heaven. He has given you the Bible, the saints, and your vocation to spur you on to know and love him more and more. He even gave you me, his own Mother, so I can watch over you as closely as I watched over him. He wants to bring you life; he wants to bring you joy. Truly you can say, even when everyone else abandons you as everyone abandoned him, "I am not alone."*

CHRIST IN MY LIFE Teach me to pray, Lord. Teach me to pray in your name, to pray with faith, to pray unceasingly. Teach me to pray for the people you have entrusted to my care. You want to shower your graces down upon them, and you are just waiting for me to open up the faucet by my sincere, trusting prayers. In your name, Lord Jesus, I beg you to send the Father's blessing and the Spirit's grace into their hearts...

I am such a product of my times, Lord. I am a coke-machine Christian: I want to put the dollar in the slot, press a button, and have holiness pop right out. I still resist the cross. No more, Lord. You have promised that if I trust in you and follow you, all my sorrows will change into the kind of joy that nothing on earth can taint. I cannot say that I like to suffer, but I can say that I trust in you, Jesus...

I am never alone. You have made sure of that by giving me your friendship. I am sorry for being so closed in on myself at times. I spend most of my day living as if I were alone. In my heart I monologue with myself, while on the outside I bustle and chat. And where are you? I don't want to relegate you to a few minutes in the morning and a few at night. I want to live in your presence, because I know that's what you want...

Questions for
SMALL-GROUP DISCUSSION

1. What struck you most in this passage? What did you notice that you hadn't noticed before?

2. What can we do to become more and more aware of God's constant, active presence in our lives? What has helped you to become more aware?

3. Jesus seems to contradict the apostles' expression of faith when he tells them that they will be scattered during his Passion. Does their scattering mean that they didn't really believe? If not, what did it mean?

4. What lessons have you learned from sorrow and difficulty in your life? What lessons have you learned from easy success?

Cf. Catechism of the Catholic Church, 2734-2741 on filial trust in our relationship with God; 2742-2745 on perseverance in prayer and fidelity; 571-573 on the suffering of Jesus; 30, 163, 301, 1804, 1829, 2015, and 2362 on the sources of joy in the Christian life

THE GOSPEL OF JOHN
Chapter 17

"He said to me, 'My divine heart is so in love with people, and with you in particular, that it can no longer contain the flames of its ardent charity. It needs you to spread them. It must manifest itself to people and enrich them with the precious treasures that I will reveal to you. These treasures are the graces of salvation and sanctification, necessary to rescue people from the abyss of perdition....' This divine heart was shown me on a throne of flames. It was more resplendent than the sun and transparent as crystal. The heart had its own adorable wound, and was surrounded by a crown of thorns, signifying the stings caused by our sins. And there was a cross above it."

– ST. MARGARET MARY ALOCOQUE

290. CASTING OUT THE DEVIL — FOREVER (JN 17:1-11)

"It is clear to me that if we wish to please God and to receive graces in abundance from him, it is God's will that these graces should come to us through the hands of Christ in his most holy humanity." – St. Teresa of Avila

JOHN 17:1-11
"Father, the hour has come: glorify your Son so that your Son may glorify you; and, through the power over all mankind that you have given him, let him give eternal life to all those you have entrusted to him. And eternal life is this: to know you, the only true God, and Jesus Christ whom you have sent. I have glorified you on earth and finished the work that you gave me to do. Now, Father, it is time for you to glorify me with that glory I had with you before ever the world was. I have made your name known to the men you took from the world to give me. They were yours and you gave them to me, and they have kept your word. Now at last they know that all you have given me comes indeed from you; for I have given them the teaching you gave to me, and they have truly accepted this, that I came from you, and have believed that it was you who sent me. I pray for them; I am not praying for the world but for those you have given me, because they belong to you: all I have is yours and all you have is mine, and in them

I am glorified. I am not in the world any longer, but they are in the world, and I am coming to you. Holy Father, keep those you have given me true to your name, so that they may be one like us."

CHRIST THE LORD This is God speaking to God, Jesus the eternal Son praying to God the Father for you and me just moments before he begins the final act in his drama of the Incarnation. By sharing this prayer with us, he lets us in to the deepest recesses of his soul. What is on his heart? The Father's glory, the souls he came to save, the successful fulfillment of his life's mission—these things were always on his heart. This discourse is traditionally referred to as Christ's priestly prayer, since it contains an extended petition to God for the Church and the world and contains inexhaustible treasures. (And like him, the main function of a priest is to intercede for others before God.)

Jesus asserts once again that he has received "power over all mankind,"—absolute authority, universal kingship. In the very next clause, he shows what kind of a King he is: "Let him give eternal life to all those you have entrusted to him." God's glory, as St. Irenaeus puts it, consists in "man fully alive" (Gloria Dei, vivens homo). Jesus Christ is a Lord completely at the service of his subjects, a King who exercises power not for selfish aggrandizement, but for the greater good of his subjects. Christ is the Leader par excellence and the model of all Christian leadership—and every Christian is called to be a leader, in one form or another.

CHRIST THE TEACHER Throughout his life and ministry, Jesus reiterated the lesson of unity. "Blessed are the peacemakers, for they will be called the children of God" (Mt 5:9). "By this they will know you are my disciples, if you love one another" (Jn 13:35). One of the biblical names for the devil, diabolus (whence "diabolical"), means "divider." The devil sows division, anger, envy, hatred, suspicion, resentment, and confusion. Christ came "to destroy the works of the devil" (1 Jn 3:8), to bring unity back to the human family, the unity that mirrors the perfect unity within God himself, who is three persons and one God. It is on his heart even at this culminating moment before his Passion: "So that they may be one like us," he prays.

On a global level, his prayer has been answered; the Catholic Church has remained one in faith, one in worship, and one in organization through twenty long and difficult centuries. But on a personal level, attacks against unity have never ceased. Schisms and divisions litter the path of Christian history. Sterile criticism divides parishes and dioceses; it separates people from priests and priests from bishops. How this must pain the Sacred Heart of Jesus! Have we ourselves learned the lesson of unity? Do we know how to make peace? Or are we unsuspecting undercover agents of the devil, the "divider"?

As Christ raised his eyes to heaven and uttered these words, how much did the apostles understand? We can only guess. We can say with certainty, however, that the prayer before Christ's Passion must have often come to the apostles' minds later, when they were spreading the gospel throughout the world. Jesus had asked the Father to keep them "true to his name." In the face of persecution and martyrdom, how much comfort must they have derived from these words! His prayer applies equally to us, who have received the same vocation to holiness. Through the sacraments, we have inherited the apostles' mission, along with their union with Christ's heart. We belong to him, and he is faithful—we have nothing to fear.

CHRIST THE FRIEND The greatest joy of human existence is relationships of love. What would mansions and yachts, works of art and mountain cottages, sunrises and ocean voyages be without others to share them with? Love, in its various forms (parental, filial, spousal, friendship) can make the most mundane experiences into thrilling adventures, the simplest places into fairylands, the humblest activities into noble deeds. In this prayer, Jesus explains that heaven is nothing more than a perfect relationship of love. We will know God and Christ (and all the saints). We will spend eternity getting to know the One who can never be fully known. If the best of human friendships never grow old, how indescribable will be our eternal friendship with God, from whom all good things come!

Mary: My child, I never preached to the crowds, I never founded universities, I never wrote best sellers, I never established international apostolates, and yet Jesus made me Queen of the Universe. Why? Because his Kingdom isn't made up of flashy achievements. His Kingdom is the unbreakable and contagious bond of love for God and love for neighbor. And so he chooses as Queen his Mother, who had learned the lesson of love, who had learned through the grace of God to be a peacemaker, as all mothers must learn. Seek greatness, because you were created for greatness—no one else can know and love Jesus the way you can—but seek true greatness, and seek it in the only place it can be found, in the Kingdom of Christ, who loved you and gave himself up for you.

CHRIST IN MY LIFE Jesus, you only cared about fulfilling the Father's will and leading me to eternal life. You only cared about others. You didn't just call yourself a servant—you lived like a servant. Dear Lord, I want to live as you lived. But I need your help. Purify my heart. Teach me to forget myself, to give myself, to lose my life in your service, so that I will find the life you want me to have...

You spent your years of ministry casting out demons, healing, and preaching the good news to those who were in need. You finished your life by paying the price for our sins, by laying down your life as a bridge between us rebels and the God who loves us. Thank you, Lord. Teach me to be like that! Make my every word, decision, and action build up my neighbor and your Kingdom. Never let me sow division...

Help me think about heaven, Lord. You are leading me there. You went to prepare me a place there. What will it be like? You came to earth, lived, suffered, and died so that I would have the possibility of going there, of spending eternity with you there. Whatever I can imagine, you can outdo. Increase my hope, Lord, and draw many others to you through me...

Questions for
SMALL-GROUP DISCUSSION

1. What struck you most in this passage? What did you notice that you hadn't noticed before?
2. Why do you think Christ would have spoken this prayer out loud to his disciples?
3. How can we be better agents of unity in the Church and in the world?
4. What effect has the promise of eternal life and the reality of heaven had on your life? What effect does Christ want it to have?

Cf. Catechism of the Catholic Church, 813-822 on the unity of the Church; 1023-1029 on heaven

291. TRUTH AND JOY (JN 17:12-19)

"But whenever we think of Christ, let us always bear in mind that love of his which drove him to bestow upon us so many gifts and graces." – St. Teresa of Avila

JOHN 17:12-19
"While I was with them, I kept those you had given me true to your name. I have watched over them and not one is lost except the one who chose to be lost, and this was to fulfil the scriptures. But now I am coming to you and while still in the world I say these things to share my joy with them to the full. I passed your word on to them, and the world hated them, because they belong to the world no more than I belong to the world. I am

not asking you to remove them from the world, but to protect them from the evil one. They do not belong to the world any more than I belong to the world. Consecrate them in the truth; your word is truth. As you sent me into the world, I have sent them into the world, and for their sake I consecrate myself so that they too may be consecrated in truth."

CHRIST THE LORD Jesus Christ did not hoard his power. He did not reserve his greatness just for himself. He was indeed the Savior sent by God into the world, but he chose to carry out his saving mission through the ministry of his followers: "As you sent me into the world, I have sent them into the world." In the Liturgy, the Church puts this thought before our minds as the Easter season is drawing to a close. We have received its message of hope, of triumph, and of everlasting life; now our Lord is counting on us to broadcast that message throughout the world, by means of our words, our example, and our actions. He was sent, and he has in turn sent us.

A core principle of human leadership is delegation: good leaders know that they cannot do everything alone, so they find qualified people and divide the tasks among them. The case of Christ and his Church is analogous, except for one key difference. Jesus Christ delegates not because he is unable to run his Kingdom without our assistance, but because he wants to give our lives eternal resonance by entrusting to us a mission that has real, everlasting consequences. He is the head who rules through the different members of his body, not because he has to, but because he wants to. In taking up the invitation to become his ambassadors, we come closer to him. We get to know him better, just as you always get to know people better when you work on a project together. We get to know ourselves better, and under his guidance we are able to develop all the qualities he has given us, qualities we may not even know we have (but he knows, since he gave them to us). The chance to work with Christ and for his Kingdom is one of his greatest gifts. It's how we become not just subjects of the Lord, but friends of the King.

CHRIST THE TEACHER The world gets bad press in this passage. Christ asserts that he does not belong to the world, and neither do his disciples, who have been "consecrated," which literally means "set apart," just as he has been. The world "hated" Christ and his followers, and yet it was that very world which Jesus came to save.

The "world" in this passage refers not to the created universe, which comes forth from God's hand as something "very good" (Gn 1:31), but to the forces of human society that have been corrupted by sin, the tendency of many social and cultural norms to lure us away from the steep but liberating path of fidelity to Christ and his friendship. In this sense, the world is one of the Christian's traditional enemies; it is the kingdom of the devil as opposed to the Kingdom of God, the city of fallen man as opposed to the city of God. As St. Augustine described them, the former is ruled by love for self to the point of despising God, while the latter is ruled by love for God to the point of self-sacrifice.

A Christian can never be completely at home in this world, never completely happy or comfortable. We are pilgrims traversing a dangerous route to heaven, soldiers marching from battle to battle in defense of our King. We must never be surprised at the challenges and opposition that we encounter; indeed, every obstacle should boost our hope, reminding us that just ahead we will find home.

CHRIST THE FRIEND Before he returned to his Father, Jesus prayed for his disciples. He prays that we may be consecrated in the truth, just as he is consecrated in the truth. He asks the Father to transplant our lives so that they may become rooted in the lasting, dependable, and rich soil of the truth. He is praying that we be given the grace to build our lives on the solid foundation of God's Word, so that when the storms come (the hatred of the world, the attacks of the evil one), we will stand strong.

What is the truth? What is the word of the Father? Pilate will soon ask the same question, and Jesus will give the definitive answer: he is the Truth; he is the Word. And when we look at him, what do we see? Love. Total self-giving and total concern for others, even to the point of self-annihilation on the cross. This is where Jesus wants us to root our lives—in love. And this consecration to the truth of love is the secret to lasting joy, to sharing in Christ's own joy: "I say these things to share my joy with them to the full."

Jesus: My child, I know what will fill your heart—love. I know what's at the bottom of your soul because I created you. It is the need to love and be loved, to discover that another person is delighted that you exist, and to be glad in the existence of that other person. This is the deepest truth of your being, because I made you in my own image, and this is the deepest truth of my being. That night when I prayed for my Apostles to be consecrated in the truth, I was asking my Father to keep the flame of love alive forever in the heart of the Church, so that it can continuously spread love among all people, and so that it would eventually kindle that flame in your heart. I need to remind you that I am glad that you exist. Not because of what you can do for me, but just because you are. You don't need to earn my love; you just need to enjoy it. And if you do, you will be true to the mission I have given you, the same mission I have given to the whole Church: distributing the embrace of my love to every heart. Know that when I see you (which I always do), I smile, because I am pleased that you exist.

CHRIST IN MY LIFE You have sent me out, just as your Father sent you out. You have sent me into the lives of those around me, into this society and this culture, just as your Father sent you into the world. You want me to be true to your will, to love my neighbor as you have loved me, just as you were true to the Father's will. You have put your mission into my hands. Thank you, Lord! With you at my side, I have nothing to fear...

Why am I still surprised when things go wrong, when tragedy strikes, or when failure brings me to my knees? Why do I keep thinking earth should be heaven? O Lord, shine your light into my mind. Give me the mind and heart of a pilgrim, a soldier, a missionary. Remind me everyday that this life is a journey, a battle, and a mission. Remind me that with you in my heart I can travel and fight and work with joy and peace, no matter what...

Everything around me reminds me of your love. Every sunset is a gift flowing from your love. All the little pleasures of the day, all the beautiful memories of my life, all the hopes that fire my heart, all the goodness I receive from those who love me: all these remind me of your love. It all comes from you. You shine your love all around me, showering me with your light. Keep me aware of your goodness, Lord. Jesus, never let me forget your love...

Questions for
SMALL-GROUP DISCUSSION

1. What struck you most in this passage? What did you notice that you hadn't noticed before?

2. Theoretically, should it be possible to tell just from the way a Christian treats other people that he or she is a disciple of Christ?

3. How much is our concept of happiness dependent on having a good supply of the world's comforts and pleasures, and how much is it dependent upon knowing that we are following the narrow and hard path blazed by Jesus Christ? What should the ratio be like for a mature Christian?

4. What can we do to be more effective agents of unity in the Church, working for the fulfillment of Christ's prayer without compromising our adherence to the true Catholic faith?

Cf. Catechism of the Catholic Church, 813-822 on the mystery of the Church's unity; 405, 2015, 2516, 2725 on life as a spiritual battle; 164, 408, 1869 on the contrary influence of the "world"

292. ONE LOVE, ONE GLORY (JN 17:20-26)

"The whole Blessed Trinity dwells in us, the whole of that mystery which will be our vision in heaven. Let it be our cloister." – Blessed Elizabeth of the Trinity

JOHN 17:20-26

"I pray not only for these, but for those also who through their words will believe in me. May they all be one. Father, may they be one in us, as you are in me and I am in you, so that the world may believe it was you who sent me. I have given them the glory you gave to me, that they may be one as we are one. With me in them and you in me, may they be so completely one that the world will realise that it was you who sent me and that I have loved them as much as you loved me. Father, I want those you have given me to be with me where I am, so that they may always see the glory you have given me because you loved me before the foundation of the world. Father, Righteous One, the world has not known you, but I have known you, and these have known that you have sent me. I have made your name known to them and will continue to make it known, so that the love with which you loved me may be in them, and so that I may be in them."

CHRIST THE LORD Christ's final words before his Passion, words which the Church puts before us each year during the Easter season, bubble up from the depths of the Trinitarian conversation. Jesus is addressing his Father; we are privy to God's interior dialogue—we can read into his mind and heart. We glimpse the love that exists in God, the love that links the Persons of the Trinity, the love that God is. This love is the theme of Christ's prayer. Love was the content of his new commandment. Love, true, self-forgetful love, self-sacrificing love, was the lesson he left when he gave himself up to death on the cross.

One other thing is clear as well: Christ is speaking to the Father like one who knows him as well as we know our own fathers. It is as if a noble prince had gone into the countryside and befriended a band of peasants, then brought them into the palace and, in their presence, begged the King to grant them royal favor. He reminds the Father that he loved him "before the foundation of the world," that "the world has not known you, but I have known you," that they are "in" each other in an inexpressible way, that the Father's glory is his glory. And Jesus asks his Father to let these simple, peasant friends of his into this ineffable closeness, this eternal union. Christ is the only Son of the Father; he is the Lord. Thanks be to God he is our Lord!

CHRIST THE TEACHER By praying out loud, Christ teaches us how to pray. A Christian is another Christ, and so our prayers ought to follow the lines of his prayer. How does he pray? In an atmosphere of assurance that he is being heard by the Father. Whenever we pray, this must be our foundation: we are in conversation with God—with a real, personal God who cares about us more than we care about ourselves. The traditional acts of faith, hope, and love that Christians have long used as reference points in their prayer life are meant to activate this awareness, to enable us to enter into an intimate contact with the one we know loves us. What does Jesus pray for? For us and for all people to enter into the everlasting divine life—and for the Church, that all believers may be united among each other and in him. So, too, we must pray for the unity of Christians and for all men and women to come to know Christ, so that through him they can enter into the life of God as well. And how does he pray? With intimacy (note how often he says "Father"!) and with reverence, "Father, Righteous One." When we approach God, we should follow in his path, opening our hearts in utter confidence, but adoring him in utter humility.

CHRIST THE FRIEND On the night of that first Holy Thursday, Christ not only prayed for his Twelve Apostles, but he also prayed for those who "through their words will believe in me." In other words, he prayed for us. We have directly received faith through our parents, or perhaps through a friend or a priest, but ultimately, all Christians trace their lineage of faith back all the way to the Apostles, because they were Christ's original messengers. Even then, so long ago in the perspective of history, yet so recent from the perspective of love, Jesus had us in mind. He was thinking of each of us during every moment of his life. Each one of us, everyone who would come to believe in his name has a claim on his heart. If there's nothing else the gospel teaches us, no one can deny that it reveals God's personal love and concern for every human person. Only God's love can be like that, simultaneously intimate and global, personalized and universal, and only in God can we find ourselves so bathed in the purest of loves, with absolutely no strings attached.

Jesus: I prayed for all of you to be one, to be united. This is life as I meant it to be: unity, charity, one heart, and one mind. Every sin causes division. Every sin hammers a wedge of discord. How I long for you to experience the joy of living in the unity and communion of true love! You were created for that. Learn from my example. Live in harmony with everyone, loving everyone as I have loved you. Put no conditions on your love, no limits. Guard your words. Speak only what will build up, never what divides. Find ways to knit hearts and lives together, to bridge gaps, to turn differences into mutual enrichment. Be of one heart and one mind—with me, with those closest to you, with those you work with, with those who are difficult to bear with. This is what it means to be my follower and to be created in the image of God.

CHRIST IN MY LIFE You have given me a glimpse of your own nature, of your relationship with the Father. I can't fully understand that, Lord. Why did you reveal it to me? You want to be known by me. You want me to enter into your friendship—even more, into your family. So I have to know the Father, the Son, and the Holy Spirit! I want to know you. The better I know you, the better I will be able to reflect your goodness in all I do...

You want me to pray well and often. It's something you want but can't get unless I give it to you. You have limited your omnipotence out of a desire for my friendship: only I can decide to give you my attention and my affection in prayer. Thank you for the gift of prayer, for this chance to show you that I love you and that I am grateful for all you have done for me. Teach me to speak to you intimately, simply, and honestly...

I believe in your personal, determined love for me. I believe that you were thinking of me during the Last Supper. I believe that you are always thinking of me. It pains me to think that I don't live with a keener, more constant awareness of this. I am always aware of what time it is, what the weather is like, who I'm with—why can't I be more aware of this much more significant truth? Lord, increase my faith...

Questions for
SMALL-GROUP DISCUSSION

1. What struck you most in this passage? What did you notice that you hadn't noticed before?

2. Why do you think Christ prayed this prayer out loud? What does this prayer reveal about the Father?

3. What do you imagine the apostles were thinking as they listened to this prayer?

4. How, practically speaking, can we deepen our appreciation of God's personal love for each one of us?

Cf. Catechism of the Catholic Church, 232-260 on the relationship between the three divine persons of the Trinity; 813-822 on the unity of the Church

"Oh, the new and ineffable mystery! The Judge was judged. He who absolves from sin was bound. He was mocked who once framed the world. He was stretched upon the cross who stretched out the heavens. He was given up to the tomb who raises the dead. The powers were astonished, the angels wondered, the elements trembled, the whole created universe was shaken, the sun fled away... because it could not bear to look upon the crucified Lord."

– ST. ALEXANDER OF ALEXANDRIA

293. Traitors, Troops, and Triumphs (Jn 18:1-11)

"God offers himself to us; there is no need to offer us more." – St. Augustine

JOHN 18:1-11
After he had said all this Jesus left with his disciples and crossed the Kedron valley. There was a garden there, and he went into it with his disciples. Judas the traitor knew the place well, since Jesus had often met his disciples there, and he brought the cohort to this place together with a detachment of guards sent by the chief priests and the Pharisees, all with lanterns and torches and weapons. Knowing everything that was going to happen to him, Jesus then came forward and said, "Who are you looking for?" They answered, "Jesus the Nazarene." He said, "I am he." Now Judas the traitor was standing among them. When Jesus said, "I am he," they moved back and fell to the ground. He asked them a second time, "Who are you looking for?" They said, "Jesus the Nazarene." "I have told you that I am he," replied Jesus. "If I am the one you are looking for, let these others go." This was to fulfil the words he had spoken, "Not one of those you gave me have I lost." Simon Peter, who carried a sword, drew it and wounded the high priest's servant, cutting off his right ear. The servant's name was Malchus. Jesus said to Peter, "Put your sword back in its scabbard; am I not to drink the cup that the Father has given me?"

CHRIST THE LORD St. John gives us a more complete view of this encounter in the Garden of Gethsemane than the other Gospel writers. He skips over Jesus' agony and prayer and moves right on to the arrest. The night was bright, lit by a full moon — the Passover always took place during the first full moon of the spring equinox. John details the makeup of this dispatch. It includes a cohort and a detachment of Temple police, all of them armed. The Greek word translated cohort (speira) can refer to three different units of soldiers (during the Passover extra soldiers were always stationed in Jerusalem). It can either be a normal Roman cohort of six hundred men, or it can refer to a cohort of non-Roman auxiliary troops numbering twelve hundred men, or it can sometimes refer to a maniple of soldiers, which consisted of two hundred men. Any way we take it, even if St. John is using the term loosely, the picture it paints shows the lone Jesus flanked by his frightened eleven Apostles courageously facing a small army.

The tough soldiers and Temple guards were made more confident by their own numbers, though perhaps irritated at being sent out in the cold late at night, and they certainly felt assured that they would soon have the famous rabbi under lock and key. But when they got to the spot and declared their purpose, it only took a word spoken by the Lord to push back the entire throng and knock them to the ground: "When Jesus said, 'I am he,' they moved back and fell to the ground." Indomitable authority and power exuded from the Lord. Peter was so invigorated by this show of force that he brandished his own sword to join the attack. But Jesus wasn't going to conquer that way. Simply destroying his enemies was too easy. He wanted to convert them instead. And so, he freely "drinks the cup" of suffering that his Father has prepared for him. All that follows throughout the Passion will display not the weakness of an inept Galilean rabbi, but the intrepid and unconquerable love of the Lord, always in control of himself and the situation surrounding him.

CHRIST THE TEACHER St. John makes a point of explaining that Judas was right in the middle of this tragic encounter, even though in John's account Judas doesn't actually do anything. Each time he mentions his fellow apostle in this passage, St. John calls him "Judas the traitor." This epithet contrasts starkly with how St. John described Judas back in Chapter 6, as "one of the Twelve, who was to betray him." This small change illustrates a big lesson:

Our spiritual life, our friendship with Christ, is intricately connected to our moral life, the choices we make regarding right and wrong. Jesus is the Creator and Redeemer of the universe, so when we choose to act in accordance with his design for that universe (morally good choices), we deepen our friendship with him—or lay the groundwork for it if it does not yet exist. When we choose to act against his design (morally evil choices), we set ourselves up as rebels against him, which can hardly be a good thing for our friendship. Every individual moral choice, therefore, affects not only its particular situation, but also the kind of person we are and the kind of friend we can be to Christ. When we choose to lie, we become the kind of person who lies. When we choose to use other people as means to selfish ends, we become the kind of person who destroys and discards our fellow man.

Before Judas' betrayal, he is still one of the Twelve; he is a follower of Jesus, however imperfect he may be. After his betrayal, he has become a traitor. He is now the kind of person who is willing to climb the ladder of success by stepping on his friends. The drama of Judas's betrayal exemplifies, lucidly and tragically, the uniquely Christian vision of human dignity: the human person's every choice and action matter. People are not recycled bits and pieces of the universe inevitably making their way back to nothingness, as eastern mysticism and modern nihilism would have it. No, people are God's children, free to be faithful to this sublime vocation of glorifying God and living in communion with him or free to betray it. Every person is created with this indestructible core of dignity, because every person is created by God in God's image. Wherever we see a fellow human being, whether on the most mundane of subways or in the most exquisite of palaces, every single one of them bears in their soul this weight of eternal glory.

CHRIST THE FRIEND Modern existential philosophers criticize Christianity for being a religion of the weak. For them, gentle Jesus being overpowered by the cruelty of Roman might was a repellant display of feeble ineptitude. But they got it all wrong. Probably they hadn't read the Gospels, and certainly they hadn't read this passage. Jesus shows more strength and authority than anyone in history. He destroyed his enemies, not by annihilation but by turning them into his friends and disciples, and he did it by freely letting them do their worst to him, continuing to love them, and staying faithful to the truth of his mission all the same.

Jesus: You are used to hearing that I love you. But you still think of love in too limited a way. Think for a moment of the whole universe. Now think that I have given it all to you. Really, it is all yours, because when you receive me in Holy Communion, you receive the whole of my Kingdom. Think for a moment of what you would be willing to do for someone you love. Think how hard it is sometimes to offer even the smallest sacrifice for their sake, especially when they show no appreciation. I offered the sacrifice of the cross for you, before you even knew me, let alone loved me. And I did it with total freedom. I didn't have to, I chose to, just because I can't bear the thought of spending eternity without you.

CHRIST IN MY LIFE I wonder if I really believe in the power of love, Lord. You did. It was your one and only weapon, and with it you have established a Kingdom that has outlasted the world's mightiest empires. What about the battles I have to fight? My responsibilities, my relationships, my temptations — have I really learned to fight as you did? Am I wielding the sword of love? I think I need more lessons, Lord...

Father, when you look upon the world, you see the same people I see, but you see them differently. You see each one as your beloved child. When parents go to a school play, they see crowds of kids, but when they behold their own children something entirely different happens in their mind and heart. That's what you are like with each of us. Lord, teach me to see and love my neighbor as you do...

Lord Jesus, thank you for becoming my Savior. I am sorry that my heart is so hard, so insensitive. Soften it, Lord, so that I can truly appreciate all that you have done for me. Teach me to feel sincere sadness for my sins and the sins of everyone, but at the same time to feel the joy you want me to feel always, the deep joy of knowing that I am loved so purely, completely, personally...

Questions for
SMALL-GROUP DISCUSSION

1. What struck you most in this passage? What did you notice that you hadn't noticed before?

2. Why do you think St. John made a point of telling us the name of the man whose ear Peter cut off with the sword?

3. Judas' betrayal is dramatic, but it is also possible to betray Jesus in subtler, more hidden ways. How are we tempted to betray him in our own life-situations?

4. Why do you think Jesus let loose his authority to the point of knocking the battalion to the ground, when he knew all along that he was going to let himself be arrested by those same men?

Cf. Catechism of the Catholic Church, 1730-1742 on morality and human freedom; 1749-1756 on the morality of human acts; 599-600 on Jesus' Passion as being ordained by the Father

294. THE POLITICAL TEMPTATION (JN 18:12-27)

"Behold, God the Father has sent down to earth as it were a bag filled with his mercy; a bag to be rent open in the passion so that our ransom which it concealed might be poured out; a small bag indeed, but full." – St. Bernard of Clairvaux

JOHN 18:12-27

The cohort and its captain and the Jewish guards seized Jesus and bound him. They took him first to Annas, because Annas was the father-in-law of Caiaphas, who was high priest that year. It was Caiaphas who had suggested to the Jews, "It is better for one man to die for the people." Simon Peter, with another disciple, followed Jesus. This disciple, who was known to the high priest, went with Jesus into the high priest's palace, but Peter stayed outside the door. So the other disciple, the one known to the high priest, went out, spoke to the woman who was keeping the door and brought Peter in. The maid on duty at the door said to Peter, "Aren't you another of that man's disciples?" He answered, "I am not." Now it was cold, and the servants and guards had lit a charcoal fire and were standing there warming themselves; so Peter stood there too, warming himself with the others. The high priest questioned Jesus about his disciples and his teaching. Jesus answered, "I have spoken openly for all the world to hear; I have always taught in the synagogue and in the Temple where all the Jews meet together: I have said nothing in secret. But why ask me? Ask my hearers what I taught: they know what I said." At these words, one of the guards standing by gave Jesus a slap in the face, saying, "Is that the way to answer the high priest?" Jesus replied, "If there is something wrong in what I said, point it out; but if there is no offence in it, why do you strike me?" Then Annas sent him, still bound, to Caiaphas the high priest. As Simon Peter stood there warming himself, someone said to him, "Aren't you another of his disciples?" He denied it saying, "I am not." One of the high priest's servants, a relation of the man whose ear Peter had cut off, said, "Didn't I see you in the garden with him?" Again Peter denied it; and at once a cock crew.

CHRIST THE LORD Power in the world often comes at a high cost. Those who are powerful constantly face the temptation to compromise their integrity in order to maintain their influence. Plenty of excuses can be found to justify such compromises: I can do more good if I stay in office, the good I do outweighs the evil, etc. When Jesus was brought before Annas, it was because the devil was presenting him with this temptation.

In those days, the high priest was both the highest authority in Israel and the closest collaborator with the Roman overlords. In previous eras, the office was held for life, but the Romans wanted to keep the high priests under control, so they imposed term limits, never letting one person get too powerful. Annas had been high priest during the years A.D. 6-15. Since then, his four sons had each served as high priest, and the current holder of the office, Caiaphas, was his son-in-law. Clearly, Annas was the real power broker, the most influential of the Jewish leaders who continued pulling the strings behind a façade of propriety. He had recognized the threat posed by Jesus and was probably involved in the machinations against him. It is logical that he would have the Lord brought to him first. He wanted to gauge Christ's moral metal. If Jesus could be persuaded to join forces with Annas—if he could be corrupted—this would give yet more influence into his hands, most especially influence with the common people, something he didn't have. If not, and if Jesus truly were as influential as everyone said, he would have to be destroyed.

So Annas initiates talks with Jesus before sending him to any kind of an official trial, even before letting the others know that he has been successfully apprehended. And he questions him about his teachings. Jesus knew very well that it was against Jewish law to force a man to bear witness against himself—only third parties could speak evidence against a man on trial. If he were to answer Annas' questions, therefore, he would be breaking this law and putting himself on the side of Annas' corruption. It was the moment in which he could have compromised his integrity in order to protect his power. But Jesus' Kingdom is no earthly kingdom. He has no truck with evil. Knowing the mind of Annas, he merely reminds him of the law, perhaps hoping to stir the old conniver's conscience.

If all Christians—or even if half of all Christians—followed their Lord's example of unstinting integrity, the world might have more martyrs, but it would also have more justice.

CHRIST THE TEACHER Jesus teaches us how to respond to unreasonable blows. The guard who slapped the Lord after his response to Annas was acting unreasonably. Jesus had done nothing wrong; he had only reminded Annas of the law and refused to play his political game. But the guard saw a chance to demonstrate his loyalty to the powerful old man. He made a show of it, not because it was the morally right thing to do, but because it served his personal agenda. Many times in life we suffer similar blows. We are treated unfairly or uncharitably because others are out to use us as tools to satisfy their own passions and desires.

When the guard strikes the Lord, Jesus doesn't join the fray. He doesn't respond to an unreasonable blow by giving an unreasonable blow in return. He keeps his composure because, unlike the guard, he is not interested in satisfying self-centered desires; he is interested in fulfilling his mission and being faithful to the Father. Jesus will let his enemies drag him through the streets of Jerusalem, but not through the moral mud of impassioned physical or verbal fisticuffs. The more we can learn to seek first the Kingdom, as Jesus did, the freer we will be to parry wild thrusts of injustice with the sturdy two-edged sword of love and truth.

CHRIST THE FRIEND *Peter: After that night, for the rest of my life, people who didn't believe in Christ mocked me by imitating a cock crowing when I would walk into a room. At first it galled me. I always hated being made fun of. But as the years passed, I was glad of it. That night was the greatest night of my life. For the first time, I discovered that someone loved me, not because of what I could do for them or because I was so full of loveable traits, but simply because I was me. Jesus knew all along that I was too weak to follow him and fulfill my mission by leaning just on my own natural strength. But I didn't know it. I thought I could earn the honor he showed me by choosing me and inviting me to be his friend and build his Kingdom. How wrong I was! Who can earn honor from God? God is the one who confers honor. That night shattered once and for all the arrogance I had cultivated my whole life long. It taught me the most valuable lesson of all: when I am weak, then I am strong, because I have to lean on the strength of the Lord.*

CHRIST IN MY LIFE I am sorry for the times I cut corners on my conscience. My heart is still divided, Lord. I am your disciple, but I still seek the benefits of other kingdoms in addition to yours. I know that my life will never bear the fruit you and I both want it to bear until I seek first and uncompromisingly your Kingdom in all that I do. Purify my heart, Lord. Make me strong; give me courage...

I have so much trouble controlling my emotional reactions, Lord. I want to contemplate your composure, your inner strength, the balance and harmony and peace that flow from having your heart entirely engaged in your Father's will. I know that you can teach me to arrange the sail of my fidelity just right, so the wind of every emotion will drive me further into your Kingdom...

Why am I afraid of failing, Lord? You failed in the eyes of the world. Peter failed. The other apostles failed. Can my successes increase your love for me? Can my failures decrease it? The only reason I fear failure is because I value my own achievements too much. O Lord, what good are my achievements if they flow from fear and not from love? Teach me to love, Lord, to live from your love...

Questions for
SMALL-GROUP DISCUSSION

1. What struck you most in this passage? What did you notice that you hadn't noticed before?

2. Which do you think pained Christ's heart more, Peter's betrayal, Judas's betrayal, or Annas' connivance? Why?

3. Only Peter and the "other disciple" (tradition claims it was John, the author of this Gospel) followed Jesus from a distance to his trial. Where do you think the other apostles went after the arrest, and why do you think they didn't go with Peter and John?

4. In what situations are we most easily tempted to deny Jesus by word or action?

Cf. Catechism of the Catholic Church, 601-605 on God's love as shown in the Passion; 595-598 on the trial of Jesus; 1897-1904 on the proper understanding of political authority; 2465-2470 on the importance of honesty

---

295. TWO KINGS, TWO KINGDOMS (JN 18:28-40)

"Jesus responded to the questions of the Roman governor affirming that he was King, but not of this world. He did not come to dominate peoples and territories, but to free men from the slavery of sin and be reconciled with God." – Pope Benedict XVI

JOHN 18:28-40
They then led Jesus from the house of Caiaphas to the Praetorium. It was now morning. They did not go into the Praetorium themselves or they would be defiled and unable to eat. So Pilate came outside to them and said, "What charge do you bring against this man?" They replied, "If he were not a criminal, we should not be handing him over to you." Pilate said, "Take him yourselves, and try him by your own Law." The Jews answered, "We are not allowed to put a man to death." This was to fulfil the words Jesus had spoken indicating the way he was going to die. So Pilate went back into the Praetorium and called Jesus to him, "Are you the king of the Jews?" he asked. Jesus replied, "Do you ask this of your own accord, or have others spoken to you about me?" Pilate answered, "Am I a Jew? It is your own people and the chief priests who have handed you over to me: what have you done?" Jesus replied, "Mine is not a kingdom of this world;

if my kingdom were of this world, my men would have fought to prevent my being surrendered to the Jews. But my kingdom is not of this kind." "So you are a king then?" said Pilate. "It is you who say it," answered Jesus. "Yes, I am a king. I was born for this, I came into the world for this: to bear witness to the truth; and all who are on the side of truth listen to my voice." "Truth?" said Pilate. "What is that?"; and with that he went out again to the Jews and said, "I find no case against him. But according to a custom of yours I should release one prisoner at the Passover; would you like me, then, to release the king of the Jews?" At this they shouted: "Not this man," they said, "but Barabbas." Barabbas was a brigand.

CHRIST THE LORD As the liturgical year reaches its conclusion with the Solemnity of Christ the King, by presenting us with this passage the Church shows us the stark contrast between Christ's Kingdom and all other kingdoms. Pilate is the Roman Emperor's representative in Palestine. His career as procurator had been marked by violence and political blunders, by which he alienated the Jews he was supposed to be ruling. Though he recognized Jesus' innocence, he feared further conflict with the Jewish leaders, since that could cause them to denounce him to the emperor. Pilate is the typical earthly king, interested more in his personal career, prestige, and success than in what is true and right. Even when he finds himself face-to-face with the light of Truth itself, his own worldly ambitions blind him to it. We are sympathetic to him because we share his weakness.

Jesus, on the other hand, is fully identified with his Kingdom, the eternal Kingdom, established on the solid but hidden foundations of truth and divine love. His Kingdom is demanding but lasting. It involves obedience to the Father's will, even at times to the point of sacrificing one's earthly life. But it is the true Kingdom, the realm of meaning—deep, existential meaning—that abides. For the sake of this Kingdom, Jesus is willing to suffer rejection and injustice at the hands of an earthly king because he knows that such a crime will only reveal more brilliantly the splendor of his Lordship. We are inspired by him because we know in our hearts that we are called to the same kind of nobility of spirit. We recognize that we cannot serve both Christ the King and the kings of this earth, and we are often torn between the two. Every such moment of decision (and there are plenty of them every day) presents us with a chance to renew our option for Christ, to confirm our citizenship in the Kingdom of God.

CHRIST THE TEACHER Pilate stands face-to-face with the Lord of the universe. They are having a conversation. No one can interrupt them. The cool morning air is refreshing. Pilate is agitated by the circumstances, but he is thinking clearly because it's still early in the day. Jesus is exhausted from the first twelve hours of his Passion, but his eyes glow with the love and determination that had led him to this hour. His love for Pilate is no less because of his tiredness. He came to earth in order to save Pilate's soul. Providence has brought them together. Jesus is eager to draw this Roman patrician close to his heart. All the conditions are right for Pilate to detect in Jesus the God for whom his heart longs. Yet he doesn't. He is in the same room with Jesus, speaking with him, but he remains unmoved. Why?

"Everyone who belongs to the truth listens to my voice." Here Jesus teaches us the secret to intimacy with God. Whoever lets himself be led by what is true will be drawn into communion with Christ and will hear and heed God's ceaseless invitations to follow him more closely. But being led by truth requires humility. It requires recognizing a higher authority than oneself: if I am obliged to discover, accept, and conform to what is objectively true (morally, physically, historically), then I am not autonomous, I am not the master of my universe, I am not God. That act of humility, which frees us from the enervating bonds of selfishness, is hard to make. Our fallen human nature tends toward pride, toward self-sufficiency, control, and dominance. To resist that tendency requires courage. It takes courage to obey the truth and expose oneself to the burning love of God. May he grant it to us all in abundance.

CHRIST THE FRIEND "Mine is not a Kingdom of this world." If it were, our friendship with Christ would be a lot easier than it sometimes is. He wants to lead us along the journey of life in this world toward our eternal home in heaven. Therefore, he often urges us to get up and move along when we are tired. He often asks us to take steep, demanding paths that we would prefer to avoid. But he knows the way, and he knows the destination. Like a true friend, he will never rest until we have reached the fullness of life – even if he has to put up with our complaining along the way.

Pilate: Many things confused me that day, but nothing confused me more than the crowd's choice to free Barabbas. Barabbas was a typical hotheaded revolutionary, a man who would kill or maim as easy as he would break a stick for the fire. But that Jesus was a noble man, a temperate man, a wise man. He had done nothing wrong. They were envious of him, that's all. But why did the crowd choose Barabbas? How could they not see that Jesus was a worthy man? I can say this now, but the fact is that I acquiesced to their choice; I made the same horrible mistake. If I had been in Jesus' place and he had been in my place, I know he never would have turned me over to that crowd. But he wasn't in my place; I was in my place. Why did I give in? Why didn't I stand my ground? I wish he hadn't brought up all that talk about the truth. That disconcerted me. No one believes in truth anymore—that went out of fashion long ago. But when he said the word, it rang in my ears like the single clap of a small silver bell, clear and penetrating. It is still ringing. I can't stop thinking about it. Why did I not listen to him? Why did I not trust him? Why did I not follow that voice that was speaking so clearly in me? Everything would be different if I had just done what I knew was right! Yet I know I can never undo what I did.

CHRIST IN MY LIFE Who is my king? Whom do I serve? I want to serve you, Lord, because you truly are the King. But I still tend so much to serve myself. I want people to do things my way—I want to have what I want, when I want it. I want my plans to work out exactly as I plan them. I guess all of this is natural, but you want to lead me to the supernatural realm. Renew my mind and heart, Lord; Thy will be done, not mine…

Every time I have followed your voice resounding in my conscience, I have experienced the peace and the satisfaction that comes from living in harmony with the truth. And every time I haven't, I writhe and agonize. And yet I still haven't learned, Lord. I still waffle. How do you put up with me? O Jesus, purify my heart, pour your love into my heart; with the courage of your heart, strengthen my heart…

Mary, I don't want to be like Pilate. Why am I such a reluctant disciple? I know Jesus; I have been given a share in his mission—what greater privilege could I desire? And yet, sometimes I look at it as if it were a burden. The spirit of self-centeredness and fascination with the trinkets of this world still pulls at me. Mary, teach me to be his faithful friend, his brave soldier. Mother most pure, pray for me…

Questions for
SMALL-GROUP DISCUSSION

1. What struck you most in this passage? What did you notice that you hadn't noticed before?

2. What do you think was in Christ's mind and heart during this interchange with Pilate? What do you think he was hoping for?

3. Pilate committed an injustice in order to protect his personal ambitions. In what ways are we tempted to do the same?

4. Christ tells Pilate that his Kingdom is "not of this world." Does this mean that our faith shouldn't affect our lives on earth? How should being a citizen of Christ's Kingdom affect our interaction with earthly realities? What exactly did Jesus mean by saying this?

Cf. Catechism of the Catholic Church, 668-682 on Christ's second coming and the last judgment; 595-598 on Jesus' trial; 2816-2827 on "Thy Kingdom Come, thy will be done…"

THE GOSPEL OF JOHN
Chapter 19

"How great the cross! What blessings it holds! He who possesses it possesses a treasure. More noble, more precious than anything on earth, in fact and in name, it is indeed a treasure, for in it and through it and for it all the riches of our salvation were stored away and restored to us. If there had been no cross, Christ would not have been crucified. If there had been no cross, Life would not have been nailed to a tree. If he had not been nailed, the streams of everlasting life would not have welled from his side, blood and water, the cleansing of the world; the record of our sins would not have been cancelled, we would not have gained freedom, we would not have enjoyed the tree of life, paradise would not have been opened. If there had been no cross, death would not have been trodden under foot, the underworld would not have yielded up its spoils."

-ST. ANDREW OF CRETE

296. A Reluctant Sinner and a Willing Lamb (Jn 19:1-16)

"In the cross every apostle has gloried; by it every martyr has been crowned and every saint made holy." – St. Theodore the Studite

JOHN 19:1-16

Pilate then had Jesus taken away and scourged; and after this, the soldiers twisted some thorns into a crown and put it on his head, and dressed him in a purple robe. They kept coming up to him and saying, "Hail, king of the Jews!"; and they slapped him in the face. Pilate came outside again and said to them, "Look, I am going to bring him out to you to let you see that I find no case." Jesus then came out wearing the crown of thorns and the purple robe. Pilate said, "Here is the man." When they saw him the chief priests and the guards shouted, "Crucify him! Crucify him!" Pilate said, "Take him yourselves and crucify him: I can find no case against him." "We have a Law," the Jews replied, "and according to that Law he ought to die, because he has claimed to be the Son of God." When Pilate heard them say this his fears increased. Re-entering the Praetorium, he said to Jesus,

"Where do you come from?" But Jesus made no answer. Pilate then said to him, "Are you refusing to speak to me? Surely you know I have power to release you and I have power to crucify you?" "You would have no power over me," replied Jesus, "if it had not been given you from above; that is why the one who handed me over to you has the greater guilt." From that moment Pilate was anxious to set him free, but the Jews shouted, "If you set him free you are no friend of Caesar's; anyone who makes himself king is defying Caesar." Hearing these words, Pilate had Jesus brought out, and seated himself on the chair of judgement at a place called the Pavement, in Hebrew Gabbatha. It was Passover Preparation Day, about the sixth hour. "Here is your king," said Pilate to the Jews. "Take him away, take him away!" they said. "Crucify him!" "Do you want me to crucify your king?" said Pilate. The chief priests answered, "We have no king except Caesar." So in the end Pilate handed him over to them to be crucified.

CHRIST THE LORD Those who insisted on crucifying Jesus revealed the reason behind their blindness in the very accusation they leveled against him: "Anyone who makes himself king is defying Caesar." This was the clincher. It convinced Pilate to betray his own conscience because Pilate wanted nothing more than to stay in the emperor's good graces. If the Jewish leaders sent a report to Rome claiming that Pilate was neglecting to rein in rebels and usurpers, it could mean the end of Pilate's career. Pilate cared more about the passing kingdom of this world than his moral integrity, the ticket to eternal life. And so did the Jewish leaders who clamored for Christ's crucifixion. They, too, were so attached to their status and their desires for earthly pomp and success that they shut their eyes and ears to Jesus' message of a Kingdom of Heaven. They wanted God to provide a Messiah according to their own contaminated expectations; they refused to adjust and elevate those expectations in accordance with the Messiah God had sent.

Still today, among believers and unbelievers, Christ's message of a Kingdom of the heart and spirit, a Kingdom for which it is more than worthwhile to sacrifice earthly glamour and wealth, meets with stubborn resistance. We cling so much to our hopes for heaven on earth, to Caesar's power, prestige, and possessions, that we decline the Lord's unceasing invitation to leave behind everything and follow him. Like Pilate, we crucify Jesus to keep our jobs. And what fools we are when we do; Caesar went to dust long ago, but Christ reigns forever.

CHRIST THE TEACHER During the Last Supper, Jesus bequeathed his new commandment to his apostles, his Church, and the world: "This is my commandment: love one another, as I have loved you. No one can have greater love than to lay down his life for his friends" (Jn 15:12-13). Since that moment he has been engaged in showing what he meant. His whole Passion is the laying down of his life for his friends – for every human being ever created. By laying down his life in such a dramatic way, Jesus demonstrates with equal drama the great revelation of Christianity: "God is love" (1 Jn 4:16). This revelation brings hope to the human heart, which ever since original sin had doubted God's goodness and been reluctant or unable to trust him. Throughout all of pre-Calvary human history, God had been looking forward to the chance to make this definitive revelation of his love. He had been looking forward to offering himself as the saving sacrifice and thus winning back the trust of his beloved but estranged humanity. St. John highlights this long-standing desire by telling us exactly when the condemnation of Jesus occurred: on the Passover Preparation Day, at the sixth hour.

The sixth hour (about noon) of Preparation Day was the hour when the Passover lambs began to be sacrificed. The lamb was bound, as Christ had been bound. It was taken to the center of the Temple, as Jesus was taken to the hill of Calvary. It was put on the altar, as Christ was nailed to the cross. It was slaughtered quickly and all its blood was drained away, just as Christ was to pour out all his blood, even to the point of letting them pierce his heart with a spear.

The Passover lamb commemorated the lambs that had been killed by the Israelites at the time of the original Passover, when Moses led the Jews out of Egypt. To convince Pharaoh to let his people go, God had sent a plague on the land, killing every firstborn son throughout Egypt. But instead of killing the Israelite children, God instructed every family to sacrifice a lamb and mark their doors with the lamb's blood. Thus, God killed the Passover lambs in order to save the lives and the freedom of his Chosen People. That Jesus' condemnation to death occurred at the very hour commemorating that ancient, ritual sacrifice is no coincidence. It finally reveals in brilliant fullness the heart of God. God, incarnate in Jesus Christ, takes upon himself the punishment due to fallen humanity; he dies for us, laying down his life for us in order that through faith in him we may enter into the fullness of life. With his words, with his life, and finally with his death, Jesus offers us the richest lesson in the history of the world: God is love, and love is the way to God.

CHRIST THE FRIEND *One of the soldiers: I was there that day. I watched it all happen. I watched the crowd and the Jewish leaders turn from calm and law-abiding docility to frenzied, violent hatred, as does everyone who tries to build their lives on selfish lies. I watched Pilate squirm like a cornered animal, desperately trying to have his cake and eat it too, until he caved in, just like everyone who puts personal ambition above duty and truth. I watched my fellow soldiers take ribald pleasure in humiliating* *and victimizing a man just like them, and I saw how it left them empty and disgusted with themselves, as sensual indulgence always does. But above all, I watched Jesus. The whole universe caved in on this man and he stood firm, not just physically, which was miraculous enough, but in his mind and his spirit. I have seen criminals go insane after scourging. I have seen fearless prisoners beg and whimper for mercy under the shadow of the cross. I have seen pagan kings prostrate themselves like sycophants at the feet of our Roman governors. But I have never seen a man withstand such a raging storm of malice with such inner strength and outward composure. No, "withstand" is not the right word. It was as if he were commanding that storm. It broke upon him because he wanted it to.*

The more I watched, the more it mesmerized me. And then he caught my eye. They were taking him away to pick up his cross. He passed beside me. He turned to look at me. I froze. I had never spoken to or laid eyes on him before that morning, but when he saw me, somehow, I knew that he knew my name. And his gaze addressed me in my conscience, where no one goes but me. It said, "Don't you know me? Don't you recognize me yet? I am the one you have been looking for, the one you can trust."

CHRIST IN MY LIFE I know you want me to be a saint, Lord; you created me for that. The restlessness I feel in my heart comes from my implacable need to live in an ever-deeper communion with you. But for some reason I keep trying to relieve it with man-made tranquilizers. O Lord, you know I believe in you. Make your will and your example more and more attractive to me, and the world's false promises will simply fade away...

Open my eyes, Lord; I want to see everything you want to show me. By your wounds I am healed. What does that mean? It means that each one of your countless wounds whispers to my heart the words I most long to hear and have the most trouble believing: "No matter what you do, I still love you." Every wound testifies to your love for me. Open my eyes, Lord; open my heart...

You embraced suffering. You were able to see your Father's will in everything that happened. Help me to do the same. Help me to live on the level of purpose, recognizing your providence in every event and relationship. Help me to walk in the light of your love, focused on my life's mission, spreading your love through my fidelity and prayer. Kindle in my heart the unquenchable fire that burns in yours...

Questions for
SMALL-GROUP DISCUSSION

1. What struck you most in this passage? What did you notice that you hadn't noticed before?

2. All the people around Jesus during his Passion reveal the state of their souls—what they really want—by their reaction to him. But what about Jesus, what does he want?

3. Jesus says that the sin of those who handed him over to Pilate is greater than Pilate's sin. Why do you think that is so?

4. What do you think Jesus means when he says that Pilate only has authority because it was given him from on high?

Cf. Catechism of the Catholic Church, 2771-2774 on bearing witness to the truth; 595-598 on the trial of Jesus; 608-614 on Jesus as the Lamb of God and the definitive sacrifice; 2234-2246 on the authorities of civil society and our duties toward them

297. A Parting Gift (Jn 19:17-30)

"Mary has truly become the Mother of all believers. Men and women of every time and place have recourse to her motherly kindness and her virginal purity and grace, in all their needs and aspirations, their joys and sorrows, their moments of loneliness and their common endeavors." – Pope Benedict XVI, Deus Caritas Est, 42

JOHN 19:17-30

Then they took charge of Jesus, and carrying his own cross he went out of the city to the place of the skull or, as it was called in Hebrew, Golgotha, where they crucified him with two others, one on either side with Jesus in the middle. Pilate wrote out a notice and had it fixed to the cross; it ran: "Jesus the Nazarene, King of the Jews." This notice was read by many of the Jews, because the place where Jesus was crucified was not far from the city, and the writing was in Hebrew, Latin and Greek. So the Jewish chief priests said to Pilate, "You should not write 'King of the Jews,' but 'This man said: I am King of the Jews.'" Pilate answered, "What I have written, I have written." When the soldiers had finished crucifying Jesus they took his clothing and divided it into four shares, one for each soldier. His undergarment was seamless, woven in one piece from neck to hem; so they said to one another, "Instead of tearing it, let's throw dice to decide who is to have it." In this way the words of scripture were fulfilled: They shared out my clothing among them. They cast lots for my clothes. This is exactly what the soldiers did. Near the cross of Jesus stood his mother and his mother's sister, Mary the wife of Clopas, and Mary of Magdala. Seeing his mother and the disciple he loved standing near her, Jesus said to his mother, "Woman, this is your son." Then to the disciple he said,

"This is your mother." And from that moment the disciple made a place for her in his home. After this, Jesus knew that everything had now been completed, and to fulfil the scripture perfectly he said: "I am thirsty." A jar-full of vinegar stood there, so putting a sponge soaked in the vinegar on a hyssop stick they held it up to his mouth. After Jesus had taken the vinegar he said, "It is accomplished"; and bowing his head he gave up his spirit.

CHRIST THE LORD Even as Jesus' last drops of strength ebb away on the cross, he shows once again that he is the Lord of life and history. "To fulfill the scripture perfectly," St. John tells us, Jesus said, "I am thirsty," and a sponge full of vinegar (the Greek word can also refer to cheap wine) was lifted up to his lips on a hyssop stick.

The flexible, willow-like wood of the hyssop plant was expressly designated for ritual purification in the Old Covenant. God had commanded his people to spread the blood of the Passover lambs on the lintels of their houses using a hyssop stick (Ex 12:22). He had commanded Israel to purify lepers and houses where leprosy has sprung up with sacrificial blood sprinkled by a hyssop stick (cf. Lv 14, Nm 19). Moses had used a hyssop stick to distribute the sacrificial blood during the ceremony that established the Old Covenant at Sinai (Heb 9:19).

Is it only a coincidence that at the time when Jesus' blood is being poured out to purify the world itself from its sin, a hyssop stick is used to hold a sponge to his parched, cracked, and blood-stained lips? If it were, St. John would not have made a point of identifying the type of wood. It was no coincidence. It is yet another sign, given for our sake, to convince us that the Crucified One is exactly who he claimed to be: the Son of God, the Word of Life and Redeemer of the world who governs and orders the universe in all its grandeur and in the tiniest details. Jesus Christ is Lord; nothing escapes his rule.

CHRIST THE TEACHER Jesus' final words were, "It is accomplished." It sums up what St. John has repeated again and again throughout his Gospel: Jesus lived life focused on his mission. As his life draws to its close, he declares that that mission has been fulfilled. He had given himself completely—even to the point of sharing the very clothes on his back.

Jesus is the model for every Christian. He is also our Savior, Lord, brother, and companion, but he is still our model. And so, if he lived life focused on his mission, so should we. In this fallen world, the human family has forgotten who they are. They have come to think of themselves as autonomous mini-gods, instead of as God's stewards. In the original plan of Creation, the human family had been given the task of cultivating and protecting the Garden of Eden. We were created "to live in communion with God, in whom we find our happiness," as the Catechism reminds us (45). But that communion was never meant to be something passive. It is a relationship in which we glorify God through discovering his goodness in prayer and in action—as we do the work we were created to do, we become the saints we were created to be.

Jesus restores the possibility of that communion through reversing Adam's rebellious disobedience. He also points the way for us to partake of that restoration: by learning once again to see our lives as a mission. In this epoch of Redemption, the mission is not merely to cultivate and protect the garden, but to build the Kingdom of Christ, which we do the same way Jesus established it, seeking and fulfilling God's will: "I seek to do not my own will but the will of him who sent me" (Jn 5:30).

CHRIST THE FRIEND The beloved disciple mentioned in this passage is commonly considered to be the author himself, St. John. Only he records Jesus' final will and testament, in which Jesus places his mother, Mary, under John's care and John under hers. St. John was writing his Gospel later in life, when he was already an old man. For him to emphasize this detail means that it was significant not only for him personally, but for the whole Church. And indeed, the Church has always considered this gesture of Jesus to be much more than a practical arrangement.

Jesus is on the verge of completing his earthly mission. As he does so, the mission of the Church (represented in a special way by the "beloved disciple" because the Church is Jesus' beloved) is just beginning. By explicitly transferring the care of the Church (the beloved disciple) to Mary's motherly attention and entrusting Mary to John in a filial way, Jesus extends Mary's mission. She had been the Mother of Christ, the head of the Church, and now she is to be the Mother of the whole body, the members of the Church. Christ had only one thing left to give as he breathed his last breath—his own Mother, and he didn't grudge us even that. Each follower of Christ, to enter fully into God's family and to have Christ as a true brother, has to follow John's example: "And from that moment the disciple made a place for her in his home."

Mary: I didn't choose to become Jesus' mother; that was God's choice. How could I have ever chosen for myself such an exalted role when I always knew that I was only a blade of grass in the foothills beneath the mountain of God? Only God in his wisdom and goodness can give one of his creatures such a sublime mission. And though I didn't choose it, how much joy it gave me! Even the sorrow of his pain on Calvary filled me with a certain spiritual joy because it allowed me to suffer too; it showed him in a new way that I would never leave him or doubt him. And I didn't choose to become your Mother either; that, too, was his choice. How could I have presumed to take upon myself such an exalted task, to be mother to a child born of water and the Holy Spirit? Only God in his goodness could give me such a joyful and worthy mission. And now I watch over you just as I watched over him; I accompany you just as I accompanied him; I love you just as I loved him. He made me Queen of Heaven so that I could be your refuge and solace.

CHRIST IN MY LIFE Nothing escapes your rule. Down to the tiny detail of a hyssop stick on Calvary, you govern every speck of the cosmos and every wrinkle of human history. You are the Lord. You are my Lord. Increase my faith, Lord. I want to rejoice in the peace of knowing you more deeply and trusting you more unconditionally...

For so many people, life is only a mystery, Lord. They don't know that it is a mission. They seek to refresh their souls at empty wells. Teach them about your Kingdom! Call out to them so that they stop spiraling further down into sterile self-absorption! In you, Lord, life takes on the dimension of adventure that we all know it should take on. Ring out your message, Lord, louder and clearer...

Mary, how do you guide me? I don't see your face or hear your voice. But I know you are faithful to God's will, and it is his will for you to teach and nourish me as my mother in grace. How do you do it? You instruct me by your example: you stood at the foot of the cross, firm and faithful because your love was true and total. Teach me how to embrace fully the will of God, even when it means embracing the cross...

Questions for
SMALL-GROUP DISCUSSION

1. What struck you most in this passage? What did you notice that you hadn't noticed before?

2. Why do you think these three women were at the foot of Christ's cross while the other disciples kept their distance? Why do you think St. John was the only one with them?

3. Why was St. John so impressed by the exact fulfillment of the prophecy from Psalm 22:18, "They divide my garments among them and cast lots for my clothing"?

4. What do you think the expression on Jesus' face was as he uttered his last statement, "It is accomplished"? Was he grimacing, relieved, smiling, or something else?

Cf. Catechism of the Catholic Church, 599-605 on Christ's redemptive death in God's plan of salvation; 606-618 on Christ's self-offering to the Father for our sins and our participation in it; 487-507 on Mary's role in God's plan of salvation; 963-972 on Mary as Mother of the Church

298. A BITTER END AND A SWEET BEGINNING (JN 19:31-42)

"The Lord is the goal of human history, the focal point of the longings of history and of civilization, the center of the human race, the joy of every heart and the answer to all its yearnings." – Gaudium et Spes, 48

JOHN 19:31-42

It was Preparation Day, and to prevent the bodies remaining on the cross during the sabbath–since that sabbath was a day of special solemnity–the Jews asked Pilate to have the legs broken and the bodies taken away. Consequently the soldiers came and broke the legs of the first man who had been crucified with him and then of the other. When they came to Jesus, they found he was already dead, and so instead of breaking his legs one of the soldiers pierced his side with a lance; and immediately there came out blood and water. This is the evidence of one who saw it–trustworthy evidence, and he knows he speaks the truth–and he gives it so that you may believe as well. Because all this happened to fulfil the words of scripture: Not one bone of his will be broken; and again, in another place scripture says: They will look on the one whom they have pierced. After this, Joseph of Arimathaea, who was a disciple of Jesus–though a secret one because he was afraid of the Jews–asked Pilate to let him remove the body of Jesus. Pilate gave permission, so they came and took it away. Nicodemus came as well–the same one who had first come to Jesus at night-time–and he brought a mixture of myrrh and aloes, weighing about a hundred pounds. They took the body of Jesus and wrapped it with the spices in linen cloths, following the Jewish burial custom. At the place where he had been crucified there was a garden, and in this garden a new tomb in which no one had yet been buried. Since it was the Jewish Day of Preparation and the tomb was near at hand, they laid Jesus there.

CHRIST THE LORD Once again St. John mentions that the details surrounding his death (no breaking of his bones, being pierced...) coincided with Scriptural prophecies. He notes that the day Christ died was Preparation Day. This was the day on which the Jews sacrificed their Passover lambs and prepared to begin the eight-day festival of Passover, commemorating their miraculous liberation from slavery in Egypt.

It is possible to misunderstand the meaning of these coincidences. Jesus, the Lamb of God, as St. John the Baptist had called him back in Chapter 1 of this Gospel, didn't die on Preparation Day in order to associate himself with the past. Rather, the ancient events of the Passover had occurred and been commemorated in light of Christ's future sacrifice on Calvary. From God's perspective, Christ's self-immolation on the cross, the everlasting reversal of Adam's disobedience that brings salvation to the human race, was the fulcrum, the center—the very heart of human history. Everything that had come before was, in God's providence, leading up to it. All that has come after and is still to come flows from it. Jesus is not following a script; Jesus is the script that all history follows.

CHRIST THE TEACHER St. John gives special emphasis to the blood and water that flowed out of Jesus' side when they pierced him with the lance to make sure he was dead. Why? He sees it as the fulfillment of the prophesy of Zechariah 12:10, "They will look on the one whom they have pierced," but considering that the details of his death fulfilled many other prophecies as well, that hardly merits the climactic testimony John gives us: "This is the evidence of the one who saw it... so that you may believe as well." Why is the flow of blood and water so important to John?

A dead body doesn't bleed. And yet, when they pierced Jesus' breast, blood and water flowed out. The scientists tell us that this may be explained by Jesus having died, literally, of a broken heart, instead of suffocation or loss of blood, as normally happened with crucifixion victims. If Jesus had died of suffocation, he most likely would not have had sufficient breath to utter the loud cry or prayer that preceded his death, nor the final words that John records. If he had died of blood loss, there most likely would not have been enough blood left inside the chambers of his heart to actually flow out when his heart was pierced with the lance. If Jesus' heart had simply broken to cause death, however, the blood in those chambers would have been mixed, as oil and water is mixed, with the watery fluid of the chest cavity around the heart, the pericardium. When the soldier pierced his side with the lance, he would have punctured the pericardium (a wider target than the heart itself), releasing the mixed liquid. This seems to go along with the timing of Jesus breathing his last breath, which happened right after he said, "It is accomplished," as if he willingly ended things at that moment, letting his divine love for sinful man burst his human heart. Maybe John knew these medical details and maybe he didn't.

The more obvious reason behind John's spotlighting the water and blood comes from the roles those two elements would take on in the life of the Church. The water of baptism was to become the gateway into sharing in Christ's death—dying to the ways of sin—and the blood of the Eucharist was to become the door to sharing in Christ's own life and thus becoming "children of God" (Jn 1:12). But that could only happen for those who believed in the

270

Lord, the Word of God made flesh for our salvation, and that same blood and water flowing from Christ's heart was also an invitation to faith. For St. John, they showed without any shadow of doubt that the Lord was true man, just as the new life in the Spirit that was to come through those sacraments showed without any doubt that the Lord was true God. In Christ's final gesture from the cross, the whole Gospel blazes forth and cries out to be believed.

CHRIST THE FRIEND *Joseph of Arimethea: I gave him my tomb – what irony! He was the one who had given me life and hope! He was the one who had loved me and let me taste the joy I had longed for all my life, and all I could do for him was supply a grave.*

That day something broke inside of me. Up until then, I had been so fearful of associating with him publicly. I was always watching my back, wondering what the other members of the Sanhedrin were saying. I was so cautious and tentative in coming to his defense! When he died – when we killed him, rather – all the convoluted excuses I had made for myself to justify that posturing and measuring and calculating just disintegrated. I wept. My entire soul collapsed. It was as if my old self died when I saw him die.

And then, in the midst of that collapse of my old self, I suddenly felt a change. I was freed. Finally I was free from worrying about what the others said behind my back and how they might crimp my position and reputation. I didn't know what to do at first, there was such calm in my heart. I went and searched for Nicodemus. We looked at each other and we didn't need to say a word – I knew that the exact same thing had happened to him. And we went to Pilate without even a trace of fear. We took the Lord and buried him before sundown. There was such a sadness of loss in our hearts, but at the same time such a jubilation to finally be his true and undivided disciples, to finally bear witness to our love for him without hesitation. Why did we wait so long to trust him? We could have done so much more!

CHRIST IN MY LIFE You are the focal point of history, but are you the focal point of my life? I want to believe in you with a faith that gets brighter and stronger every day. I want to trust in you with total abandonment, like diving into the vast ocean. I want to love you with the simplicity and purity and humility of a young soldier in his first battle, of a bride on her wedding day, of a child in its mother's arms...

Thank you for the sacraments, Lord. They prove every day that your life and your death were for me. How could you have been thinking of me then? But I know you were. Your Church teaches that you were. You had me in mind. You eagerly laid down your life so that you could come and cleanse my soul in baptism and nourish it with the Eucharist. Teach me, Lord, to love my neighbor as you have loved me...

When my life comes to an end, what will my regrets be? That I didn't make enough money? That I didn't win enough awards? That I didn't pray enough? That I didn't follow my conscience more? That I didn't strive with all my heart, soul, mind, and strength to know, love, and imitate you? Give me wisdom, Lord. I want no more regrets. Life is too short. I want to invest all that I am in fulfilling your will...

Questions for
SMALL-GROUP DISCUSSION

1. What struck you most in this passage? What did you notice that you hadn't noticed before?

2. What can we do to find in our community those "secret disciples" of Christ who, like Joseph and Nicodemus, may need a boost in order to take that next step of faith to follow Christ more closely?

3. Why do you think St. John didn't spend more time at this point of his Gospel criticizing those who condemned, tortured, and murdered Jesus? What lesson does his example of restraint have for us?

4. Jesus saved the world through self-sacrifice. What role should self-sacrifice have in our Christian lives? What should self-sacrifice look like in our life-situations?

Cf. Catechism of the Catholic Church, 1734, 2015, and 2340 on the role of self-sacrifice (ascesis) in the spiritual life; 1114-1126 on the sacraments in general and their relationship to Christ, the Church, and faith; 1213, 1322-1323 on the sacraments of baptism and the Eucharist in general; 624-628 on the significance of Christ's burial

"Come then, all you nations of men defiled by sin, receive the forgiveness of sin. For it is I who am your forgiveness, the pasch of your salvation, the lamb slain for you; it is I who am your ransom, your life, your resurrection, your light, your salvation, your king. I am bringing you to the heights of heaven, I will show you the Father who is from all eternity, I will raise you up with my right hand."

-ST. MELITO OF SARDIS

299. SON RISE (JN 20:1-10)

"So on Sunday we all come together. This is the first day, on which God transformed darkness and matter and made the world; the day on which Jesus Christ our Savior rose from the dead." – St. Justin Martyr

JOHN 20:1-10
It was very early on the first day of the week and still dark, when Mary of Magdala came to the tomb. She saw that the stone had been moved away from the tomb and came running to Simon Peter and the other disciple, the one Jesus loved. "They have taken the Lord out of the tomb" she said "and we don't know where they have put him." So Peter set out with the other disciple to go to the tomb. They ran together, but the other disciple, running faster than Peter, reached the tomb first; he bent down and saw the linen cloths lying on the ground, but did not go in. Simon Peter who was following now came up, went right into the tomb, saw the linen cloths on the ground, and also the cloth that had been over his head; this was not with the linen cloths but rolled up in a place by itself. Then the other disciple who had reached the tomb first also went in; he saw and he believed. Till this moment they had failed to understand the teaching of scripture, that he must rise from the dead. The disciples then went home again.

CHRIST THE LORD Easter Sunday, when the Liturgy presents this passage to the Church, brings Holy Week to its glorious climax. Indeed, this week, which ranks highest among the periods of the liturgical year, is made "holy" precisely by the Lord's Resurrection. Imagine how a Good Friday without Easter Sunday would alter the Christian message: Jesus would be no more than another Socrates. His teaching would perhaps be remembered, but his outlandish claims to be the Messiah, the Son of God, and the Light of the World would be invalidated. The apostles would have remained passive and frightened, and the Church would never have come into existence. The Eucharist would be, at best, a mere myth, an empty ritual. The martyrs, virgins, and other saints who have flooded these last twenty centuries with such revolutionary holiness would have remained mere citizens of the earth...

Jesus Christ was Lord of heaven. By his Resurrection, he has conquered this fallen world's reigning powers of death. Now he is Lord of heaven and earth; the Kingdom of God is close at hand—among us, in fact, through the Church, which is the Risen Lord's body. There is only one Lord, Jesus Christ, crucified for our sins, risen for our redemption, and present through his Church. If now we embrace him there, he will make sure that we rise to embrace him forever in heaven.

CHRIST THE TEACHER St. John's attention to detail is meaningful. He records how he himself ran to the empty tomb faster than St. Peter, but waited for Peter to go in first. His reward: "he saw and believed"—faith. What could these minutiae have to teach us? Peter was the leader of the Twelve Apostles. Christ had dubbed him the rock upon which he would build his Church. At the Last Supper, he had commanded him to strengthen his brethren in the Faith. Soon after his Resurrection, he specially commissioned him to feed and tend his sheep. St. John, the "beloved disciple," follows Peter into the empty tomb instead of rushing in ahead of him, and he receives the gift of faith; he comes to believe in the risen Lord.

The Church is not a conglomerate of individual believers all living out their own inspirations from the Holy Spirit. The Church is the unified Body of Christ and the organized people of God. It is the New Israel, and like the old Israel, it has a structure, and God has chosen to work through that structure. When we responsibly live out our membership in the Body of Christ, we stay in step with the Church, under the guidance of Peter's successor, the pope. We neither lag behind nor run too far ahead, and in that way Christ pours out upon us a strong and vibrant faith, just as he did for his beloved disciple, John.

CHRIST THE FRIEND He rose for us. He came to earth for us, he suffered for us, and he rose for us. Nothing in Christ was for himself. Nothing. He is all love, all self-giving, all obedience to the Father's will for the sake of our salvation. He rose so that we might rise with him. In his Resurrection, we see what he is preparing for us. How eagerly he looks forward to that day when he will "wipe away every tear" (Rv 7:17) from our eyes and welcome us into the fullness of life that is his eternal kingdom! The more faithful we are to him now, the more we will share in his glory when he raises us from the dead. Good friends fill our lives on earth with joy and comfort; only Christ can offer a joy that will keep growing forever.

Jesus: I know it's hard for you to feel the power and the joy of my Resurrection. You still need to grow in your faith and humility to be able to feel it. But you don't need to feel it in order to believe in me. Think of my Resurrection often. The more you turn the eyes of your heart toward it, the more its light will illumine and warm your heart, until your whole life is gradually bathed in its power and joy. And I have given you a reminder – the sunrise. Each day, the sun comes up and brings light to the world, just as I rose from the darkness of death in order to conquer it forever with the light of my life.

CHRIST IN MY LIFE I believe that you have risen from the dead, Lord, though I still tend to live as if this life were all there is – but you know that in my heart I am seeking your will and your Kingdom. Help me to seek them as I ought. Why do I keep thinking that the broken shards of happiness that sparkle in this fallen world can have any meaning – for me or anyone – apart from a living friendship with you?...

Have mercy on your Church, Lord. In this day and age, it is so hard to trust in authority, even in your divinely established authority. But I want to. Teach me to discern your presence and your will in the words and indications of the pope, as all the saints have done. Teach me to see you in him, and to love you by serving the Church through obeying him. May I, too, become a saint...

I know that you lived your life for my sake, for my salvation, and for my instruction – and to comfort me, so that I never have to suffer alone. I want to live my life for your sake, building up your Kingdom, obeying your will, making you known and loved by everyone around me. What else would be a worthy response to all that you have done for me? With the love of your heart, inflame my heart...

Questions for
SMALL-GROUP DISCUSSION

1. What struck you most in this passage? What did you notice that you hadn't noticed before?

2. What might the emotional and intellectual reaction of the apostles and other disciples have been as they gradually began to understand that Jesus had risen from the dead?

3. Why would Christ have instituted a Church to mediate his saving grace, instead of just inspiring individuals directly?

4. If a non-believing acquaintance sincerely wanted to know why you believe that Jesus rose from the dead, what would you tell them?

Cf. Catechism of the Catholic Church, 880-887 on the role of the pope and bishops in the life of the Church; 651-655 on the meaning of Christ's Resurrection

300. TAKING THE JESUS RISK (JN 20:11-18)

"Our Lord was trodden underfoot by death, and in turn trod upon death as upon a road." – St. Ephraem

JOHN 20:11-18

Meanwhile Mary stayed outside near the tomb, weeping. Then, still weeping, she stooped to look inside, and saw two angels in white sitting where the body of Jesus had been, one at the head, the other at the feet. They said, "Woman, why are you weeping?" "They have taken my Lord away," she replied, "and I don't know where they have put him." As she said this she turned round and saw Jesus standing there, though she did not recognise him. Jesus said, "Woman, why are you weeping? Who are you looking for?" Supposing him to be the gardener, she said, "Sir, if you have taken him away, tell me where you have put him, and I will go and remove him." Jesus said, "Mary!" She knew him then and said to him in Hebrew, "Rabbuni!" – which means Master. Jesus said to her, "Do not cling to me, because I have not yet ascended to the Father. But go and find the brothers, and tell them: I am ascending to my Father and your Father, to my God and your God." So Mary of Magdala went and told the disciples that she had seen the Lord and that he had said these things to her.

CHRIST THE LORD The first time Jesus speaks in the Gospel of John, he asks Peter and John a question: "What do you want?" In the Greek, his question to Mary Magdalene on the morning of his Resurrection (here translated "Who are you looking for?") uses the same verb and the same pronoun. Only the case of the pronoun is different, turning the "what" of Chapter 1 into the "who" of Chapter 20. The verb has multiple shades of meaning, but most translations use "look for" or "seek" in both instances. The distinction between "want" and "seek" is subtle; you would never seek something that you don't want, and if you really do want something, you will naturally seek it out.

And so Jesus' question to Mary Magdalene, though he asks it after his Resurrection, brings us full circle, back to the beginning of the story. He asked the same question of his first followers as he did of Mary after the Resurrection: "What do you want? Who are you looking for?" It shows that Jesus always cares about the same thing—the state of our hearts. In the depth of our souls we decide the direction of our lives by deciding what we are going to look for. And this is what matters to Jesus. He is the Lord, the King, but he doesn't rule governments or boards of trustees—he rules hearts (and those in turn rule governments and boards of trustees). He asks us each day, in the inner sanctuary of our consciences, what we are looking for, what we desire, and what we want. If we truly want the fullness of life that he came to bring us, he will be able to give it to us because we will be willing to take the risk of leaving behind the comfort of self-centeredness to launch out on the adventure of self-giving.

On the first Easter morning, Mary Magdalene might have thought that the risk she had taken wasn't panning out, but then the Lord appeared and ended her search. Trusting in Jesus Christ the Lord is a risk that always pans out.

CHRIST THE TEACHER Christ rose so that we, too, may someday rise. He conquered death so that we could look forward to everlasting life in the intense and indescribable excitement of heavenly fulfillment. In his post-Resurrection appearances, he gives us clues about what that fullness of life will be like. One thing we notice right away is that his resurrected body, though a real body (St. John will tell us later that the apostles can see and touch the wounds in his hands and side), has been somehow transformed. Mary Magdalene doesn't recognize him at first. He seems to appear and disappear at will and even pass through walls and doors.

Theologians call the resurrected body a "glorified body." A popular but mistaken idea among many Christians is that life in heaven is purely spiritual.

After the last judgment, however, when we all have been raised ("Those who did good will rise again to life; and those who did evil, to condemnation"—Jn 5:29), those who are welcomed into heaven will receive the fullness of life, which, for human beings, includes bodily existence. Just as Jesus and Mary are right now, at this very moment, physically present in heaven, so we will enjoy everlasting life not only with our souls but with glorified bodies. Much theological speculation has gone into describing the characteristics of our glorified state, but suffice it to say that it will be exempt from the physical sufferings and limitations of life on earth and will far surpass—very far—the physical delights of life on earth. It is something we should look forward to, something we should hope for, because it is something God wishes to give us.

CHRIST THE FRIEND Before Mary Magdalene was searching for Jesus, he was already watching over her. He lets her search, sorrowing, only so that the joy of their reunion will be that much more intense. It seems, in fact, that he wants to give her a chance to believe in the Resurrection before experiencing it. And so, the angels announce to her the Good News. But neither the daunting presence of the angels nor their remarkable announcement satisfied Mary. For her, nothing but the Lord himself, his very presence, would do. She turns away from them because they can't give her that presence. But she perseveres in her search—asking the gardener for what the angels couldn't give. This perseverance moves the heart of Christ, and the first recorded appearance of the resurrected Lord ensues.

Jesus came to earth in search of our love. So if we truly love him, and if we show it by seeking him in spite of obstacles and failures, how can he resist rewarding our desire? To experience the revolution of Christ in our lives, it is enough to want to do so—and to keep on wanting to.

Jesus: My child, while you are searching for me, I am already at your side. I never abandon you. Where can you hide from my love? Where can you flee from my presence? If you rise up on the wings of the dawn and set down across the farthest sea, my hand will still be guiding you, my strong arms will still be holding you fast. All that your heart seeks you will find in me. But you have to keep looking, because you're not ready to receive everything right away. If only you knew how much I long to fill every moment of your life with the light and warmth of my divine heart! I am always knocking at the door of your heart—my knocks give rise to your weeping and searching, just as they did with my faithful friend Mary Magdalene…

CHRIST IN MY LIFE What am I looking for? What do I want? You know, Lord. I want to follow you. I believe in you. My faith is puny and impure, but it's there. A myriad of other wants and desires swarm around my heart, and sometimes I let them get the upper hand, but even so, Lord, without you in my life, what direction, what hope could I possibly have? Keep me faithful to your will; never let me be separated from you...

Lord, increase my hope! You have revealed to me the truth about my final destiny. You have gone to prepare me a place in heaven. You want me to spend eternity in your company and in the company of all the saints. There the fullness of life that I have always longed for and have begun to taste here on earth will surpass my greatest longings. Lord, make these truths come to life for me...

Why do you let me weep and search? Why don't you show yourself to me always? Your ways are beyond me, Lord. But I know that they are wise. You are Wisdom and Goodness and Power and Love. It is enough for me to know you, to believe in you. That is already a gift far beyond what I deserve! O Lord, open my eyes to see your hand at work in all things, and strengthen my will to follow you more closely...

Questions for
SMALL-GROUP DISCUSSION

1. What struck you most in this passage? What did you notice that you hadn't noticed before?

2. When Jesus let Mary experience his presence, he didn't let her remain there long. Instead, he gave her a mission to share the good news with others. Why do you think Jesus did that (he could have gone himself to make the announcement), and how does this example apply to our lives?

3. Both the angels and Jesus ask Mary why she is weeping. Don't you think they should have known the reason? Why do you think they asked her that question?

4. Mary recognizes Jesus as soon as he says her name. Why do you think she did so at that point? What do you think this exchange teaches us about Christian prayer?

Cf. Catechism of the Catholic Church, 1718-1729 on our search for happiness; 631-658 on the nature and meaning of the Resurrection

301. THE CHURCH GETS GOING (JN 20:19-31)

"Christ who is God, supreme over all, has arranged to wash man clean of sin and to make our old nature new." – St. Hippolytus

JOHN 20:19-31

In the evening of that same day, the first day of the week, the doors were closed in the room where the disciples were, for fear of the Jews. Jesus came and stood among them. He said to them, "Peace be with you," and showed them his hands and his side. The disciples were filled with joy when they saw the Lord, and he said to them again, "Peace be with you. As the Father sent me, so am I sending you." After saying this he breathed on them and said: "Receive the Holy Spirit. For those whose sins you forgive, they are forgiven; for those whose sins you retain, they are retained." Thomas, called the Twin, who was one of the Twelve, was not with them when Jesus came. When the disciples said, "We have seen the Lord," he answered, "Unless I see the holes that the nails made in his hands and can put my finger into the holes they made, and unless I can put my hand into his side, I refuse to believe." Eight days later the disciples were in the house again and Thomas was with them. The doors were closed, but Jesus came in and stood among them. "Peace be with you," he said. Then he spoke to Thomas, "Put your finger here; look, here are my hands. Give me your hand; put it into my side. Doubt no longer but believe." Thomas replied, "My Lord and my God!" Jesus said to him: "You believe because you can see me. Happy are those who have not seen and yet believe." There were many other signs that Jesus worked and the disciples saw, but they are not recorded in this book. These are recorded so that you may believe that Jesus is the Christ, the Son of God, and that believing this you may have life through his name.

CHRIST THE LORD We call St. Thomas the Apostle "doubting Thomas"; we may be off the mark in doing so. Jesus did not ask the other apostles to believe in his resurrection without showing them the wounds in his hands and sides. Thomas was merely demanding his rights as an apostle when he demanded the same privilege. And none of the others responded to the risen Christ with a faith as complete and firm as Thomas': "My Lord and my God!" Thomas knew what this meant. He knew that if Christ had come back from the dead, then everything he said about himself, everything he claimed to be, was true. Jesus blessed him for his faith.

Our faith, and the faith of all Christians throughout the centuries, is built upon the solid foundation of the apostles' testimony to the risen Christ, a testimony validated by twenty uninterrupted centuries of Church life, of saints and martyrs, of sacraments, Liturgy, and a college of bishops that links us directly, even physically, to that little group of frightened apostles who encountered the Risen One. Blessed indeed are we who have believed: although we have not seen Christ in the flesh, we have seen, experienced, and benefited from the undeniable work of his Spirit. In times of darkness and doubt, we know where to look to recover the light.

At the beginning of creation, "the earth was a formless wasteland, and darkness covered the abyss, while a mighty wind swept over the waters" (Gn 1:2). When God created man and woman, he "formed man out of the clay of the ground and blew into his nostrils the breath of life, and so man became a living being." The word for "wind" in Hebrew (and in Greek, the language of the New Testament) is the same as the word for "breath" and "Spirit." Thus, when St. John points out the detail of Jesus breathing on the disciples as he gives them the gifts of the Holy Spirit and the commission to carry on his work of evangelization, he is calling to mind the "wind" and the "breathing" of the first creation. The Fathers of the Church understood this first post-Resurrection appearance to the apostles as the start of a new creation. Jesus has won the forgiveness of sin, which marred the first creation, and dubs his apostles messengers and distributors of this forgiveness. As they spread it throughout the world and build up the Church, all mankind is to be renewed, elevated to a more sublime intimacy with God. As St. Paul put it, "So whoever is in Christ is a new creation: the old things have passed away; behold, new things have come" (2 Cor 5:17).

CHRIST THE TEACHER Jesus Christ is the only Savior, the only Mediator between sinful, fallen mankind and the one God who can give them eternal life. He achieved his mediation by his loving obedience to God's will even through humiliation, torture, and death on a cross. This obedience reversed the disobedience of Adam, and reestablished communion between God and men; it opened once again the flow of God's grace. In his first appearance to the confused group of apostles on the first Easter, he teaches us how he wants that flow of grace to irrigate the human family: through the ministry of the Church guided by the Twelve Apostles. He bequeathed his peace to them; he sent them on a mission just as his Father had sent him; he breathed his Spirit into them; he transferred to them his divine power of absolving from sin, the very thing that obstructs our communion with God. Do we wish to find Easter joy, won for us at such a terrible price? We need only dip into the flowing fountain of God's grace, which is his one, holy, Catholic, and apostolic Church.

At the beginning of his Gospel, St. Matthew told us why Jesus came among us: "He will save his people from their sins" (Mt 1:21). In this first meeting with his apostles after his atoning sacrifice on the cross, Christ eagerly begins the fulfillment of that mission. His first post-Resurrection deed is to "breathe" on the Twelve, inaugurating as it were a new creation (God had "breathed" into

Adam's nostrils to give him life at the first creation), one that will rise up from the first creation that had been so disfigured by sin. And with that breath, he delegates to them his power to wipe sins away, to administer the forgiveness from sin that he won through his self-oblation on Calvary. Ever since, that ministry has been carried out through the sacrament of Confession. How eager Christ was to grant this surpassing grace to his Church! How close it must be to his heart if it was one of the first things he did after coming back from the dead! If he cares about it that much, then so should we.

Often we look for extraordinary and emotional encounters with the Holy Spirit. Sometimes we think that unless we experience a special feeling or perceive a supernatural phenomenon, the Holy Spirit is not at work. Yet, Jesus shows us that the primary mode of operation followed by the Holy Spirit is the same one he followed in his Incarnation: he turns normal realities into vehicles of grace. The Holy Spirit acts in our lives powerfully through the sacraments of the Church, through the preaching and teaching of the Church's ministers, and through our own prayer and reflection on the Scriptures. If we are ready to find the Holy Spirit in these ordinary channels that Christ has established, he will readily fill our lives with the extraordinary fruits of his action.

CHRIST THE FRIEND St. John tells us why he wrote his Gospel: he wants us to believe in Jesus Christ, so that we may "have life through his name." Life. We cherish life, and yet we sense that there is more to it than the limited version we experience. Our hearts seem unsatisfied even by all that life offers us. We always want more. God made us like that. He made us thirsty for a happiness that only he can give in order to make sure that we would seek him. Our life is a quest for Jesus Christ, a quest of which he is the author, the companion, and the end. He wants to give us what we most want; he asks only that we believe in him, that we trust and follow him.

Thomas: When Jesus turned to me and told me to touch his wounds, his eyes were merry. I had been stunned when he appeared, but then I felt ashamed when he made reference to my earlier comments. But his eyes were so bright, so inviting, that I stepped forward. He held out his hands, those same hands that had cured so many sick and crippled people, those strong, carpenter's hands that had multiplied the loaves and commanded the sea. He held them out to me. They were pierced through, but he was smiling. I looked at them. They were wounded hands; I held them, and I felt the wounds. Then he took my left hand and brought it to his side. He was really there. The Lord had returned – the same Lord. It was no ghost, no vision. It was the Lord, the Teacher. And I looked back into his eyes, and it was as if I had seen him for the first time. That's when I knew. I knew in an instant that it was true, that he was not simply a rabbi, a prophet, or a king. I knew that he was Yahweh himself. Yahweh himself had come to visit his people, to save them. I fell on my knees. I cried with joy. Emmanuel! Really, truly... The New Covenant had finally come.

CHRIST IN MY LIFE Why don't I trust you more? If you were to let me see the wounds in your hands and feet and sides, would that be any more evidence than you have already given me of your greatness, your goodness, your presence, and the transforming power of your love? Lord Jesus, I want you to be in the center of my life. You are God, and you know my name, and you call to me. I want to hear you, Lord...

How passionately I should love your Church! It is your chosen instrument for reaching out and touching each one of your beloved brothers and sisters everywhere in the world. How would I have found you if it were not for your Church? Bless your Church, Lord. Make it grow, make it flourish; fill it with saints. Teach me to be a joyful, faithful child of the Church. To build it up right here, right now...

I have tasted the life you have in store for me. I know the difference you have made in my life. I know that I need your grace, and I know where to find it and how to cooperate with it: by seeking out and fulfilling your will. But what about all the people in the world who don't know what a difference you can make, who don't know where to find the grace they thirst for? Make me a channel of your peace...

Questions for
SMALL-GROUP DISCUSSION

1. What struck you most in this passage? What did you notice that you hadn't noticed before?

2. Why do you think Christ waited until eight days after Easter Sunday to appear to Thomas?

3. St. John puts Christ's conferral of peace on the apostles in the same sentence as "and he showed them his hands and his side." Do you see any connection between these two realities?

4. How would your faith change if Christ appeared to you physically, as he appeared to the apostles? What are the most meaningful signs God has already given to you personally that have made the most difference in your faith? How have you responded to those signs?

Cf. Catechism of the Catholic Church, 1076, 1086-1087 on the sacraments and the Church as the channels of God's saving grace; 731-741 on the meaning of Pentecost and the Holy Spirit's role in the Church; 694-701 on the Holy Spirit's individual action in each soul; 1849-1851 on the definition of sin; 1440-1449 on the sacrament of Penance and Reconciliation

THE GOSPEL OF JOHN
Chapter 21

"Here, in Krakow, the beloved city of my predecessor John Paul II, no one is astonished by the words 'to build with Peter and on Peter.' For this reason I say to you: Do not be afraid to build your life on the Church and with the Church. You are all proud of the love you have for Peter and for the Church entrusted to him. Do not be fooled by those who want to play Christ against the Church. There is one foundation on which it is worthwhile to build a house. This foundation is Christ. There is only one rock on which it is worthwhile to place everything. This rock is the one to whom Christ said: 'You are Peter, and on this rock I will build my Church' (Mt 16:18)... You know well the Rock of our times. Accordingly, do not forget: Neither that Peter who is watching our gathering from the window of God the Father, nor this Peter who is now standing in front of you, nor any successive Peter will ever be opposed to you or the building of a lasting house on the rock. Indeed, he will offer his heart and his hands to help you construct a life on Christ and with Christ."

– POPE BENEDICT XVI

302. Fishing for Humility (Jn 21:1-14)

"Consider, children, a Christian's treasure is not on earth, it is in heaven. Well then, our thoughts should turn to where our treasure is." – St. John Vianney

JOHN 21:1-14
Later on, Jesus showed himself again to the disciples. It was by the Sea of Tiberias, and it happened like this: Simon Peter, Thomas called the Twin, Nathanael from Cana in Galilee, the sons of Zebedee and two more of his disciples were together. Simon Peter said, "I'm going fishing." They replied, "We'll come with you." They went out and got into the boat but caught nothing that night. It was light by now and there stood Jesus on the shore, though the disciples did not realise that it was Jesus. Jesus called out, "Have you caught anything, friends?" And when they answered, "No," he said, "Throw the net out to starboard and you'll find something." So they

dropped the net, and there were so many fish that they could not haul it in. The disciple Jesus loved said to Peter, "It is the Lord." At these words "It is the Lord," Simon Peter, who had practically nothing on, wrapped his cloak round him and jumped into the water. The other disciples came on in the boat, towing the net and the fish; they were only about a hundred yards from land. As soon as they came ashore they saw that there was some bread there, and a charcoal fire with fish cooking on it. Jesus said, "Bring some of the fish you have just caught." Simon Peter went aboard and dragged the net to the shore, full of big fish, one hundred and fifty-three of them; and in spite of there being so many the net was not broken. Jesus said to them, "Come and have breakfast." None of the disciples was bold enough to ask, "Who are you?"; they knew quite well it was the Lord. Jesus then stepped forward, took the bread and gave it to them, and the same with the fish. This was the third time that Jesus showed himself to the disciples after rising from the dead.

CHRIST THE LORD Christ's authority is absolute. He is God's anointed, and he has risen from the dead: his Kingdom will stand forever. And yet, he shares that authority with others; he extends his Kingdom through the free collaboration of his followers. First among them is Peter. During his public ministry, the Lord repeatedly pointed out that Peter would have a unique role among the apostles and in Christ's Kingdom (e.g., Mt 16). This mysterious encounter on the shores of Lake Tiberias was a replay of Christ's original call to Peter three years earlier, when he also worked a miraculous catch of fish. The renewed encounter confirms Peter (and his successors, as the Church teaches us) as leader of this little band of Christians—a little band that would, through God's grace, rock the world. It was Peter whom Jesus was about to command to "feed his sheep," and it is through union with Peter and his successors, the popes, that we will be able to receive food for our own souls, as well as dish it out to others.

Peter dived into the water, even though the boats were close to shore and full of fish. The Lord has come looking for him again, and this time Peter has no objections, no comments of his own, no hesitations, and no fears. Jesus has finally won Peter's heart. Once so self-reliant and independent, so authoritative and in control, now Peter climbs onto the shore wet and bedraggled, overjoyed to kneel at Jesus' feet and embrace his Lord. Jesus had been patient with Peter, never giving up on him, and now his patience was paying off. Christ's love was now Peter's only nourishment, and so now he was ready to begin his career of fishing for men. His apprenticeship was over; the Lord was about to send him out.

CHRIST THE TEACHER Christ only asks for one thing from us: our trust. If we trust him, as the apostles did by throwing their nets over the starboard side, he will fill our nets. If we trust him, we will have everything we need to fulfill our life's mission, even a mission as grand as Peter's. During Christ's Passion, Peter had wavered in his trust. Now Jesus gives him a chance to renew it. And Peter is ready to trust more because has experienced his own weakness and so has grown in humility.

At the beginning of Peter's discipleship, he resisted the Lord's entreaty to throw out his net after a fishless night. Now, after the Resurrection, Peter voices no objection to the stranger's suggestion, even though Peter was an expert fisherman and the hour for catching fish had passed. But he is docile. He has grown in humility. Humility is the hardest but most necessary lesson that every Christian apostle has to learn. Many times, we wonder why God permits so many hardships and failures in our lives. Many times, he does so because it's the only way we will learn that we are limited, that we are not God. Substantial humility is the habitual and joyful awareness that we are utterly dependent on God for all things, from the most sublime to the most mundane. Jesus knew where the fish were; Peter didn't. Jesus still knows where the fish are; we don't. We need to trust in him and in the instruments he chooses to use—a confessor, a spiritual director, a superior in the apostolate. If we work hard doing all we can and then throw out our nets wherever Christ tells us to, he will surely never leave us empty-handed.

CHRIST THE FRIEND *Jesus: Begin again, as many times as necessary. With me, you can always begin again. The world doesn't let you do this. Other people often don't let you. With them, once you fail, it's over. But with me, you can always begin again. That morning on Lake Tiberias was just like a morning three years ago on the same lake. Both times they had spent the whole night working their nets and caught nothing. Both times I approached them—because they didn't know how to come to me. I told them to cast out their nets. And both times they pulled in a huge catch. Peter needed to begin again. How much this pleased me! Begin again: in your efforts to follow me, to be like me, to build my Kingdom, in your attempts to repair broken relationships, to succeed where you have already failed, to form virtue where you have vice—in all these things you will need to begin again a thousand times. And though it may seem that you are starting from scratch each time, as it seemed to Peter, you're not. Each time you look at me, each time you hear my voice, each time you trust me after a failure, all the important virtues (humility, faith, hope, love) are stronger.*

If ever you feel discouraged when you should just be dusting yourself off and beginning again, I can guarantee that your discouragement doesn't come from me. I came not to condemn, but to save. *My love for you doesn't depend on your impeccability – in fact, it doesn't depend on anything. My love for you is total, a waterfall that never stops flowing. You can always begin again.*

CHRIST IN MY LIFE I believe in your Church, Lord, and in your vicar on earth, the pope. You have chosen to continue to walk with me through him. I wish I had more time to study all that he says, to keep up with his words and actions, to second them more completely in my own life and community. Show me how I can be more faithful to your vicar. Show me how I can love him as you want me to...

I have to be honest, Lord: humility is a mystery to me. I keep thinking I'm humble, mainly because I see so many people who are more arrogant or vain than I am, but then you remind me that I'm not really humble yet. Make me humble! Give me the docility I need so that I can give you a chance to fill my nets with hundreds of fish! Please do, Lord; all I long for is to be your faithful and fruitful apostle...

How can I help feeling discouraged? Lord, I will never give in to discouragement again. Maybe I can't help feeling the emotion, but when I do, you will remind me that it doesn't come from you, that with you I can always begin again, and that you can bring good even out of the worst failures, the worst evils. Thy will be done, Lord; I trust in you...

Questions for
SMALL-GROUP DISCUSSION

1. What struck you most in this passage? What did you notice that you hadn't noticed before?

2. Our adherence and obedience to the vicar of Christ reflects our dedication to Christ himself. How can we increase the former in order to intensify the latter?

3. Do you think Christ's hopes for us are being fulfilled? If not, why not?

4. What has helped you most in your efforts to grow in the crucial virtue of humility?

Cf. Catechism of the Catholic Church, 25, 49, 68 on the primacy of love in the Church's mission; 2559, 2631, 2713, 2546 on the role and nature of humility; 871-933 on the nature of the Church and the authority it has received from Christ

303. KEEP FOLLOWING ME (JN 21:15-25)

"What matters above all is to tend one's personal relationship with God, with that God who revealed himself to us in Christ." – Pope Benedict XVI

JOHN 21:15-25
After the meal Jesus said to Simon Peter, "Simon son of John, do you love me more than these others do?" He answered, "Yes Lord, you know I love you." Jesus said to him, "Feed my lambs." A second time he said to him, "Simon son of John, do you love me?" He replied, "Yes, Lord, you know I love you." Jesus said to him, "Look after my sheep." Then he said to him a third time, "Simon son of John, do you love me?" Peter was upset that he asked him the third time, "Do you love me?" and said, "Lord, you know everything; you know I love you." Jesus said to him, "Feed my sheep. I tell you most solemnly, when you were young you put on your own belt and walked where you liked; but when you grow old you will stretch out your hands, and somebody else will put a belt round you and take you where you would rather not go." In these words he indicated the kind of death by which Peter would give glory to God. After this he said, "Follow me." Peter turned and saw the disciple Jesus loved following them – the one who had leaned on his breast at the supper and had said to him, "Lord, who is it that will betray you?" Seeing him, Peter said to Jesus, "What about him, Lord?" Jesus answered, "If I want him to stay behind till I come, what does it matter to you? You are to follow me." The rumour then went out among the brothers that this disciple would not die. Yet Jesus had not said to Peter, "He will not die," but, "If I want him to stay behind till I come." This disciple is the one who vouches for these things and has written them down, and we know that his testimony is true. There were many other things that Jesus did; if all were written down, the world itself, I suppose, would not hold all the books that would have to be written.

CHRIST THE LORD One of our most frequent and intense temptations is to try and control other people's lives. Like Peter in his relationship with John, we often let our laudable affection and interest in others override our humility. We cannot control other people's lives. Only Christ is Lord; only Christ governs hearts. The only heart we can govern is our own. Our task in life is to gradually train our own wild, rebellious hearts to run freely and fruitfully under the guidance of the Lord. That is more than enough to keep us busy. When it comes to other people, the most we can do is love them – but even that may not change them. Loving means treating them with respect, being attentive to their needs, seeking ways to make them happy, forgiving them without limit, refraining from judging and criticizing them, praying for them sincerely and continually, and encouraging them to pursue goodness by creating an environment where goodness is easier to pursue than selfishness—both by the power of our own example of seeking to follow Christ before all else and also, when the time is right, by our words. We can do no more. Only God can touch them more deeply.

Our relationships with others constitute one of the most difficult arenas in which to let the Lord be Lord. By not relinquishing our sense of control in this area, we heap huge quantities of fruitless frustration and needless suffering onto our already overburdened souls. By releasing this illusion of control, we find greater interior peace, finally get out of God's way, and please the heart of Christ immensely, because it shows that we trust him with what matters most—the ones we love. Every Christian should always keep these words of Jesus, with which St. John concludes his Gospel, on the screensaver of their mind: "If I want him to stay behind till I come, what does it matter to you? You are to follow me."

CHRIST THE TEACHER This after-breakfast conversation between Peter and Jesus is a curious one. Peter had betrayed Jesus verbally three times the night before Good Friday. He is sorry for his infidelity, as he has shown clearly by his eagerness to be near the Lord during his post-Resurrection appearances. Even so, Jesus gives him a chance to reverse his betrayals by verbally professing his love. Jesus wanted to give him this opportunity. Even though it makes Peter uncomfortable, Jesus knows that he needs it. The same dynamic is at work in the sacrament of Confession. When we enter the confessional, we are already sorry for our sins (otherwise we wouldn't go), but Jesus knows that we need to express this in words to his chosen representative. Human beings are like that. We are not angels, who are pure spirits; we are incarnate spirits. Through all the sacraments, Jesus continues to come to us in the very same way he came to Peter on that cool spring morning at the shore of Lake Tiberias, where he served him a meal and then spoke with him heart-to-heart.

Another lesson is at work in this exchange, however. Peter may have been doubting whether after his failure he was still worthy of the mission Jesus had entrusted to him. He was called to be the visible head of the Church, the instrument of Church unity—a mission that Peter's successors, the popes, continue to carry on until Christ's return in glory. In this conversation, Jesus reinstates Peter in this critical role. He commands him three times (just to make sure Peter won't have any doubts): "Feed my sheep." The context of this renewed commission, however, reinforces the lesson Peter had learned on Good Friday. The key to Peter's ability to resume his role and fulfill his mission will not be his natural capacities, however notable and apt they may be. Rather, what will enable him to stay faithful and succeed in his God-given task is his personal union with Jesus, his love for and dependence on Christ. "Peter, do you love me?" Jesus asks him, and on the heels of his profession of love, he commands him to lead the Church.

We all fall, as Peter did, and we all are subsequently approached by the Lord, who wishes to reinstate us in our place in the Church, to recommission us in our vocation. Christ's grace and our response of love, feeble and inconstant thought it may be, are more than sufficient for such a reinstatement and recommission—they are more than sufficient for everlasting success. We simply have to renew that response of love in prayer and then live it out by obeying his will.

CHRIST THE FRIEND "Follow me" are the last words that Christ speaks to Peter. How would he have said them? Would the tone have been harsh, commanding, military? Perhaps. But maybe it was warm, inviting, and excited. "Follow me, Peter! I have great things in store for you! Stick by my side; trust me; do whatever I ask of you, and you will come to share in my glory." The heart of Christ is full of hopes for each of us. First among them is his hope that we will stay close to him even if he leads us down difficult paths, which he will. Peter and all the other apostles except for John followed Christ down the path of martyrdom; every Christian must be led by the Lord "where we would rather not go" in one form or another. Otherwise, how could we prove our friendship, our loyalty, and our love? That's what Jesus wants—our friendship. This is the only reason he came to "dwell among us"—to be able to offer his friendship and ask for ours in return. And he asks for it every day by speaking those same words deep within our hearts in myriad ways, ways that each one of us can hear, if we keep on listening: "Follow me."

John: We didn't see him again until the day he ascended into heaven, but we didn't need to. He had shown us everything. He had shown us that nothing we would ever do could lessen his love for us or increase it. He had shown us that he knew us through and through, and still he loved us, wanted to walk by our sides, and entrusted his Kingdom into our care.

Many times later in life I cast my nets and came up with nothing. Many times I told people about the Lord only to have them smirk and then belittle me. I was arrested, just as he had predicted. I was tortured and exiled because I refused to stop believing in his love and truth. Yes, there were many nights without a single catch. But there were also many mornings like that one on Lake Tiberias. He surprised me time and time again.

Things I said or did without even thinking became occasions of conversion, moments of inspiration for people I didn't even know. Cities we visited almost by mistake became centers of thriving Christian communities – full nets. We made our plans and did our best, and always the Lord showed that his plans were bigger and that his grace would multiply our efforts. The longer I lived, the more confident I became in the power of his grace. He was always one step ahead of us, eager to show us his love. How I wish I could tell all his followers to simply trust him! He is the Lord and he is your Friend – why do you fear? Why do you hesitate? Why do you fret? Courage! Be brave, because you bear his name. Be patient, because the morning is coming. He is with you. He is calling to you from the shore of eternity, telling you to cast out your nets, preparing to welcome you home.

CHRIST IN MY LIFE You are the Lord. Everyone I love, everyone I care about, everyone I am afraid of – they are all under your Lordship. Nothing they do escapes your gaze, your justice, or your mercy. You are more interested in their salvation and happiness than I could ever be. O Lord! Grant me the peace that comes from trusting in you. You went to the cross to show that you deserve unshakable confidence...

You know everything, Lord, so you know that I love you, even though I have failed you so many times, Lord. I get so wrapped up in secondary things. I go through my day and compromise my commitments, letting myself get swept into the self-seeking ways of the world. But you never fail to search me out, to feed me with your Word and your Eucharist. You are always faithful. Your grace is always there. Renew me again now, Lord, and accept my renewed profession of love...

If I try to imagine a more marvelous, wonderful, astonishing plan than the one you have given to my life, I can't. You, Creator, Redeemer, the all-powerful, all-knowing, all-loving God, have come into the mundane circumstances of my life, called out my name, and invited me to be your companion and your ambassador. And even that wasn't enough – you have even become my brother. Thank you, Lord...

Questions for
SMALL-GROUP DISCUSSION

1. What struck you most in this passage? What did you notice that you hadn't noticed before?

2. Why do you think John got up and followed Peter and Jesus while they were having their talk? Why do you think Peter asked about John's future? Why didn't Jesus give him an answer?

3. What do you think are some of the many things that Jesus did that were never recorded?

4. The first time, Jesus asked Peter if he loved him "more than these others do." The second and third time, he just asked him whether he loved him. Why the change?

Cf. Catechism of the Catholic Church, 1423-1433 on the sacrament of Confession and the nature of ongoing conversion; 874-896 on the hierarchical constitution of the Church; 813-822 on the unity of the Church; 2015 on the necessity of the cross for spiritual growth

APPENDIX 1

UNITS LINKED TO PARTICULAR POINTS OF SPIRITUAL WORK

APOSTOLIC ZEAL: 239, 240, 241, 243, 245, 249, 250, 253, 255, 256, 260, 262, 264, 265, 268, 269, 271, 276, 277, 281, 283, 285, 286, 287, 290, 291, 296, 297, 298, 299, 301, 302, 303

CHARITY/LOVE FOR NEIGHBOR: 252, 253, 255, 258, 262, 263, 264, 268, 269, 271, 274, 276, 278, 279, 280, 281, 283, 284, 285, 286, 290, 291, 292, 294, 296, 298

CONFIDENCE IN GOD (FAITH, HOPE, LOVE) (This point of spiritual work is the bedrock of Christianity. Almost every passage in the Bible can be read as a revelation of God's trustworthiness): 239, 241, 242, 243, 244, 245, 246, 248, 249, 250', 251, 252, 254, 255, 256, 257, 258, 259, 262, 263, 264, 265, 266, 267, 268, 269, 270, 271, 272, 273, 274, 275, 276, 277, 278, 279, 280, 281, 282, 283, 284, 285, 286, 287, 288, 289, 291, 292, 293, 294, 296, 297, 298, 299, 300, 301, 302, 303

DEATH/HEAVEN/HELL/JUDGMENT: 253, 261, 265, 267, 273, 274, 278, 282, 285, 298, 300

EUCHARIST: 244, 255, 256, 257, 258, 259, 277, 284, 285, 298

FORGIVENESS/MERCY/REPENTANCE/CONFESSION: 241, 261, 263, 280, 294, 302, 303

HUMAN RESPECT/VANITY: 242, 245, 248, 250, 251, 254, 260, 263, 267, 276, 294, 295, 296, 298

HUMILITY/OBEDIENCE: 240, 242, 243, 244, 246, 248, 251, 252, 253, 254, 255, 257, 259, 261, 265, 266, 267, 270, 272, 276, 277, 278, 279, 280, 282, 283, 285, 294, 295, 298, 302

LOVE FOR THE CHURCH AND THE POPE: 239, 240, 242, 243, 245, 256, 264, 268, 269, 270, 271, 272, 285, 288, 290, 291, 292, 293, 297, 298, 299, 301, 303

MARY: 244, 281, 283, 284, 286, 287, 288, 289, 290, 295, 297, 298

PATIENCE/FORTITUDE/PERSEVERANCE: 250, 251, 269, 275, 277, 287, 289, 293, 294, 300

POVERTY/DETACHMENT: 246, 259, 276, 279

PRAYER: 243, 244, 245, 249, 260, 262, 273, 274, 276, 277, 283, 285, 286, 288, 289, 290, 291, 292, 297, 299, 300, 303

PURITY/CHASTITY: 249, 263

PURITY OF INTENTION/SPIRITUAL SIMPLICITY: 242, 245, 248, 250, 254, 260, 266, 267, 279, 294, 300, 302

SIN/TEMPTATION: 239, 253, 259, 263, 265, 266, 267, 269, 270, 272, 276, 280, 281, 285, 290, 294, 295, 296

SINCERITY/HYPOCRISY/CONSCIENCE: 242, 245, 252, 261, 267, 269, 276

SUFFERING/SACRIFICE: 251, 260, 268, 269, 271, 273, 274, 275, 278, 285, 287, 288, 289, 291, 293, 294, 295, 296, 297, 298

VOCATION: 240, 241, 242, 243, 246, 250, 255, 258, 259, 260, 262, 264, 270, 278, 280, 281, 282, 285, 286, 287, 288, 291, 292, 295, 301, 302, 303

APPENDIX 2

BOOKS ON PRAYER AND THE SPIRITUAL LIFE

Navigating the Interior Life, Daniel Burke
This Tremendous Lover, Eugene Boylan
The Secrets of the Interior Life, Luis Martinez
Difficulties in Mental Prayer, Eugene Boylan
Talking with God, Francois Fenelon
How to Pray Always, Raoul Plus
Spiritual Combat, Lorenzo Scupoli
Weeds among the Wheat, Thomas H. Green, SJ
When the Well Runs Dry, Thomas H. Green, SJ
Opening to God, Thomas H. Green, SJ
A Vacation with the Lord, Thomas H. Green, SJ
Darkness in the Marketplace, Thomas H. Green, SJ
Prayer and Common Sense, Thomas H. Green, SJ

Sophia Institute

Sophia Institute is a nonprofit institution that seeks to nurture the spiritual, moral, and cultural life of souls and to spread the Gospel of Christ in conformity with the authentic teachings of the Roman Catholic Church.

Sophia Institute Press fulfills this mission by offering translations, reprints, and new publications that afford readers a rich source of the enduring wisdom of mankind.

Sophia Institute also operates the popular online resource CatholicExchange.com. *Catholic Exchange* provides world news from a Catholic perspective as well as daily devotionals and articles that will help readers to grow in holiness and live a life consistent with the teachings of the Church.

In 2013, Sophia Institute launched Sophia Institute for Teachers to renew and rebuild Catholic culture through service to Catholic education. With the goal of nurturing the spiritual, moral, and cultural life of souls, and an abiding respect for the role and work of teachers, we strive to provide materials and programs that are at once enlightening to the mind and ennobling to the heart; faithful and complete, as well as useful and practical.

Sophia Institute gratefully recognizes the Solidarity Association for preserving and encouraging the growth of our apostolate over the course of many years. Without their generous and timely support, this book would not be in your hands.

www.SophiaInstitute.com
www.CatholicExchange.com
www.SophiaInstituteforTeachers.org

Sophia Institute Press® is a registered trademark of Sophia Institute.
Sophia Institute is a tax-exempt institution as defined by the
Internal Revenue Code, Section 501(c)(3). Tax I.D. 22-2548708.